DOWNTON SHABBY

HOPWOOD
DEPREE

WILLIAM MORROW
An Imprint of HarperCollins*Publishers*

DOWNTON

ONE

AMERICAN'S

ULTIMATE

DIY

SHABBY

ADVENTURE

RESTORING

HIS FAMILY'S

ENGLISH CASTLE

This book is a memoir and as such, it reflects the author's recollections of experiences over time. Some names and characteristics have been changed, some characters and events have been combined and created, some events have been compressed or expanded, and some dialogue has been re-created.

HarperCollins books may be purchased for educational, business, or sales promotional use. For information, please email the Special Markets Department at SPsales@harpercollins.com.

FIRST EDITION

Designed by Elina Cohen
Key art courtesy of Shutterstock / AVA Bitter and Vector Tradition

Library of Congress Cataloging-in-Publication Data

Names: DePree, Hopwood, 1970– author.
Title: Downton Shabby : one American's ultimate DIY adventure
   restoring his family's English castle / Hopwood DePree.
Description: First edition. | New York : William Morrow, [2022]
Identifiers: LCCN 2021034447 | ISBN 9780063080850 (hardback) |
   ISBN 9780063080874 (ebook)
Subjects: LCSH: Hopwood Hall (England) | Middleton (Greater
   Manchester, England)—Buildings, structures, etc. | Historic
   buildings—Conservation and restoration—England. | DePree, Hopwood,
   1970—Homes and haunts—England. | Actors—Dwellings—England. |
   Actors—Family relationships—United States.
Classification: LCC NA7512.4.M53 D47 2022 | DDC 942.7/3—
   dc23/eng/20211115
LC record available at https://lccn.loc.gov/2021034447

ISBN 978-0-06-308085-0

22 23 24 25 26 FRI 10 9 8 7 6 5 4 3 2 1

This book is dedicated to my father, my grandfather, and all those who came before me

DOWNTON
SHABBY

CHAPTER 1

LONG LOST HOPWOOD

*I*t was one of those nights when you hope your biggest responsibility will be uncorking a bottle of wine. Little did I know that an internet search was about to change my life, upending my entire understanding of my purpose on this planet, my place in the bigger continuum of history, and what a home improvement project can really mean.

It was spring 2013, and I was at home in Los Angeles in the Hollywood Hills. There was only one helicopter circling overhead, so it was quieter than usual. Outside the window, daylight was fading into dusk, and the desk lamp glowed amber next to me as I sat down at my laptop.

That evening, as had become my new secret wine-time relaxation habit, I started clicking around on ancestry sites: WikiTree .com, Ancestry.com, Myheritage.com. I was familiar with all of them.

Whenever I had a half hour or so to spare, I'd dig a bit further along the twists and turns of my ancestral tree. If you've never been on one of these sites, let me warn you: They are seriously addicting. A half hour can easily turn into a few hours or all night, so I often had to limit myself. Find a copy of some yellowed document you've never seen before and then you're clicking on another link, which takes you to proof of an unknown second cousin four times removed, and before you know it you've found an old black-and-white photograph of some long-deceased great-aunt. It can be dizzying. Spend enough time on these sites, and you'll start to feel like a detective on the trail, following breadcrumbs of evidence, except in this mystery most of the people in the story are already dead and have been for decades.

Until recently, it was true that I'd always been the kind of person who focused on the future; I didn't spend much time looking behind me. But lately, that had changed. I was becoming more and more curious about the past. How had I gotten sucked into genealogy searches? I know it wasn't thanks to the shows on TV featuring celebrities tracing their family history, because I didn't watch those. And it wasn't that I hoped to find some lost relative or uncover a family secret. If I had to say exactly why I was willing to spend hours of my life learning about people I didn't know and was never going to meet, I would say a lot of it had to do with loss. Loss, and probably some regret too.

Until recently, my grandfather on my mother's side had been our family genealogist. His name was Herbert Hopwood Black, but I called him Pap. He had an infectious grin and was over six feet tall, so when I was a little kid, he always looked like a smiling giant. As I was growing up, Pap used to love to tell me stories about our Hopwood ancestors and how they had founded the small town of Hopwood, Pennsylvania, in 1791. Pap should know. He had been born and bred in Hopwood. The only reason he left his beloved hometown in the 1920s was because he was offered an opportunity in Michigan to get involved with a rapidly growing company called General Motors. To the end of his days, he couldn't have been prouder of our connection to Hopwood and that we could trace our family tree there back eight generations. Or was it seven?

The problem was, as a kid, I'd never really listened.

From my perspective, anything to do with Hopwood was problematic. Yes, my name is Hopwood, just like my grandpa, but from a very early age, I hated my name. Calling me Hopwood had been my mom's idea—she chose it as a tribute to her father and his side of the family. When I was a baby and toddler, it was fine: Hopwood got shortened to "Hoppy" or "Woody," which in preschool was considered pretty cute. It was only when I got to kindergarten that the teasing began. The other kids thought "Hopwood" was hilarious. They said I should have been called John. Or Steve. Things got so bad that I came home from school one day and told my parents I'd had enough.

"I don't want to be Hopwood anymore!" I declared as I pushed over a wooden plant stand, hearing it crack as it hit the ground. I felt bad looking at the damage I'd caused, the fern tipped over with dirt spilling out of its side.

My dad, always a loving pragmatist, had seen this outburst coming. When I was born, he insisted at the last minute that my mom also give me the name Tod as a backup to Hopwood in case I didn't like it. (My dad's initials were T.O.D.)

Being Tod was a major relief. The kids stopped teasing me. I got on with life. But this didn't stop my grandfather from drilling me about the Hopwoods of generations long ago. He loved anything to do with family history.

My mom was cut from the same cloth. When I was six years old, she dragged me and my two sisters to Hopwood, Pennsylvania, to visit the town of our ancestors. She was serious about giving us an education in the past. I remember on that trip she marched us around graveyards, where we were forced to do creepy gravestone rubbings alongside thorns, poison ivy, and dried bird poop. To this day, I can picture my mom wearing her signature stylish pantsuit, with stacked black hair, lipstick, and cat-eye sunglasses, as we tackled an array of educational adventures. At one point, Mom made us pose in front of the town sign: HOPWOOD. I refused to smile.

After lunch, in front of one of our ancestors' nineteenth-century houses, she was able to coax a momentary grin out of me by promising me a new Batman costume.

Hopwood and sisters visiting Hopwood, Pennsylvania, 1976
Photo by Deanna DePree

"Someday, you'll be glad you took this photo," she added.

Still scarred from my kindergarten experience, I remember being terrified that someone from my class was going to drive by and see me. (This was unlikely, as our hometown of Holland, Michigan, was about five hundred miles away, but even so.)

In high school, I continued to go by Tod. My high school yearbook lists me as Tod H. DePree, which was horrifying to me at the time because it meant everyone asked what the *H* stood for. I refused to tell them. Not even my closest friends knew I was Hopwood. Apparently, at graduation I was called out onstage as "Tod Hopwood DePree," giving the game away, but I think I must have blocked out the memory because I don't remember it. Even the sound of the word *Hopwood* was enough to make me wince. And so, when my grandfather gave me his history lessons, I'd pretty much tune them out.

All these years later, sitting at my laptop, I knew bits and pieces of our family chronology, although there were some big holes in my understanding. I knew that my Hopwood ancestors came to these shores from England sometime in the 1700s, founding the town of Hopwood soon after. Then, at a certain point in the 1800s, the American side of the Hopwood line came close to dying out when my grandfather's grandmother—Alcinda Hopwood—got married. Alcinda was the last to carry the Hopwood name since, once married, she would take her husband's last name, and the Hopwood line would be over. This bothered her for much of her life, and so when her grandson—my grandfather—was born, she demanded his parents give him Hopwood as a middle name. Which is how the name was passed down to me.

But there was one more piece of information my grandfather told me that had lodged in my childish brain.

When Pap sat me on his knee and told me stories about my

5

Hopwood ancestors, he'd always talked about how there was also a vast area of land called Hopwood in England where our ancestors had built a magnificent castle.

"When your Hopwood ancestors came to America, they left behind the grandest castle you've ever seen," he'd say lowering his voice. *"Hopwood Castle."*

Despite my embarrassment about my name, I secretly loved the idea that somewhere across the ocean, there was a fairy-tale castle with the same name as me. In my mind, it looked like a cross between the one at Disneyland and my favorite childhood toy, the Fisher-Price Play Family Castle.

Where was this castle? Did it even exist? I wasn't sure. Maybe Pap had made the whole thing up, creating an exciting story in the hope that his stubborn grandson would finally fall in love with his Hopwood name.

As much as I hoped it was real, looking around at the 1970s brightly colored orange and green kitchen in our suburban Michigan home that was barely thirty years old, I couldn't help but think, *No way is that true.*

As it happened, after high school and college, I slowly learned to accept—and even appreciate—the name that had once caused me so much embarrassment and pain. I started working as an actor and comedian. I found success as a writer and producer in TV and film, founding my own production company. I realized that in Hollywood, being Hopwood might have a serious advantage over being Tod: It could help me stand out in a crowd. That Tod guy is forgettable. But Hopwood? He's someone who gets a second meeting! When I was about twenty-five, I switched my name back to Hopwood. My mom and grandfather were thrilled.

I spent the rest of my twenties and thirties getting roles and projects, enjoying my success and the special attention. I received more invitations to parties, and it even seemed as if people began to find me more intriguing. *I should've skipped the gym and gone with the weird name years ago,* I thought. Despite my newfound appreciation for my name, however, I didn't spend a lot of time thinking about my family's history. I was too busy getting on with my life to look behind me.

Then around the time I turned forty, two events happened that changed my perspective completely.

The first was that my grandfather passed away.

Pap had been the foundation of our family. Even though he was in his nineties when he died and had lived a good long life, his loss felt like the shifting of the tectonic plates. He had been the keeper of our history, the one who knew all the stories. After his death, I truly regretted not spending more time with him talking about where the Hopwoods came from and what it all meant.

About two years later came the second event: My dad died suddenly of a massive heart attack. He was seventy-five and had only recently been given a clean bill of health by his doctor. No one saw it coming. If my grandfather was the ground beneath our feet, then my dad was a pillar holding us all up. I remember leaving the hospital after his death, and Mom turning to me and saying, "It's just too soon." She had lost her husband and her father within a period that felt like the blink of an eye. I could only imagine how hard it must be for her—I knew it was hard enough for me.

The back-to-back deaths of the two most important men in my life left me reeling. Not only that, now I needed to come to terms with the fact that I was the next generation on the chopping block. *Where did everyone go, and how did we get here so quickly?*

Outside my office window at my home in Los Angeles, I had a

Spanish courtyard. A spiral staircase went up to an old weathered wooden door. Bright fuchsia bougainvillea and ivy covered the stucco walls and cacti were in pots dotted around. To one side of the courtyard was a big outdoor terracotta chiminea where I would light fires whenever I had parties at my house, usually after an event, a premiere, or night out at the clubs in Hollywood. That night at my laptop, I remember looking out and seeing a crack in the chiminea that ran up the side that I hadn't noticed before. It was how I felt about every aspect of my life: Nothing looked the way it used to anymore.

Until that point, I had never asked questions about who I was or what my purpose in life might be. I was the son of Thomas O. De-Pree and grandson of Herbert Hopwood Black. I was a filmmaker and an actor. I was Hopwood, and I was okay (well, most of the time). None of those old assumptions seemed true anymore. Without my dad and my grandpa, who was I? It was as if the seawall standing between me and my mortality had collapsed.

As I entered my forties, many of my friends were already married, having kids, settling down. Meanwhile, I was childless, in on-again-off-again relationships—most recently off again, with a model who, in a heated argument, would not hold back from pointing out the fact that I'd gained a bit of weight. It was all causing me to drink too much, which indeed made me gain weight, which in Hollywood is akin to a criminal act. Not only that, but I was struggling in my work. I'd always loved being an actor and producer, but I no longer felt the same passion I had when I'd first gotten into the business. I had experienced high points, like winning awards by making my own independent films, launching a respected film festival, and producing projects with recognized talent. But the introspection also made me realize that many things hadn't panned

out the way I had expected. Recently I'd been passionately working to set up a TV docuseries about inner-city gang violence that
seemed like it could make real social change. I had even managed to
get Academy Award nominee John Singleton to come onboard. So
when all the networks passed on the project, I was beside myself. I
had worked hard, but Hollywood doesn't always reward hard work.
Would my eighteen-year-old self, who wanted to make a difference
in the film capital of the world, be content with where I was today?
I couldn't answer yes.

I was questioning everything: my career, my relationships, my
entire life.

In movies, the saying goes that if a scene isn't working, then
don't focus on that scene; go back to the scene before it. There was
something about tracing my ancestors online that comforted me.
Every time I found a new link or name, I felt a tug of connection.
So many generations of our family, all their names on the site, each
one of them a leaf on a tree, recorded for the ages. Those links and
names felt like anchors, keeping me tied down to this crazy, spinning blue marble.

That fateful night, with the warm spring air wafting through
my window, I kept scrolling away on the ancestry website. Going
back further and further, trying to find something—I just wasn't
sure what. And that's when I saw it. A link I hadn't seen before. I
clicked on it.

It was a short article about a "Lord Hopwood" of "Hopwood Hall."

Wait—could Hopwood Hall be the Hopwood Castle my grandfather had always told me about?

Maybe Pap hadn't invented the castle after all.

I clicked over to Google and did a quick search for "Hopwood
Hall, England."

Several entries came up. It looked like Hopwood Hall was a vocational college somewhere near Manchester in England. Perhaps there had once been a Hopwood Castle there, but maybe it had long since fallen down, and now the college sat on the same site.

I kept scrolling, stopping for the occasional swig of wine.

A few pages into my search, I found another hit. It was some type of environmental survey by the local council that mentioned "Hopwood Woods" and "Hopwood Hall." In the description, the Hall was described as "run-down." There was also mention of the hope that someday it would be restored. Did this mean the original Hall was still standing?

Suddenly, I froze. There in front of me on the laptop screen was an old black-and-white picture of a grand English country house. It was beautiful. And stately. It looked like it must be a full city block, with about thirty chimneys and dozens of windows and doors. I was in awe. It could easily have been the castle that Pap had told me about. If only we had the internet back when I was a kid, I never would've doubted him!

Equally, had I known that clicking on the photo would lead me into never-ending sleepless nights and days of backbreaking labor, I might have slammed my laptop shut and never looked at it again. I am not what you might call handy. The last DIY home improvement project I attempted culminated in me practically bursting into tears in a Home Depot parking lot after trying to cover my 4 × 4-foot bathroom floor with self-sticking adhesive tiles. As soon as I began peeling off the protective backing of the tiles to reveal the sticky goop, I quickly realized the only thing that was stuck was me.

Of course, I had no idea that the house in the photo would one day

Hopwood Hall Estate, 1950s *Printed with kind permission of the De La Salle Trust, Oxford*

become my responsibility—that when it rained, I would be running with a bucket to catch the drips. That night of innocent scrolling in the Hollywood Hills, I just wanted to find out more. Hopwood Hall seemed to be located in a town named Middleton, just outside Manchester in the North of England. The thought crossed my mind: *What if we could go and visit it?*

For the past few months, my mom, my sisters, and I had been planning a trip to Europe to scatter my father's ashes and pay tribute to him. The last conversation I'd ever had with my father, on the night before he died, we'd talked about going to France for my parents' upcoming fiftieth wedding anniversary the following spring. My dad had been a proud US Marine and always wanted to visit the beaches of Normandy to pay his respects to those who had fallen fighting for freedom in World War II. Dad died before he could make that trip, but together with the rest of my family, we decided to make the journey to France in his honor, taking his ashes with us. It seemed like the perfect way to lay him to rest.

If Hopwood Hall was still standing, then maybe we could take a short side trip to England while we were in Europe. That way we could pay tribute to my Hopwood grandfather as well as my dad.

At the bottom of the environmental report about Hopwood Hall, I'd spotted an email address for someone at the town council, so I pulled up my email and pasted the address into the box.

> Hello,
>
> I am a descendant of the Hopwood family and am interested in the restoration of Hopwood Hall. I will be traveling to your area around May 13 and would very much appreciate meeting with you to visit the Hall. Please let me know if this is possible.
>
> Cheers,
>
> Hopwood

By the time I got up the next morning, there was already a response waiting for me in my inbox. It was from Bev Percival, a conservation project officer, explaining that she was going to be away in May when we wanted to visit, but that she was CCing a man named Geoff Wellens who knew all about the history of the Hall and might be able to show us around.

I replied to Bev right away, explaining that I'd love to be in contact with Geoff and anyone else who could help me learn more about the Hall.

Later in the day, Geoff sent me an email.

Dear Hopwood,

I look forward to meeting you. I have previously tried to get in touch with Hopwoods through their family website but, alas, they said they weren't connected with Middleton.

We have lots to tell you about, but I need to ask you a question. Was there any red hair in the Hopwood family? We had to do repairs to the Hopwood tomb as some surrounding flagstones had fallen in, leaving a gap through which we could see lead coffins. On entering the tomb, we found that one coffin had completely disintegrated leaving the skeleton exposed. The skull still had some red hair attached (I took photos).

Following "archaeological research," we reinterred the bones in a new wooden coffin and conducted a Christian committal service. Then we did the necessary work to seal the tomb.

I hope this is of interest?

Regards

Geoff Wellens

I felt goosebumps prickle on my arms. According to my mom I was a redhead until I was six months old, at which point my hair fell out and grew back blond. Somehow, that recessive gene had found its way across an ocean and the centuries to me . . .

This whole thing was surreal. I couldn't believe I was corresponding with a man who had recently been poking around in the tombs of my English ancestors.

I wrote back to Geoff, and we agreed to speak on the phone the next day.

"Hopwood?" asked the very British voice on the other end of the phone.

"Hello?" I replied.

"Is that really *Hopwood*?" Geoff asked.

"It really is!" I replied.

"Well, this is a turnup for the books," he went on. "There hasn't been a Hopwood family member that we've known of for decades. We'd almost given up hope of ever finding anyone. The Hall is in need of a bit of help, you see."

"But wait, aren't there any Hopwoods taking care of the Hall right now?"

"Not a soul!" Geoff replied. "Other than the ghosts. It's completely abandoned, didn't you know? We've been looking for a family member for years."

I told him I had no idea.

Geoff explained that the last Hopwoods to live at the Hall had left the house in the 1920s.

"It's really a tragic story," Geoff continued. "The two male heirs to the Hopwood estate were both officers and were killed in the First World War, along with twenty-four members of their staff."

The aging Hopwood parents were so devastated by the deaths of their sons and the people who worked at the Hall that they decided to move out, putting their home up for sale in May 1922. They couldn't stay there any longer without their sons or any staff to help them carry it forward. And so they left the house behind and moved to London. The two sons had died before *they* had any children, and so after that, there was no one left to carry on the Hopwood line— and no one to take care of the Hall.

"During the Second World War, Hopwood Hall was taken over by the Lancashire Cotton Corporation, who used it as a base for making uniforms, as they were afraid they would be bombed in Manchester," Geoff told me. "And then in the late forties, a group of monks moved in. They used the Hall as a training college for Catholic teachers. After the monks left, Hopwood Hall stood empty for about three decades. And unfortunately, many of the people including myself who see the importance in saving a historical building like this are all slowly dying off. It's all in a bit of a mess, you see."

I told Geoff I didn't mind what shape the Hall was in; we'd love to come and see it.

"You'd be more than welcome," he replied right away. "I can pick you up from the airport. And perhaps you can stick around for a bit afterward so we can have a pint. I have so many things to discuss with you."

Geoff explained that in addition to being a fan of the house and something of a local historian, he was also the town's longtime undertaker, recently retired. This was why he had been asked to look at the Hopwood tombs after some vandals had caused damage by breaking in and disturbing the bones. It had been his job to lay them to rest again.

We promised to speak again soon to make plans.

I hung up with Geoff and tried to make sense of everything I'd just heard. Twenty-four hours ago, I wasn't even sure Hopwood Hall existed, and now here we were, talking about airport pickups. And pints!

I called my mother and explained what had just happened.

"Mom, guess what? Hopwood Castle is called Hopwood Hall! It's in the North of England. And I've made contact with a man named Geoff who wants us to come over there. He's going to show us Hopwood Hall!"

She thought I was joking, and even after I persuaded her that I was serious, she was in shock. She had never believed my grandfather's stories either.

For her, this was even more exciting than the trip to Hopwood, Pennsylvania, that we'd taken when I was a kid. Mom was still grieving for both her husband and her father. Adding a stopover in England during our visit to France seemed like the best thing I could possibly do to cheer her up.

"We couldn't really go there, could we?" she asked.

"I think we have to," I said.

CHAPTER 2

UNEXPECTED HOMECOMING

Our plane shook from turbulence as we broke through the clouds. I could see the green and unfamiliar landscape of Northern England below, dotted with white sheep and slate-roofed buildings. The land of my ancestors.

"Flight attendants, please prepare the cabin for arrival," said the captain in the most charming English accent. Just hearing his voice made me feel "posh." I gathered my "rubbish" and handed it to the attendant as she made her way down the aisle.

It all seemed so foreign to me, but I felt lighter than I had in a very long time.

The day before, we'd scattered my dad's ashes and said a tearful goodbye on Omaha Beach in Normandy, standing at the end of a long wooden pier, looking out over the English Channel. My mother, my two sisters Dori and Dana, my uncle and aunt, my brother-in-law, and my five-year-old niece were all with me. There was a biting chill in the air, icy-gray waters surrounding us, the long stretch of the coast at our backs. Although my sisters are three years apart in age, people often mistake them for twins, with their long brown hair and big sunglasses. They had each taken one of my mother's arms as we made our way down the rickety dock. I led the way, looking for the perfect spot.

I said a few words before we scattered the ashes. I talked about Dad's kindness, his influence on me, how he had always brought people together—and how he was bringing us together again in this location. It said a lot about how much he meant to us that we'd all traveled halfway across the world to be here. I looked over at my sisters, their heads slightly bowed. They were silent, their hair blowing and covering their faces. They hid their emotions well, but I knew they were just as much of a mess as I was. My mom let the tears fall freely. Even my rambunctious five-year-old niece was quiet.

It was a windy day, but suddenly the gusts died down and things got very still. I opened the container holding Dad's ashes and shook them into the clear, cold water below. We stood, watching them float for a moment on the surface before they sank and disappeared into the sand. In many ways, it had felt like we'd been holding our breath ever since his death; now we could finally exhale. I snapped a photo of the view from the end of the pier. Even without the picture, I knew I would never forget the moment or the place where we laid my father to rest.

Our brief time in Normandy had been filled with emotion and sadness, but the English leg of our European tour began in a very different spirit. We were going to see the mythical—or not so mythical—Hopwood Castle. This was the wildcard part of the trip,

Luc-sur-Mer pier, Normandy, France *Courtesy of the author*

and we were all excited. It felt daring—and a little nuts, exactly the way my father would have wanted it. He always got a kick out of our strange travel adventures, like the time my mother organized a North–South road trip to visit the birthplaces of the US presidents. My dad had a portable, worn leather whiskey kit that he would bring along to enjoy once back at the hotel each night, so I felt certain he would've brought it with us to England on the journey to Hopwood Hall.

As we said goodbye in France, my mom looked as if a weight had been lifted. She was so jazzed to see the Hall. After a period of deep mourning for my dad and grandfather, she was coming back into her old self, wearing a ladybug barrette in her hair, now showing wisps of gray. She was even carrying her purple notebook with educational pamphlets sticking out of the pages. She loved anything to do with family history, and unlike the last genealogical trip we'd taken to Hopwood, Pennsylvania, when I was six years old, at least this time she knew *I* was just as excited as she was. It felt good to do something to make her smile.

My mom, my sister Dana, my brother-in-law, and my niece had already planned to take a passenger boat across the Channel to Southampton on the south coast of England, and they would drive up to Manchester from there. My sister Dori, who is three years older than me and frequently my partner in crime, was going to take a train to the airport with me and then fly to Manchester, where we'd all be reunited again. Dori and I made our way to Paris, where we caught our flight to Manchester. A few hours later, we landed at Manchester Airport and hurried through customs into the airport terminal greeting area.

I looked around for Geoff, who had promised to come and get us. Right away, I spotted a familiar-looking older man, about seventy, with white hair and glasses, smiling widely. Even from a distance he gave off the specific glow of a kind soul. He was wearing a long, tan raincoat and holding a plaid flat cap. He looked very British and exactly as I had expected. As we walked toward him, he stretched out his hand to shake mine.

"Hi, I'm Hopwood," I said.

"And so you are," Geoff said. "The return of the golden son."

My sister tapped me on the arm. "Oh, and this is my sister Dori," I said.

Geoff shook her hand too.

"We've been waiting a long time for you," he told us. "And so has the Hall."

I couldn't quite tell if he was joking or serious.

Outside the terminal, it was pouring rain, the kind of cold, wet, driving rain that in Los Angeles would have been a major weather event. Offices and schools would have been closed. All the TV and radio stations would have been talking about "Rainmageddon." It only rains about thirty-four days a year in LA (we count .01 inch of precipitation as a "rain day"). In Manchester, it's about 140 days—and this major storm seemed to be business as usual. As Geoff walked us toward the car, he didn't even mention the weather.

"Climb in while I put your bags in the boot," he told us.

By now I was too wet and cold to ask exactly how and why he was going to put our bags in his boot. How big *was* his boot? Instead, I sprinted to the front of the car and let myself in, sinking into the seat with relief.

Seconds later, Geoff appeared at the car door. "Are you going to drive?" he asked.

In my excitement to get out of the rain, I'd forgotten that the driver's seat is on the opposite side in England. I apologized, got out, raced around to the passenger side, and clambered in.

Once at the wheel, Geoff turned to me and smiled.

"You're going to have a lot to learn," he said.

We chatted happily with Geoff for the next thirty minutes until we reached our hotel. He dropped us off, informing us he'd pick us up in the morning.

We were staying on the edge of Middleton at a place called the Norton Grange Hotel. Geoff explained it was an old miller's home that had once stood on the Hopwood property. Built in the 1800s, it was a big stone house that had been added onto, eventually being converted into a hotel.

At check-in, the receptionist, a rosy-cheeked young woman with her hair in a ponytail and an enthusiastic smile, greeted us.

"Ya alright?" she asked.

Why is she asking if I'm all right? I thought. *Do I look that tired and disheveled? Maybe my eyes are bloodshot.*

"Hello!" I replied.

"Ya alright?!" she said again.

". . . I think I'm all right. Do I not look all right?"

She just stared at me like I was crazy.

She got in even more of a fluster when she looked at the booking and realized my name was Hopwood. The hotel was located a few miles away from Hopwood Hall—it even had a Hopwood Suite—and now here she was, faced with an actual Hopwood. The poor woman got increasingly overwhelmed as she filled out our forms. She kept calling me "sir" to the point that I wondered if she thought she should be calling me "lord." I reassured her it would be fine to call me by my preschool nickname, Hoppy.

Soon enough, she gave me my key and directed me toward room 210, which she said was on the first floor.

"Wouldn't room 210 be on the second floor?"

"No, that would be 310."

Soon enough I would learn that the British first floor is the American second floor, but right then, it was like I had entered an alternate universe. I must've looked utterly confused, so she clarified.

"Just get in the lift and push 1," she said, gesturing to the elevator.

As the elevator doors opened, I passed another hotel employee.

"Ya alright?" he said.

My gosh, I thought. *I must really look terrible.* Other than one time when I had fallen down a flight of stairs, I'd never had so many people in a row ask me if I was all right. Hopefully I would be.

. . .

*T*he next morning, we got up bright and early to meet with our mom and the other family members who had arrived the night before. As we stood in the lobby waiting for Geoff to pick us up, everyone was doing his or her best to ignore the jet lag that had kept us up half the night.

Despite the early hour, Geoff arrived full of smiles and humming a little tune. I introduced him to my mom and family. Years of dealing with the bereaved in his work as an undertaker had clearly left Geoff an expert in meeting with people who feel out of place, slightly stunned, and unsure of what to do next. He took my mother's arm as we left the hotel. He did magic tricks for my niece, pulling out a shiny coin from behind her ears and giving it to her.

As we were leaving, another woman who worked there looked at me and said, "Ya alright?"

I wanted to spin around and scream "I'M FINE!!!" What the heck was going on?!

I told Geoff that I must look incredibly jet-lagged or ill because everyone in the hotel kept asking me if I was all right.

"Hopwood," Geoff said, smiling and shaking his head. "Almost everyone in the North of England says 'Ya alright?' instead of saying hello. It's nothing personal."

"Oh," I replied. "Well, that's a relief."

Although I couldn't help but think that if Lionel Richie had been from here, his song would've been very different.

My brother-in-law Erik had rented a large van so we could get around. We all climbed in, Geoff included. It had started to rain again, a sort of misty drizzle that would continue for the rest of the day. Compared to Rainmageddon, it was a relief.

In the van, Geoff explained that we were going to meet Bob, the caretaker of Hopwood Hall, who would give us a tour. He also warned us that we couldn't take the original entrance lane to the house because the access was closed off, full of potholes and mud. We would have to go around the back way through the campus of Hopwood Hall College. He said the college had been founded in the early 1990s in some of the training buildings that the De La Salle order of monks had built on part of the estate. After the monks left, the town council took possession and then split off the educational buildings into their own entity to open as a small college that was named after the Hall.

"Queen Elizabeth actually visited in 1992 to celebrate the opening of the college," Geoff told us proudly.

We drove through the college campus and up to a gate where a representative from the council was waiting to let us in. We said our hellos/"ya alrights," and the gate opened. I felt my heart skip a beat as we slowly drove forward. I could feel we were getting closer, and for some strange reason the landscape around me seemed incredibly familiar. We could see a stream, lush fields, and hills beyond that. Cows were grazing. It looked like a painting.

"I can't believe how green it all is!" I kept repeating.

Then we came around a curve in the road. Suddenly, the trees thinned out.

"And there she is," Geoff said, smiling.

The Hall's facade of redbrick and buff-colored stone seemed to glow through the veil of mist and rain. Dozens of chimneys sprouted from its crenellated rooftops, soaring into the heavy gray skies above. Even under clouds, it was a magical sight—the Hall's giant windows appeared to be twinkling at us, capturing whatever light they could and sending it back in our direction. Tiny windowpanes gave the building life, as if the light sparking on them was performing some kind of ancient welcome.

Geoff explained the reason for the dazzling effect. "Those windows are actually made up of hundreds of diamond-shaped individual panes of glass," he told us. "That's why they glimmer like that."

My five-year-old-niece, Jetsen, stared, mesmerized. "Wow . . . those windows look like they're made of jewels," she said.

Geoff also pointed out that above the front of the house, mounted into the brick just below a dramatic row of castellations, there was a large sundial, which was how our ancestors would have told the time in the days before clocks and watches.

We pulled around to the original entrance and got out of the car, unable to go any farther. Between us and the Hall was a thirteen-foot-high security fence topped with razor spikes. Hanging from the fence was a sign that read KEEP OUT: DANGEROUS BUILDING.

Geoff told us the fence had been erected by the town council to deter vandals who broke into the Hall on a regular basis. People had stolen the lead from the roof and precious carvings from the walls, or smashed windows and mirrors.

"Not that the fence has stopped them," Geoff said. "People still try to get over it. Some of them get caught on the spikes, which tends not to be pretty. That's why the locals nicknamed it the Scrotum Shredder."

Waiting for us on the other side of the fencing was a short, stocky man in his fifties with a trimmed beard and messy hair sticking out of a hard hat. He was wearing a bright yellow construction vest.

"You're late!" he barked.

CHAPTER 3

HOPWOOD HALL

Are these the Americans?" the man in the hard hat asked in a gruff, thick-accented voice, adding, "I assumed you would be late . . . since you're Americans."

"Manchester humor," Geoff reassured us before introducing Bob, the caretaker of Hopwood Hall.

"There's nothing humorous about it!" Bob snapped back. "This is the second time the council has asked me to open up this month. I'll be lucky to get paid for it."

With a loud clanging, Bob unlocked the huge padlock holding the security gate shut and let us through.

We shook hands and nodded nervously at Bob, who clearly didn't feel much need to make small talk.

"Let's get on with this tour then," he said.

Bob handed out hard hats and what he called "high-vis" yellow vests. Geoff had already warned us to wear "sturdy shoes" in one of his emails. We hadn't been entirely sure what this meant, but we packed sneakers and hiking boots and hoped for the best.

"Only a third of the building is safe to walk through," Bob warned us. "It's about sixty rooms in total, but just so you know, we can't go in all of those.

"A few rules before we go in," Bob went on. "Don't go running off, and only walk where I tell you to. If you don't listen to me, you may fall through a floor and die. If that does happen and you are wearing a watch, please hold your arm up when you're falling so that when you land, I can easily collect your watch to sell it later."

My mother looked at me, a bit baffled.

"Manchester humor!" I whispered, in an attempt to clarify Bob's rules for her.

We followed Bob as he clomped toward the Hall. From a distance, Hopwood Hall had looked spectacular, but on closer inspection, it was clear it had seen better days. Its sparkling windows were cracked and broken. There were small trees growing out of the chimneys. Out front, a giant dumpster overflowed with debris and garbage.

This should have been my first clue that Hopwood Hall wasn't going to look much like the stately homes I'd seen on *Masterpiece Theatre*. In my mind, however, I was still picturing some kind of Downton Abbey. This was more like Downton Shabby.

After Bob's somewhat rude welcome, I had to hold myself back from asking him: "If you're the caretaker here, what exactly are you taking care of?!"

"Okay," Bob declared. "Let's gather 'round."

We did. Bob was standing in front of a pair of giant wooden double doors.

"You're looking at the old carriage entrance to the Hall," he told us.

Bob pointed to the thick, rough pieces of dark wood joined together with battered-looking steel rivets and metal clasps and decorations.

"Carpenters on the estate would have built these doors from timber chopped in the Hopwood Woods, and then the resident blacksmiths would have forged the rivets and the hinges," he continued. "Everything would have been made right here on the estate. You can still see the hammer marks."

He showed us the tiny indentations made by a blacksmith five hundred years ago. We all made appreciative "wow" and cooing noises.

"And here, you can also see where someone from the gas company drilled a hole in the door when they installed a dehumidifier to try to help with the damp, circa 2012," Bob continued, bringing us all back down to earth. "Just one of the many things at Hopwood Hall that needs fixing."

Then he braced his shoulder against the ancient entranceway and gave a shove until the doors swung open, making a deep creaking noise.

We stepped inside the hall. Ahead of us was a high limestone archway leading into a courtyard with soaring redbrick walls and more leaded glass windows filled with square-shaped panes on three sides. Thick flagstones were under our feet. Bob told us that this was where the carriages would have come in, dropping off passengers, before turning around and exiting again.

"If you had come here in the eighteenth century," Geoff described, "there would have been more people working on the estate than the entire population of Middleton. All the staff would have come out to greet you when you arrived."

I tried to picture butlers, footmen, and maids peering out the windows, then rushing outside to line up and welcome us. A prettier picture for sure than Bob glaring at us in his hard hat . . .

To our left was a small chapel, built in 1690, where the family worshipped when they didn't feel like making the trek to the local church, said Geoff. To the right was a part of the house Bob described as the Guards' Room.

"These are actually the newer parts of the Hall," he told us. "They were built during the reign of King James II."

Newer? He was talking about buildings that were a century older than America! I wondered if Bob was uninformed and had somehow gotten his timeline wrong.

Geoff and Bob led the way and we followed, walking into the Guards' Room.

We found ourselves standing in a large empty space, an ornate plaster ceiling over our heads decorated with flowers and other patterns and cracked and peeling walls painted in a faded mint green.

"During the 1600s, this room is where you would have been searched for weapons before being allowed to enter the Hall," said Bob.

"Kind of like a medieval TSA!" I laughed, pleased with my joke. Bob didn't smile, but I felt the need to keep the mood light.

Ahead of us was a giant, imposing stone fireplace with columns on either side. Bob pointed out that there were dogs' heads carved into the tops of the columns, their noses protruding as if they were about to bite.

"The dogs look quite angry," Bob told us. "No one is sure why. Maybe they had to get up early to greet visitors at the Hall!"

"It's beautiful," I told Bob, who seemed to visibly soften with the compliment.

We walked up a couple of steps into an even grander room, painted the same shade of green, that Geoff described as the Reception Hall.

"This is where guests would have met the family and been offered something to eat," he explained.

The room was large, with high ceilings and a long bank of tall windows with stone mullions at one end looking out over the courtyard. I tried hard to picture the Hopwoods greeting their guests in grand *Downton Abbey* style, but it wasn't easy. Old paint unfurled forlornly from the walls, damp patches seeped from the plaster, and electrical cables dangled from the ceilings. A lonely ladder was propped against the windows, black plastic trash bags filled with who knows what were dumped on the floor, and there were various unidentified tools lying around covered in a coat of dust. Bob led us toward another stone fireplace—this one decorated with one of the Hopwood family coat of arms and emblazoned with the motto "By Degrees" on either side. The coat of arms was in the shape of a shield with an adjacent stag.

We had no idea that we had a motto, let alone a coat of arms! We snapped photos eagerly with our phones.

"Maybe we should all get matching tattoos," I whispered to Dori, who laughed.

Then Bob showed us what he described as his "pride and joy." These were long tables in the middle of the Reception Hall covered with bits and pieces of debris and rubble. Anytime anything fell from the walls or the ceilings—a shard of molding, an ancient chunk of wood—he would pick it up and put it here, along with little maps indicating where the pieces originated from. Bob seemed to derive a lot of pleasure from his tables and maps, but what he was showing us seemed to be a kind of artifact graveyard.

"One day, maybe we'll have the money and support to put all of these bits back where they came from." Bob sighed.

Next, Geoff and Bob led us into what they called the Gallery,

The fireplace in the Reception Hall, Hopwood Hall Estate *Matt Wilkinson*

The Hopwood family motto inscribed on the Reception Hall fireplace
Courtesy of the author

which was a long corridor lined with dark wood paneling and the same square-shaped leaded glass windows we had seen from outside in the courtyard. Geoff asked us to imagine the place as it would have been: an elegantly furnished space, its walls hung with oil paintings of our ancestors, some of them dating back centuries.

I looked around me, trying to follow his prompt, imagining how sumptuous it would have been in its heyday, and doing my best to ignore the giant yellow damp patches making menacing patterns on the intricate plasterwork on the ceiling. What would this place have looked like with some lavish velvet drapes in front of the leaded windows, instead of the broken panes letting in rain, I wondered?

"On days when it rained or it was too hot to go outside," Geoff explained, "this was where the family would take their daily walks, up and down the corridor instead of 'taking a turn' in the gardens. See the large alcove midway down, with the tall windows? That would have provided a perfect well-lit spot to sit and read a book or perhaps to study sheet music or do embroidery."

Then Bob warned us to watch our heads as we ducked under a low wooden beam to access a small, partially hidden recessed sitting area at the far end of the Gallery that he called the inglenook.

This was the smallest area we'd been in so far, lined with the same kind of dark wood paneling as the Gallery. Although the inglenook was small in scale, it was dominated by another stunning stone fireplace, this one with a crest hanging over it painted in stripes of blue, gold, and red.

"You're now looking at the Lord Byron fireplace," Geoff declared. "See how the left corner of the fireplace is marked with the number 16 and the right corner with 58? This means the fireplace was made in 1658. Back then, your America was just a cluster of British colonies."

Even my niece Jetsen was hanging on his words. Geoff explained that it was called the Byron fireplace because it was thought to belong to the famous Romantic-era poet Lord Byron.

"In 1811, in the early days of his career, Byron was a guest of the Hopwood family and stayed at the house," Geoff recounted. "At the time, he was trying to sell off parts of his estate in nearby

Rochdale, possibly including the enormous stone fireplace you see before you."

During Byron's visit, the Hopwood family must have agreed to take the outsized fireplace, because it had been here ever since.

"Some people think the fireplace was a thank you gift to the Hopwood family for letting Byron stay and finish work on his world-famous poem 'Childe Harold's Pilgrimage.'"

I didn't like to admit that I hadn't heard of the poem. Luckily, Geoff was there to give us a potted history.

"During his stay, Byron liked to wander through the nearby Hopwood Woods, waiting for inspiration to strike. Which must have happened, because by the time he left Hopwood Hall, he had completed 'Childe Harold's Pilgrimage,' which made his name as a poet."

But Byron wasn't the only world-famous artist to visit during the 1800s. There was even a rumor that the legendary composer and pianist Frédéric Chopin may have visited the Hall while on tour in the area in the mid-nineteenth century.

"In its glory days, it was that kind of place—it attracted the best of the best." Geoff smiled.

Next, Geoff told us to turn our attention to the plasterwork on the ceiling above our heads, shaped with rosettes and twisting vines.

"This ceiling work was installed in the early 1900s by the architect Edgar Wood, who was from Middleton and a leading member of the Arts and Crafts movement," he explained. "Designers like Wood rejected the mass production of the Industrial Revolution and wanted a return to architectural elements that were made by hand using time-honored techniques."

Geoff went on, revealing the layers of history so we could appreciate the work and care that had gone into the Hall's creation, showing us how, even in its current neglected state, there was so much to appreciate and admire.

"The inglenook would have been a very special place for the owners," our guide went on. "This is where you would come to sit and relax by the hearth and perhaps have a glass of wine or brandy. And unlike the rest of the house, which would have been cold and drafty, this actually would have been the warmest and coziest place in the Hall."

We went back into the Gallery and kept walking.

"Next, we're going to see the Oak Parlor, the oldest room in the house," Bob explained, resuming his role as tour guide. "This would have been part of the original structure back when the Hall was built in medieval times—around the 1420s."

The 1420s? I quickly did the math for Jetsen.

"That's two hundred years before the Pilgrims arrived in America," I told her. "In other words, if George Washington's great-grandparents had visited Hopwood Hall, they would have thought it was old."

Geoff quickly jumped in to explain that it was possible there was a building on this site much earlier than 1420, perhaps a previous home or hunting lodge that would likely be discovered by archaeologists in the future.

"In fact, we have written records that show evidence that your family tree goes all the way back to the 1200s and likely the Norman Conquest of England in 1066. After that, William the Conqueror divided the country into various estates, granting them to his French and Norman allies. The knights of Hopwood de Hopwood would have been given the estate sometime around then. They went on to rule over this area for many centuries—taking their name from the surrounding area, *hop* meaning a small, enclosed valley, like the one where this house is located, surrounded by woods."

In 1066? I had been impressed with the fireplace from 1658! I couldn't help but knock myself on the head for not listening more to Pap. If the kindergarten bullies had known I was related to knights, they probably would've shut their mouths! I could've challenged them to a joust on the playground.

"Your ancestor, the knight John Hopwood, is the one who built the redbrick structure you see when you approach the house today. In fact, Hopwood Hall is one of the only examples of Tudor brickwork in the North of England—John Hopwood must have visited the south and decided he wanted his own place in the latest architectural style."

We followed Geoff and Bob into the Oak Parlor. Right away, the air around us felt different, colder and damper than before, as if we'd traveled back even further in time. This was unlike anything we'd seen before. Over our heads, long, dark wooden beams met at dramatic intersections, but it was the walls in this room that really drew our attention. Made of wood paneling, almost black in color, they were decorated with incredibly intricate carvings, stretching from the baseboards to the ceiling.

Everywhere we looked, there was something else to catch the eye. Carved columns and arches held little carved figures clasping crosses and chalices, surrounded by flowers, birds, and twisting vegetation. Bob and Geoff began to point out some of the highlights: carved scenes of people playing musical instruments, including a man with a viol, an instrument from the 1500s. Geoff gestured to a figure of a bearded man who—inexplicably—was holding a pitchfork with a disembodied head on it. There were carvings of

The Jacobethan overmantel in the Oak Parlor, Hopwood Hall Estate *Andy Marshall*

pineapples and tulips, exotic luxuries of the times, signs of the Hopwoods' hospitality and success. Another series of panels featured carvings of roses, thistles, and daffodils to represent England, Scotland, and Wales.

Geoff also showed us a very special panel inscribed with the letters and numbers ES1689.

"We believe this was to commemorate the marriage of Elizabeth of Speke to one of the Hopwood sons in 1689," Geoff said helpfully. "At the time, the family built a new banquet room to celebrate the marriage."

"As one would do," I joked, adding that I couldn't believe I was standing only two feet away from what was probably one of my ancestors' wedding gifts from three hundred years ago.

"We actually had the timbers in these walls dendrodated," Bob interjected. "That's where you test the wood to find out how old it is. That's how we know there are timbers here from 1426."

The dates were just unbelievable to me. Astonished, I looked over at my mom, who seemed completely in awe as well. All I could think was that nearly six hundred years ago, this is where my ancestors ate, slept, and lived their lives. That this was where it all began.

"Before anyone invented chimneys," Geoff told us, as if reading my mind, "your ancestors would just light a fire in the middle of the room, and the smoke would escape through a hole in the thatched roof."

According to Geoff, this long history meant the Hopwood family had survived through every major event in English history, from the Crusades in the twelfth and thirteenth centuries to the Plague in the 1300s that killed millions of people across Europe to the War of the Roses in the fifteenth century. They had endured through every war, famine, and natural disaster after that, all the way until the First World War.

"Which is when we lost the Hall's two male heirs, Edward and Robert, and we feared the Hopwood line had died out forever. That is, until you came along," he said as he and Bob led us into the adjoining room.

Again, we were in a space lined with dark wood paneling, but without the detailed carving of the Oak Parlor. We picked our way carefully across the floor, which was missing many boards and scattered with chunks of plaster that had doubtless fallen from the ceiling overhead. Yet another enormous fireplace anchored the room. This one was carved from wood, stretching from floor to ceiling and decorated with rows of delicate little spindles, some of them lined up like pins in a bowling alley and others in the shape of beautiful rosettes.

"We're standing now in what would have been the birthing room," Bob explained. "This is where your fourteenth great-grandfather would have been born."

I was blown away. To be standing next to the exact same fireplace my fourteenth great-grandfather stood next to six centuries ago. How many people get to hang out in the room where their fourteenth great-grandfather was born? I put out a hand and carefully put my fingertips on the fireplace, as if I doubted any of this was real.

From there, Bob explained he had one last room to show us that was of great historic significance. What could be more important than the room where our distant ancestors had been born?

"Walk this way," Bob told us. He led us through a narrow door, stepping over missing floorboards, up a short flight of stairs, before turning down a long, wide hallway and through another large doorway.

"Ta-da! The disco!" he exclaimed, giggling when he saw the confused looks on our faces.

In front of us was a long, cavernous space. The walls were painted black and graffitied with peace signs, piano keys, and music notes. One wall was emblazoned with the words "GET DOWN AND BOOGIE!" It felt like we'd stumbled into a college dormitory bar. After the historic Oak Parlor and the birthing room, this was definitely a bit of a contrast.

"The Hopwoods had a nightclub?" I asked, flabbergasted. It was true that I had been known to enjoy a night out at the clubs of LA, but I had no idea that my aristocratic forebears felt the same way.

"The monks who lived here started it," Geoff said, confusing us even further.

"The monks?" said Jetsen, wrinkling her forehead.

"Yes, the De La Salle Brothers lived here from the late 1940s to the '80s," Geoff explained. "They ran a teacher training college in the building. The downstairs rooms were lecture rooms, and the upstairs bedrooms were split up to make dorms. But the monks knew they had to do something to generate income to help with the upkeep of the Hall. And so they installed a full working bar and nightclub in this room so that the college students could book their favorite up-and-coming bands for entertainment."

"If you can believe it," Geoff added, "Ozzy Osbourne is supposed to have played here. Of course, that probably didn't go over too well with the monks! Legend has it that Sharon Osbourne threw a beer at Ozzy onstage. UB40 and Madness performed here too. Some people even say that John Lennon once drove over from Liverpool to help out a friend's band."

My head was spinning. Lord Byron. Chopin. And now Ozzy Osbourne and John Lennon? It was almost too much for my brain to process.

We followed Bob out of the nightclub and down yet another hallway. Ahead of us was a dilapidated staircase, its banisters hanging lopsidedly and boards missing from the treads.

"We won't be able to go into this section of the house," our guide told us. "As you can see, it's not safe. And so hereby concludes our tour."

We thanked Bob for taking time out of his day to show us around. We made sure he knew about how incredible it was to be here, how impressed we were with the Hall and what an amazing historic monument it was.

"Yeah," Bob agreed. "And if nothing is done to save it, it'll be gone in five to ten years."

Wait a minute—gone? "Are you serious?" I asked him.

"Look at the place," Bob said, gesturing around him. "The stairs are falling down. There's water leaking in, vines growing through the walls. The place is full of dry rot. It's crumbling. Each winter there's more rain, more mold, more plants, more insects. I do my best, but there's only so much I can do to patch everything up. In a few years Hopwood Hall will be beyond repair. Next time you come back, it might well be rubble."

Five to ten years left? For a house that had been here for at least six hundred years? We were standing in the middle of a structure that had been built in the 1400s, where Lord Byron had stayed and wrote poems, where Sharon Osbourne threw beer at Ozzy, where countless generations of my ancestors had lived and thrived . . . This place was important to British history, to the heritage of the nation! And it was going to be nothing but dust in a handful of years?

"But that's crazy!" we told our guides.

I felt a frustration bubbling up within me that the Hall was now at this point of destruction. If there had been a plant stand nearby, I probably would've had an outburst and pushed it over.

Bob shrugged. Geoff looked at us sadly. We could tell they didn't like it any more than we did; it was just that they'd had longer to get used to the idea.

"Bob and I care about the Hall," Geoff explained. "And so do a lot of the older people around here. It's not such a stretch for us to imagine it as it once was. But I worry that a younger generation doesn't feel that same connection to the place or to its history. What's going to happen when we shuffle off this mortal coil, as Shakespeare said? Who will care then if Hopwood Hall is still standing?"

Maybe it was the jet lag, or maybe it was the fact that we had just scattered my dad's ashes, but by now I was completely spellbound by the Hall, Middleton, the whole history of the place. I told Geoff and Bob I would do whatever I could to help save the Hall from oblivion. Maybe we could make a donation, throw a fundraiser, help them write a grant proposal? I wasn't sure. Bob quickly informed us that to save a structure like Hopwood Hall would take all the above and a whole lot more. My sister Dana, a whiz at math, and her husband, Erik, a contractor, began adding up what it might cost, while my sister Dori, the researcher, began scrolling through potential grant sources on her phone. My mother put her arm around Jetsen, explaining to her the importance of saving history for future generations.

I scratched my head. I was inspired but also daunted. How many millions of pounds would it take to restore this place to some semblance of its original state? The look in my eyes must have been one that Bob had seen before in others after he'd shown them the Hall—dazzled by its beauty but overwhelmed by its current state of rack and ruin. Rather than stand there and debate the possibilities, Bob cleared his throat.

"Well, I know you Americans would like to make us poor English people keep working," he muttered, "but at some point, I need to have my dinner."

We all laughed. Except for Bob.

We knew we had stayed much longer than expected. There was no doubt that walking through the Hall surveying the degree of the decay had brought its own emotional exhaustion to all of us, including Bob.

It was time to go. We walked back through the Guards' Room and into the courtyard, through the old wooden doors and toward the steel gate with its padlocks and chains.

We said goodbye to Bob at the gate. As we shook hands, I was starting to realize I had completely underestimated Bob. What he lacked in social niceties, he more than made up for in his determination to preserve the near wreck that was the Hall. Without Bob, the house would doubtless have been rubble a long, long time ago.

I looked the savior of Hopwood Hall in the eyes.

"Bob, you rock!" I blurted out.

Bob looked back at me incredulously. His face broke into a grin. Then he started laughing.

"Who *are* you?" he asked.

CHAPTER 4

LORDS OF HOLLYWOOD

*O*nce back in LA, I quickly settled into my usual routine: a trip to the gym at LA Fitness on Hollywood Boulevard to start the day, followed by the Coffee Bean for a sugar-free skinny vanilla ice-blended, and then on to pitch meetings for work.

Back then, my life was one long to-do list, my days measured out in hours, my calendar filled with meetings and appointments. My MO in those days went something along the lines of make calls, make things happen, get a spray tan, check, check, check. This was the norm. It was how everyone I knew spent their days. In LA, if things slow down, you schedule a lunch, you talk about another project. As soon as you finish one project, you've already started another one. If you don't have something going on, you talk to someone and make something else happen.

After working long days, my busy schedule didn't stop. In

Hollywood, going to social events is part of the job—it's what you do. Besides, I knew that if I went home, I'd be alone and all the old fears about falling behind in life would start creeping up on me.

My friend Jonny, a charismatic all-American former Dolce & Gabbana model turned liquor distributor (what a combination!), always had a suggestion of an event or party or two, and so every night of the week we had a plan. Often it was the opening of a new restaurant or club, the ones that people read about in magazines that have reservation lists six months long, but somehow Jonny was able to miraculously walk in without any notice whatsoever and get seated at the best table in the house. It was his job.

In a town where many people's friendships burn out after a couple of years, I had known Jonny for thirteen. Of course, it's no surprise we met at a club. With blond spiky hair, a sleeveless shirt, and sunglasses on, my friend stood out in a room. At the time, he was dating an aspiring actress I knew named Jennie Bounce—who quite fittingly loved to get on the dance floor and jump up and down. After the club closed, somehow we all ended up in a friend's limo being driven around the streets of Hollywood while the party continued. I immediately clicked with Jonny—he was happy and fun and always up for the next Hollywood adventure. We have been friends ever since.

On a Thursday night, a few days after I returned from England, I'd arranged to meet up with him at Bootsy Bellows on Sunset and Doheny, a swanky LA hotspot founded by actor David Arquette and designed to feel like Frank Sinatra's 1940s home, with low-hanging gold lamps, indoor palm trees, and a mirrored bar.

"How was London?" Jonny shouted over the DJ.

"Great. Actually, I was in Manchester."

He furrowed his eyebrows. I think he'd only been looking for a one-word answer.

"Manchester?! Why? Did you see a soccer game?" he said.

"No. I was tracing my genealogy," I admitted.

"Is that something to do with denim?" he said with a smile.

I knew he was joking, but for some reason I felt the need to clarify.

"No, genealogy, the study of family ancestry. I went to a place called Hopwood Hall—it's my family's ancestral seat!" I suddenly found myself spilling the beans.

I could see Jonny's eyes immediately flicker as he saw someone over my shoulder.

"Hellooo!" he erupted to a beautiful young model standing behind me.

I suddenly felt like Mr. Bouman, my high school history teacher, stuck in the middle of a bumpin' club. I hastily put down my drink and joined Jonny's conversation about the details of the afterparty.

Slightly hungover the next morning, I pulled myself out of bed after staying awake most of the night due to my jet lag. I was booked for lunch with my square-jawed talent manager, Jay—a young lookalike of actor Michael Douglas. We met at Villa Blanca, with its streetside outdoor café tables perfectly perched for people-watching near the sunny corner of Rodeo Drive and Brighton Way in Beverly Hills. Although Jay is my manager, he's also my best friend. We've known each other since our teens, first meeting in the summer beach resort of Macatawa, Michigan, after we both snuck into the bar through the kitchen entrance (since neither one of us were old enough to be in a bar). Jay went on to graduate top of his law school class at Pepperdine University, becoming the youngest vice president of MGM, and then formed his own management company, ROAR, in Beverly Hills, representing well-known actors like Chris Hemsworth and musicians like the Zac Brown Band. Jay was one of my first friends to jump onboard with me dropping the name Tod and going by Hopwood.

When I began to share the details of my trip to England and the discovery of Hopwood Hall, he listened intently, shaking and nodding his head at all the right moments.

"I'm glad you're finally waking up!" he said. "Owning your past is key. How insane is it to think you spent years trying to pretend your name wasn't Hopwood, when all along there was an actual castle named after you. . . . If you'd only known!"

Although Jay was clearly more interested in my family ancestry than Jonny had been, I knew he probably had fifteen meetings lined up after mine, so we got down to business.

"We've got a new job prospect for you," he explained. "It's consulting for a production company in Chicago. They want you to come in to pitch ideas for television shows to air on a new closed-cable network that McDonald's is launching in all their restaurants."

Turns out it was called, quite fittingly, the McDonald's Channel. Apparently, McDonald's was trying to figure out a way to entertain people while they sat and ate their cheeseburgers. Obviously, McDonald's has a lot of restaurants and a lot of customers—"billions and billions served"—so as Jay pointed out, there was potential.

Jay and I said our goodbyes, and I promised I'd come up with a list of ideas in the next week or so.

But instead of having dreams about the Hamburglar, the morning after my meeting with Jay, I woke up thinking about the Hall. I decided to quickly check the weather report in Manchester. The forecast was 100 percent chance of rain, all day.

Hmm, I thought, *I wonder if the Hall is all right.*

Bob had given me his email address, so I decided to drop him a line. First, I thanked him for our tour and all the time and trouble he'd taken to show my family the house. Before I signed off, I told him that I'd noticed that the forecast was heavy rain all week.

"Will everything be okay with the roof?" I asked.

"No," Bob replied, blunt as ever. "There are massive gaps up there where we're missing the protective lead sheeting. We lost another section of the decorative ceiling just this week."

I told Bob that I was already thinking of ways to raise money to help the Hall and that I would stay in touch.

Shutting my laptop, I felt slightly devastated.

Over the next few weeks, the Hall was constantly on my mind. Then one Monday morning I received an urgent email from Bob saying there had been a terrible storm and water had leaked into the Library. Bob explained that the problem was that no one had been into the Hall for a week or so; the leakage problem had gone unnoticed, and, as a result, it was worse than it had ever been before, and may even have reactivated a patch of dry rot. Apparently, dry rot is a fungus that can lay dormant in woodwork, but once a bit of water hits it, it can act like a sponge—absorbing and growing. Sitting on my upper deck overlooking Hollywood and the skyscrapers of downtown Los Angeles in the distance, it sounded like a bizarre alien life-form I had read about in a movie script. I forwarded Bob's email to my mother and sisters knowing they would be concerned too. Then it dawned on me that I was more than "concerned." Perhaps I was becoming . . . obsessed!

I took a deep breath and walked down the narrow outdoor spiral staircase.

When I first bought my house, I'd thought it was impressively old. It was built in 1920 and designed in the Art Deco Spanish style of Hollywood's golden era. Local legend had it that Marilyn Monroe had once housesat there to care for a cat. Or maybe it was that she'd visited the house and accidentally sat on a cat? Either way, I was eager to celebrate the connection, hanging in the front bedroom a small vintage photo of Marilyn that I'd bought at a yard sale. The house's links to the past didn't end there. In the lower level was a former garage recording studio where the Top 20 hit song "The Future's So Bright, I Gotta Wear Shades" was recorded in 1986. When people came over, I used to tell them I loved the place's sense of history.

But my "historic" Hollywood home no longer felt quite so old. Even my "antique" Marilyn photo looked like a prop.

Later that day, Jay called to see how I was getting on with the McDonald's job. I told him I was making progress, although the truth was I was struggling to even start. After we hung up, I sat down with my laptop and tried to come up with five ideas. I drew a blank. Nothing. Typically, I was able to come up with ideas quite quickly. But this time, not a thing. A few hours passed; still nothing. I poured a glass of wine.

All I could think about was the Hall.

CHAPTER 5

THE BATTLE OF FLODDEN

*I*n mid-June, an email from Geoff appeared in my inbox.

> Hi Hopwood,
>
> Hope you and your family are all well and enjoying the summer weather.
>
> You mentioned about coming back. If perchance you were here in September, we are having a civic service to commemorate the Battle of Flodden Field on Sunday, 8th September, and I have been asked to invite you. I appreciate it's a big ask so just bear it in mind.
>
> Geoff

Even before I'd left the UK, Geoff had said something about the commemoration, so I was aware that the locals were going to be celebrating the anniversary of a five-hundred-year-old battle. As

Geoff kindly explained, the bloody Battle of Flodden was fought between the English and the Scottish, near the border of the two countries on September 9, 1513. The English had prevailed, helped by the famed "Middleton archers."

Geoff had filled us in: "Your Hopwood ancestors were among those archers who helped defeat the kingdom of Scotland and win the ultimate victory for the English," he told us. "Those Middleton archers could rain arrows down on the approaching enemy at a rapid rate that no one could keep up with, thereby assuring the Scots lost."

I quickly replied to Geoff's email, telling him I would consider attending.

In his follow-up email, Geoff told me that if I did come, he'd love for me to be a guest of honor and speak at the commemoration ceremony of the ancient stained-glass window in the local medieval church, St. Leonard's. The church window had been installed five hundred years ago to memorialize the events of Flodden Field, and it featured small portraits in colored glass of the famed Middleton archers. Not only that, it is generally regarded as England's oldest surviving war memorial and definitely worth commemorating. Over the centuries, the beautiful window had become dull and dirty, but with the milestone anniversary approaching, Geoff had arranged for the window to be meticulously cleaned and repaired.

Geoff also asked if we'd like to go with him to visit Flodden Field itself on the anniversary of the battle.

"It's a once-in-a-lifetime opportunity," Geoff said. "Well, unless you plan to live another five hundred years."

The more he said, the more I realized it was going to be difficult to turn down an invitation like that. Especially from an undertaker!

"It would mean so much to so many people to have a Hopwood there," he emphasized.

The whole idea of a second trip to England, and this time Scotland, quickly snowballed. Bev from the council must've heard I was considering returning for the commemoration, because soon enough, I received the following email:

Dear Hopwood,

   In my spare time I do archery and my club is organising a commemorative tournament for the Flodden anniversary. It's quite similar to the way that the archers at Flodden would have shot in battle, although we shoot at flags, not Scotsmen. So if you do decide to come to the service for the Flodden window, you would be most welcome to come to our event as well. If you're able to attend the main shoot, would you consider being our Lord Patron? You wouldn't have to do anything except open the shoot and chat to folks for awhile.

   Best regards,

   Bev Percival

   Rochdale Borough Council

Never before had I been asked to be a Lord Patron.

A chance to be the guest of honor and the Lord Patron?! Perhaps a splash of local hospitality was exactly what I needed at this point! I was suddenly fantasizing about phoning McDonald's and telling them that, as much as I loved their McNuggets and appreciated the opportunity, I would need to cancel the meeting, as I was now off to England to fulfill my destiny.

But instead of calling McDonald's, I dialed my sister Dori. I was curious to hear what she thought. After all, we'd only just gone to England, and it seemed a bit extravagant to get on a plane to cross the Atlantic for the second time in a year.

"Well, how the heck could you say no to an honor like that?!" she asked, as though I was wasting her time. "Of course you're going to do it."

I agreed. I couldn't wait to say yes to all of it.

Little did I realize that "open the shoot" actually meant "shoot the first arrow." Bev must've mistakenly assumed that, since I was a Hopwood, it went without saying that I would instinctively know how to shoot arrows.

Of course, nothing could be further from the truth.

In the coming weeks, I was regularly in touch with Geoff as we hatched the plan for the trip. My mom, Dori and Dana, my brother-in-law Erik, and Jetsen all decided that they too couldn't miss the chance and wanted to come along for the ride. Jetsen went to a school in Michigan that encouraged travel and offered online learning when students were away. Dana felt Jetsen would learn much more by actually going to Flodden Field rather than hearing about it from me later or reading about it in a book. My family would fly together from Michigan, I would fly in from Los Angeles, and we'd meet up again at the Norton Grange Hotel.

When I told Jonny I was going to Flodden Field, he said, "Is that a bar or a movie?"

Jay suggested that if I was going to spend time away from LA, I should at least use the experience to come up with a movie pitch about the ancient battle. It turns out that ROAR was already looking for a new role in a "battle pic" for Chris Hemsworth. "A working vacation," Jay called it.

As September approached, I couldn't wait to return to the land of my ancestors.

It was a little past midnight when my plane touched down in Manchester. I made my way through passport control and customs, then pulled my wheelie suitcase through a puddle and found the taxi stand. A line of English black cabs awaited, looking just like the ones in every British TV show or movie I'd ever watched. I love English black cabs and was so excited to get into one. Someone had told me that black cab drivers have to go to school for several years so they know every street and cul de sac, down to the smallest back alley. If you throw out an address, they will know where it is. No questions asked.

I jumped into one, ready to try it out.

"Hi, to the Norton Grange Hotel in Middleton, please," I said.

"Uhh . . . what's the postcode?" he asked.

"I'm sorry?"

"What's the postcode?"

"I have no idea. What is a postcode? Is that like a zip code?" I asked, confused.

"Yes."

"How in the heck would I know the hotel's zip code?"

"Well, we can't get there without the postcode."

As I would later learn, in England, somehow people make sure to know the postcode of where they are going before they go there. Meanwhile, in America, many people don't even know their own zip code, let alone someone else's! I decided to turn on my phone and incur the roaming charges so I could google search the hotel to determine the postcode. Clearly, if this was going to be a regular occurrence, I was going to need to invest in getting myself a UK phone.

"OL112XZ," I said, then paused, thinking, *Is that an O or a zero?* If the postcode is *so* incredibly important in finding a location, why on earth would they use both Os and zeros? If I accidentally said the wrong one, could it take us two hundred miles in the wrong direction!

I held my breath. I was jet-lagged and hungry, and this cab driver had somehow cheated his way through Cab College.

We drove for nearly an hour, much, much longer than when Geoff had driven us only a few months before. It was pitch-black, raining, and the only thing I could see through the windshield was solid fog. The driver cranked up the Jason Derulo on the radio and drove faster. I was terrified. I wondered if I was going to be found dead in one of those slate-roofed barns I'd seen from the plane.

Eventually, we pulled up to the Norton Grange Hotel. I was so relieved, I didn't even mind when the cabbie charged me extortion rates, since the shiny, colored British pounds felt like play money from one of Jetsen's board games.

Inside, the lobby of the Norton Grange was warm and welcoming with a plate of sugar cookies set out for arriving guests and a small Christmas tree leaning slightly askew in the corner, even though it was only September.

"YA ALRIGHT?!" The receptionist shouted at me as I walked in.

This time I was prepared.

"Yes. You?" I fired back, in the way that Geoff had taught me to do.

She smiled and gave a single head nod. Clearly, I had finally answered correctly!

Within minutes, I fell into my bed and was quickly asleep.

I awoke completely startled by my cell phone alarm. I didn't know where I was, but I did know I was incredibly jet-lagged.

Meanwhile, I had an email from my mom saying they had landed and were on their way to the hotel. They had rented a van, and Erik was driving. They would be here in a half hour. I hurriedly jumped in the shower, packed up, and headed to the lobby to meet them.

When the family arrived, everyone was buzzing with excitement. Unfortunately, the van they had ordered wasn't available and they'd been given a smaller one. It was a tight fit, but we all piled in and headed over to Geoff's house, a stately redbrick Victorian home perched atop a small hill, overlooking the road that led to Manchester. The home was what Bob would have called "modern" (meaning it was built in the 1800s).

Geoff was ready, waiting for us in front of the house. He quickly climbed in the back of the van. With all of us and our luggage, it was a very full ride. I had my suitcase on my lap, and I was so tired that I passed out drooling on the case as it propped up my head for the three-and-a-half-hour journey.

After what seemed to me like a few drowsy and bewildered head-jerking minutes later, we arrived in the twelfth-century village of Branxton, near Flodden Field in Northumberland on the border of Scotland. I had slept through the trip, waking to find myself peeking out through tinted windows of the air-conditioned minivan with Beyoncé playing in the background. Outside the window were deep green fields and hills, overcast skies, and small houses made from flint and stone. It was bleak yet undeniably beautiful.

"Your ancestors would have traveled these same two hundred miles from Middleton on foot or horseback, over the course of many days, ready for the fight but fearing for their lives," Geoff intoned, ever the historian.

We clambered out, and Geoff led the way up a sloping hill. The grass was damp, covered in dew, and ahead we could see a large stone monument erected in the distance. Geoff was like an excited kid, and he and Jetsen had an extra pep in their step to get to the top.

As we looked out over the ancient battlefield, Geoff gave us another one of his history lessons: "If you want to understand what happened here five hundred years ago, you need to start in May 1513. That was the month that King Henry VIII—the English king who liked to chop off the heads of his wives—decided to invade France. At the time, Scotland was allied with France against the English, so in retaliation for the French invasion, King James IV of Scotland decided to invade *England*. He assembled the largest Scottish army ever seen south of the border, some twenty-five thousand men or more, and got ready for the fight. The problem was, James decided to notify Henry of his invasion plan a month earlier, and so when the Scots got to England, the English were ready and waiting. Not only that, the Scots lacked artillery, having spent much of their firepower in helping the French fight. At Flodden, the Scots were met by an army of twenty thousand Englishmen armed heavily with bows and arrows."

The ensuing battle took place on September 9, 1513, and it was a disaster for the Scots. Up to ten thousand members of the Scottish army were killed, including the king.

We all stood there for a moment in silence, surveying the scene, before Geoff led us back down the hill, toward a long ditch at the bottom. He slowed his walk, speaking in hushed tones.

"This ditch was where most of the casualties occurred. In this exact spot on this exact day, five hundred years ago, about ten thousand bodies would have been laying here, moaning or already deceased. Perhaps even that of James IV."

Jetsen hid her face. The rest of us looked around, trying to take it all in.

Locations where a battle has been fought have a stillness about them, a heaviness in the air, as if the atmosphere is thick with lingering souls. I'd felt it on the sandy beaches of Normandy, and despite the vast difference in landscape, I felt the same thing standing looking out over the rolling green expanse of Flodden Field. The whole experience was chilling, and made the ancient past feel not so far from the present.

A few hours later, we settled into the Wheatsheaf Inn, a modest but comfortable bed-and-breakfast in nearby Duns, Scotland. There was a small bar off the lobby, and Geoff soon struck up conversation with a jovial group of locals. When Geoff told his new friends that our ancestors had fought at Flodden Field, they were excited to meet us. It turned out their ancestors had fought in the battle too.

"Except you're the *enemy!*" a large redheaded Scottish man declared, staring directly at me.

As I quickly glanced around for Erik to see if he might have my back in a barroom brawl, the redheaded man smiled and guffawed loudly. It was hard to believe that we shared a connection dating back five centuries.

"Perhaps we should have a toast!" our Scottish friend suggested.

Almost immediately, the finest Scotch whisky was brought out from behind the bar.

"To old enemies who are new friends!" the redheaded man said as everyone in his group raised their glasses and we raised ours.

Within a few minutes, Erik and I had pulled up chairs around their large wooden table. We learned that the best way to drink whisky was with a single drop of water to perfectly release the flavor. According to the redheaded man, who worked for a nearby distillery, the Scots like to keep their best whisky in their own country. They don't export it, and they don't give it away. We should consider ourselves lucky to be drinking from their secret stash.

"That's crazy!" Erik exclaimed. "You could make so much more money!"

"It's not about money, my American friend," the Scotsman replied. "It's about whisky. Would you like to try another?"

It's amazing how compassion, connection, and a bit of alcohol can mend the feuds that once would've cost us our lives. Perhaps a lesson we could all take into the future. As much as I wanted to stay up and savor more of the full-bodied whisky, I knew I had to shoot the first arrow in the morning, so after a sip or two, I decided to be responsible and go to bed.

I woke up at 7 A.M. We needed to leave soon for me to be on time to open the archery show. I couldn't be late. Geoff had already caught a ride back with friends since our van was overpacked. I got showered and dressed and walked down to Dana's room to see if she and Erik were ready.

"We have a problem," Dana said. She pointed at Erik, a lump under the covers.

"Why is he still asleep?" I asked. "We have to get going to make it in time."

"That group of Scottish guys kept him up drinking their special whisky all night. He just got home about twenty minutes ago."

"Oh my gosh, how is he going to drive?"

"He's not," said Dana flatly. "He's still drunk."

"Well, how are we going to get there? I can't be late! They asked me to be the Lord Patron! I have to shoot the first arrow!"

Dana just stared at me.

"I guess you're going to have to drive."

I had never driven in the UK before and wasn't sure I could even do it.

The idea of driving on the wrong side of the road on the wrong side of the car scared me. Wait—not a car, a *van*. A long, wide VAN! But there was no time to fret. I knew if we didn't leave very soon, I was going to be late—something a Lord Patron would never be!

A few minutes later we were loaded into the van, pulling away from the Wheatsheaf. I turned around to glare at Erik, who was now comfortably snoring and intermittently passing gas in the far backseat. If I could've reached back there and strangled him, I surely would have.

Dori was my copilot in the passenger seat. If you ever have to drive in Scotland, I must warn you: The roads are winding and humming with huge trucks—absolutely *huge*—stacked with bales and bales of hay in back, carelessly teetering about twenty feet high, as they scream by at ridiculous high speeds, careening down the curving narrow country roads. The morning sun was bright and blinding, glinting dazzling light that bounced off the windshield of every truck in the distance as it headed our way. *Oh no, this is it. This. Is. It!* I thought with each and every approaching truck that looked like a moving skyscraper headed straight for us. I was white-knuckled and sweating, wondering if Erik would be the only one to survive since he was so relaxed in the back. By the time we made it to the highway, I let out a sigh of relief.

"What is the speed limit?" I asked Dori. Time was running short, and I didn't see any posted signs anywhere.

"I don't think there is one!" she replied.

I assumed she was right, and in my American mind thought it must be like the Autobahn in Germany, so off we went.

Three hours later, we pulled up at Bowlee Park, where the event was taking place, making it just in the nick of time. I dashed out of the van, delighted I wasn't late.

What an honor to be here to shoot the first arrow, I thought.

And that's when the wave of panic hit me again. I need to shoot an *arrow*! In front of a crowd of people! I had never shot an arrow before. Could it be difficult? Should I have practiced? It was too late to worry about that now.

I took a deep breath, proud of the fact that I'd just managed to get us here against the odds. My dad typically would've been the one to jump in to save the day in these situations. But with him gone, I'd been forced to step into his shoes. As scary as it had been for me, I knew he would've patted me on the back.

Hopefully shooting the arrow would go well too.

CHAPTER 6

"LORD" HOPWOOD

*L*adies and Gentlemen, please welcome our Lord Patron, Hopwood DePree!" declared Bev into a microphone set up to the side of the field. I tried to casually stroll in front of the crowd as if I had a clue what I was doing.

Bev was wearing a medieval costume of a hooded tunic with a belt, which made her look like Robin Hood. Most of the people in the crowd were wearing the same, I guess making them the Merry Men.

I walked out and waved. Someone handed me a large bow and arrow. I smiled uncomfortably and closed my eyes. I pulled the string way, way back and . . . let go. The arrow went about six feet and stuck into the mushy ground. Clearly, I had not inherited the innate talent of my Middleton archer forebears. Or maybe I just needed practice. Either way, the audience clapped and cheered as if I'd hit a bull's-eye. I decided to play along, so I turned and waved, smiled, and bowed. A bit mortifying that I had traveled five thousand miles for this performance, but I made the best of it.

Bev and the Merry Men then emerged from the audience and began showing off their incredible skills shooting arrows at a series of flags. I was thankful that I embarrassed myself before, not after, their display of talent. From the crowd, we whooped and hollered at every shot.

When the show was over, Bev asked if I would also be willing to judge a cake contest. She led me to a brick fieldhouse where many of the archers had gathered to partake in refreshments. A young local girl with long brown hair pulled back and wearing her best pink dress had made a bright green cake with her favorite doll stuck into the middle of the top of the cake. Clearly, she had mistaken baking soda for flour, because when I took a bite I almost choked. I saw the little girl sitting there with her grandma, biting her lip in anticipation.

"That's the winner!" I said as she ran up and hugged my leg.

An older man, probably her father, came up and looked at me gratefully.

"You made the right choice, m'lord."

With the cake contest complete, we drove back to Geoff's house, where his wife, Lyn, had cooked us lunch.

After the stressful day of racing on the Autobahn and fulfilling my *Braveheart* duties, walking inside Geoff and Lyn's home felt like stepping inside a sanctuary. Lyn was a lovely, silver-haired English woman with a happy smile. Right away, she engaged us with her inquisitive questions and infectious laugh. Like Geoff, Lyn had an ability to immediately put people at ease, making you feel as if everything was going to be just fine and you were exactly where you needed to be.

Their house was tastefully decorated in light neutral tones, with darker-colored paintings on the walls, like one of those English interiors you might find in the pages of *Better Homes and Gardens.* There was a smell of scones in the oven and freshly brewed tea. Geoff explained that most of the artwork on the walls had been painted by Edgar Wood, the Middleton architect who had risen to national prominence during the Arts and Crafts movement in the late 1800s.

"Wood is the same man who had designed the inglenook ceiling at Hopwood Hall," he told us. "We took a shine to Edgar Wood's paintings, particularly his watercolors, when we first met, and we've been collecting since we got married."

After we had our tea and scones, Lyn offered us cucumber finger sandwiches and small glasses of sherry poured out of an antique crystal decanter set that had belonged to her mother. Over the delicious meal, we learned more about their lives.

Geoff had been born and raised in Middleton, and Lyn was from less than twenty miles away in Cheadle. Geoff's great-grandfather, Abraham, founded Wellens & Sons Funeral Home in Middleton in 1870.

"It's likely my great-grandfather would have buried members of your Hopwood family in the 1800s and early 1900s," he said.

The funeral home had stayed in the family, passed down to Geoff's grandfather and eventually to Geoff's dad. During the 1950s, Geoff's father became mayor of Middleton—as did Geoff's mother.

"It was my dad who got me interested in history and Hopwood Hall in particular," Geoff explained. "He was passionate about the past. He believed that if we could learn more about those who had gone before us, it would give us a chance to be happier in our own times."

As soon as Geoff came of age, he followed in the family footsteps, and by his midtwenties he was a regular visitor to the regional office that issued death certificates, where Lyn happened to work.

When they bumped into each other at a mutual friend's wedding, outside of work, sparks flew. Two years later, they got engaged while vacationing together in Austria, and eventually they married and had three daughters.

"We thought about trying for a fourth child in hopes of also having a son, but that wasn't in the cards for us," Geoff said as he uncorked a bottle of wine and poured my mother the first glass.

The entire Wellens family had helped out at the funeral home business, including Geoff's brother Norman and his wife, Margaret.

"In those days, before call-centers and answering services, we had to be on call twenty-four hours a day, so each night, one of us had to take a turn sleeping next to the phone. I can remember one sleepless night when I had three calls to inform me of various deaths, and then I had to officiate a big funeral the next morning. I was absolutely exhausted, but each group was mourning their loss, and I had to be there for those people. Sometimes in life we find ourselves in situations that are much greater than our own personal needs. Can you imagine if I had told any of them that I was going back to bed?"

With Geoff and his family's dedication to the locals, the funeral business grew and grew. They purposely kept their rates at a fair price so as not to take advantage of anyone in an unfortunate situation. The Middleton community was small, the kind of place where people took care of one another in that way.

"Originally the name Middleton was derived from 'middle town,' because it is located directly in between Manchester and Rochdale," Geoff told us. "Exactly seven miles in either direction. There are people from Middleton who hardly ever venture out into either Rochdale or Manchester. In fact, there are slightly different accents between the towns. Even though they are all nearby, there's a difference between the three, because they are very separate in the minds of the residents, and they are quite particular about it. It's a bit of a fun rivalry. And people from Middleton really feel that we belong here."

Geoff and his brother oversaw the business for thirty years with that ethos until the family made the decision to sell the business so that Geoff and Norman could retire.

"Was it hard to walk away?" I asked.

"Incredibly. But deep down you know when it's time to follow another path. Every dog has its day, and we decided enough is enough."

I couldn't help but think of my life in LA.

Lyn quickly pointed out, "Even though Geoff's officially retired, he still helps with several funerals a month. He receives personal requests all the time and finds it impossible to say no."

We also learned that as part of Geoff's work as the town undertaker, people would often give him their photos and papers for safekeeping before they died, and as a result, he had become Middleton's unofficial historian and archivist.

"I now have seventy thousand photographs and documents I'm preserving for posterity," he told us proudly.

After lunch, our retired undertaker friend pulled out dusty, worn logbooks he was taking care of for the church, some of them dating back to the 1500s. The books smelled like time gone by, and I thought I could detect a slight creaking noise as Geoff opened them. He gingerly showed us pages where my ancestors had signed their names—the original ink, my fingers lightly touching the same page that they would have touched. In America, this type of historic log would've been in a museum under lock and key. But here I was, carefully looking through it while enjoying a glass of sherry.

"I feel like I'm breaking the law!" I gasped, as Geoff handed me yet another ancient tome.

Next, he showed us pictures of Robert and Edward, the two male heirs of Hopwood Hall who had died in World War I, dressed in their military uniforms.

Edward was the elder son. He was a colonel in the Coldstream guards who fought in the early battles of the First World War. He was incredibly brave, critically wounded twice before he was killed in action in the trenches of Belgium in 1917 at the age of thirty-seven. Robert was a captain in the rifle brigade and the Royal Flying Corps, and he died the year before his brother. He was thirty-one.

"After the news of their deaths reached Hopwood Hall, the parents laid out their sons' dress uniforms in the Hall so that all the local people and staff could pay their respects," Geoff told us.

It was uncanny to see the youth and life in their faces despite the fading sepia of the photos. I couldn't help but think that they were much younger than I was, and at their age my life had revolved around parties, events, and filmmaking. It suddenly made it all feel trivial.

I was learning so much. I told Geoff I could listen to him talk about the Hall all day. In some way, he reminded me of Pap, with his knowledge and passion about the past and his overflowing bookshelves. In other ways, with his devotion to community and sense of civic duty, he reminded me of my dad. Thousands of miles away from Michigan, the location of my birth, I felt deeply connected to people and a place: at home.

Before long, Geoff informed us it was time to head out. The final stop on our itinerary was the commemoration of the Flodden window at St. Leonard's parish church in Middleton.

On the way over, Geoff explained that St. Leonard's had started as a Saxon timber-framed church with a thatched roof, but that it wasn't grand enough for the conquering Normans. So in 1100, a new church was constructed in its place.

"St. Leonard's is a stone church with a wooden steeple," Geoff informed us, "where generations of your ancestors are buried. And it has bells that date back to the 1600s that ring to this day."

I did a rough calculation.

"Okay, Jetsen," I said, leaning down and taking the opportunity to educate my little niece. "That means that the bells in this church are more than 150 years older than the Liberty Bell in Philadelphia!"

"Not only that," Geoff chimed in, "if we hop out of the car and walk around the side of the church, you can see the place where your ancestors, the Middleton archers, would have sharpened their arrows on the stone walls of the church before heading off to battle."

Sure enough, we got out of the car, and Geoff showed us where, on the outer wall of the church, there were scratches on the stone made five hundred years ago.

Inside, the church was dark, damp, with a chill in the air. Geoff led us to one side of the pulpit so we could see the newly restored stained-glass window memorializing the victory of Flodden Field. We stood at his side, looking up, marveling at the jewel-colored dark blues, greens, and bright yellows of the window.

"What you're looking at here is what is thought to be the oldest war memorial in England," Geoff told us in a reverent whisper.

I stared up at the row of archers depicted in the colorful stained-glass window. They had long blond hair, round faces, and blue outfits. I recognized them immediately.

"Give these guys a haircut and they look just like me!" I laughed.

Everyone agreed that they could see an uncanny resemblance.

Apparently, according to Geoff, the bones in the right arms of some of the Middleton archers were said to be thicker than those in their left, due to having been trained in archery from a very young age. This physical anomaly had been passed down for generations, giving the men an incredible strength when pulling back the bowstrings.

I couldn't help but look down and question if, beneath the skin, the bone on my right arm was thicker than my left. Given my embarrassing performance at the archery show I seriously doubted it.

Next, Geoff ushered us toward the front of the church, pointing

A panel from the Flodden commemorative window in St. Leonard's church, Middleton, thought to be the UK's oldest war memorial, dating to the 1500s *Fred Leao Prado*

out the seventeenth-century Jacobean "Hopwood pew" beneath which generations of our ancestors were interred.

"Eventually, there was no more room for everyone, so a new tomb was constructed outside in the churchyard," Geoff explained.

The Hopwood pew was much larger than any pew I had ever seen before—more like a small room with carved partitions in dark mahogany wood, big enough to hold a snug gathering of family members. "It's also where your ancestors would have sat on Sunday while they were still alive and attending church services," he clarified.

As we went to sit down, we spotted a very distinguished-looking older couple in well-tailored suits seated in a pew next to us. Geoff introduced us. They were Lord and Lady Clitheroe, whose ancestors had built the church in the twelfth century.

My mother and I looked at one another, and I knew we were thinking the same thing. *Do we need to bow and curtsy? What's the protocol here?* I was feeling nervous and intimidated when Lady Clitheroe stepped in to save us.

"We are probably related!" she declared.

Geoff smiled, informing all of us that an old family tree in his office that he had looked at earlier in the day showed that we were indeed descendants of the father of Sir Richard Assheton, who led the Middleton archers to victory. I couldn't believe it. After all those hours of scrolling online, I was in the middle of an ancestry search in real life!

I was so overwhelmed to meet people who seemed like royalty and shared a branch on my family tree that I wasn't sure what to do! So I snapped a photo of us and posted it on Facebook.

Within moments, my phone began vibrating as my LA friends went berserk. I quickly silenced the phone as messages began popping up saying "Where the f*@# are you?!"

I'm in the middle of CHURCH! I thought.

Soon enough, the commemoration ceremony began. Perhaps it was a combination of the haunting choir music, the light dimming beyond the stained-glass windows, and the medieval atmosphere, but when it came time for me to speak, I slid out of the pew feeling as if I was floating. As I walked toward the front of the church, it looked like there were tombstones with inscriptions under my feet, and I realized that I was walking on a hallowed ground—that bodies, probably including those of my ancestors, were buried below. I walked up to the microphone and took out my notes, determined to keep things short and sweet.

"I am honored to be here," I started, my voice quivering slightly. "I hope my Hopwood ancestors would have enjoyed the fact that their American cousins have come back across the pond to help commemorate their achievements. I'm excited to learn more about their extraordinary history."

In the audience, I noticed more than one lady and gentleman

Lord and Lady Clitheroe with Hopwood DePree at St. Leonard's church, Middleton, September 2013 *D. DePree*

crinkling a forehead, probably wondering why the heck this blond guy from LA was standing at the front of their church. Others seemed astonished yet pleased that a long-lost Hopwood had reappeared.

After the ceremony, the priest, a man everyone seemed to refer to as the vicar, excused us, beginning with our row since we were the honored guests. My family and I followed the choir out as they carried a slew of colorful ceremonial religious flags and banners, attached to tall crosses.

As I walked out of the church with Geoff, I spotted Bob, who had evidently seen me chatting with Lord and Lady Clitheroe, because he immediately saw the opportunity to tease me about it.

"Just so you know, if it turns out that you have a title, I am *not* going to be calling you lord," he said, jabbing me in the rib with an elbow. "I will, however, be calling you if the toilets at the Hall ever need unblocking."

Geoff quickly chimed in. "If an inherited lordship title, which occasionally includes a seat in the House of Lords, is tied to Hopwood Hall, we have yet to find it. But there are centuries of history to comb through, and you never know what we may discover. Either way, it would be perfectly acceptable for Hopwood to be considered an unofficial 'lord,' as in the 'lord of the manor.'"

Bob looked at me with a crooked grin. "Well then, m'lord better get a good plumber on speed dial."

CHAPTER 7

HOTEL
SALVATION

*H*opwood?! Wake up! ARE YOU DEAD IN THERE?!"

I could hear someone banging on my hotel room door. It was still somewhat dark, and it felt like the middle of the night.

The knocking was far too loud and eager to be the housekeeper. Groggy and confused, I stumbled to my door and opened it. It was my sister Dana, fully dressed for the day.

"W-what time is it?" I squinted in the blinding light emanating overhead from the LED fixtures in the beige hallway.

"Almost nine thirty. You better hurry up; the hotel breakfast finishes in eight minutes, and they charge you for it either way."

"Really? Even if I don't eat?" I questioned.

She nodded matter-of-factly. "Because when they asked, you told them yesterday that you were going to eat today. So now they're going to charge you. It seems like that's how hotels do it in England."

"Well, how in the world would anybody know *yesterday* if they're going to want to eat breakfast *today*?" I demanded.

She shrugged, as baffled as I was. "I don't know, but now you only have seven minutes." And with that she walked away, only turning back to let me know that Geoff had called for me and I should phone him back.

But first, the task at hand. In England, it turns out the "breakfast" part of bed-and-breakfast is actually a contractual obligation. Beware as you unsuspectingly sign for your hotel room, because you may also be signing your life away that you promise to eat. Even if you aren't hungry. Most Brits who aren't hungry would probably politely get tea and toast and call it good. But the American urge to "get my money's worth" came roaring out of me, and I was on my way to eat twice as much as I normally would. And I now had *six* minutes to do it. I threw on my stretchy jeans and headed down to the buffet.

As I descended in the elevator, I couldn't help but think it was only 1:30 A.M. in LA, and Jonny and the crew were probably still on a dance floor somewhere ordering last call.

Seated alone in the empty dining room decorated with plaid curtains, staring at portraits in ornate gold frames, I made my best attempt to successfully plow through a "full English"—eggs, sausage, bacon, toast, baked beans, mushrooms, half a tomato, and an unidentifiable dark-colored disk. I kept trying to remind myself that, as a middle-aged man, I had absolutely no right to be inhaling food like I was. But I couldn't stop. I wondered if it had something to do with feeling like I could get away with it here, unlike in LA.

"Would you like some more black pudding? There are only a few left," said the smiling waitress in a thick Northern accent, gesturing to the discarded hockey puck on my plate with a bite out of it. I had thought it was an overcooked, slightly spoiled sausage patty.

"Black pudding? What is that?"

"Pig's blood and a few other ingredients. My favorite. It's chock full of iron, so it's good for you. Would you like more before we clear the buffet?"

"Uh, no thank you," I muttered. "But it was . . . delicious," I said through a forced smile.

Fortunately, her interruption had come in the nick of time to stop me from gorging myself to the point of feeling sick. Now I only felt sick at the thought that I'd swallowed a mouthful of solidified pig's blood.

I took several gulps of tea and walked outside into the gray morning mist to get some fresh air. Looking at my phone, I noticed that Geoff had texted asking me to call him.

He answered his cell phone after a few rings. He was getting into his car after having just dropped off a casserole at the home of a widow whose husband's funeral he would be officiating later in the week.

"I bumped into Bev from the council this morning," he said. I could hear his car ignition dinging as he put the key in. "Guess what? There's a developer—Oliver someone or other—who is looking into potentially turning the Hall into a hotel. He's very interested in speaking with you as a Hopwood ancestor. If you're open to it, he would like to involve you in the project. Bev can arrange for you to meet with him."

"Well, it couldn't hurt to talk to him," I said. "And if it will help move the rescue along faster, then of course I'll do what I can."

We both agreed that with a developer interested in saving the Hall, there was the potential for the money and the momentum to finally preserve it—and to put the building to good use. As much as I'd been sincere in my offers to help fundraise to save the Hall, the reality was that it was going to take millions of pounds to complete a full restoration. Even though in the past I had found investors for movies, I couldn't think of anyone who might be willing to invest in a dilapidated six-hundred-year-old castle with dry rot.

"The only issue is that the earliest they can set the meeting is for Friday," Geoff explained. "Aren't you booked to fly home before then?"

I told Geoff I could change my flight. I'd bought it on miles, so it was flexible. The only thing that *wasn't* flexible was a lunch meeting Jay had set for me in LA on Friday to discuss a new project.

"Wonderful!" Geoff replied. "I will let Bev know and she will get back to you with details."

My family went back to the United States, and I ended up staying in Middleton for another ten days.

With my trip extended, I offered to help Bob out at the Hall. My DIY skills were limited at best, and my run-in with the sticky tiles in my bathroom in LA was still a recent traumatic memory, but at least I could provide an extra pair of hands and some company for him. Geoff had told me that Bob was only contracted by the council to work one day a month, but because of his love for the place, he ended up putting in many more hours than that, unpaid. Time spent on Hopwood Hall was time away from his own heritage restoration business. My appreciation for Bob only continued to grow.

As a result of all the damage and decay, the Hall was considered dangerous, so I had to get special permission from the council to go onsite to help.

When I arrived the first morning, Bob was waiting for me at the gates, and we made our way to the Reception Hall, the large, green-painted room with the fireplace featuring the Hopwood family coat of arms and motto.

Here, Bob handed me a broom and asked me to start sweeping up the bits of dust and detritus on the floor. I tried not to be too disappointed. I'd imagined I'd be doing something a bit more involved, maybe climbing a ladder to patch up a bit of ceiling. But no, sweeping seemed to be the task that Bob felt I might be most capable of executing.

It was a damp, gray morning, but every now and again, there'd be a brief burst of sunlight through the long bank of windows at the end of the room, and I'd want to run over and bask in it for the few seconds it lasted. While I swept, Bob worked on arranging bits of plaster and other broken and fallen moldings on the tables in the Reception Hall where he kept his "artifacts." Once again, he gleefully showed me how he was marking each piece so he could remember where it came from and so they could be put back in place at some point in the future.

"God knows when that will be if this hotel thing doesn't work out," Bob said. "I hope I'm still alive to see it."

After I finished bagging up the fruits of my sweeping in the Reception Hall, Bob told me to move on to the Oak Parlor, the room lined with intricately carved wooden panels dating back to the 1400s.

Out of pure habit, I went to check my phone, but it didn't seem like there would be any hope of getting a signal in a house with walls made of such thick stone. Instead, I resumed my sweeping. The sound of the broom brushing against the dusty floorboards had a hypnotic effect, and as I swept, I let my eyes run across the many carvings all around me: I spotted some little angels and cherubs I hadn't noticed the last time I was here among the pretty flowers and twirling shapes and patterns—not to mention the bizarre man in the corner with a pitchfork stabbed through a decapitated head. I guessed this was probably what my ancestors did for entertainment, before TV, phones, and the internet came along—they'd simply spend time looking at their lovely carvings. I chuckled as I imagined my fourteenth great-grandmother complaining to her friends, "There's so much violence in *carvings* nowadays . . . I worry about its impact on the children."

I realized that if I were in LA, I would be checking my phone every few minutes for messages and calls. Here at the Hall, lost in my daydreams, it was like I existed in another zone, one where the modern world and its demands no longer held any power over me.

As I swept, I happened to notice some funny wooden carvings near the fireplace that looked a bit like a medieval interpretation of the flying monkeys from *The Wizard of Oz*.

"What are those things?" I asked Bob when he returned to check on me.

"Believe it or not, these bizarre-looking creatures are supposed to be lions," he explained. "These are so old they were probably created by a woodworker who had never seen a lion for himself and so they were made from a written description of a lion, rather than real life. Which explains why they look nothing like one!"

I leaned in closer, observing the oddly shaped square head, tiny eyes, and huge mouth with fangs—a clear representation of why it's important we experience things for ourselves rather than simply basing our reality on what others tell us.

"You'll never be bored spending time here," Bob said. "There's always something new to discover, something you've never seen before."

Bob explained that because he was always having to pull up floorboards due to dry rot, which would spread unless you removed it, he'd often find things hidden beneath them.

"One time I found a pair of old cloth shoes under some floorboards by the fireplace in the Morning Room," he told me. "Geoff thinks they would have been placed there to ward off witches. Another time, I was prizing up the boards in the same room and I found a rusted old gas mask at the bottom of a small pit that had been dug to provide a concealed bomb shelter from the Second World War."

Perhaps as a reward for my diligent sweeping, Bob took me over to see the gas mask for myself. To get there, we passed through what Bob described as the Georgian rooms—all of which were added to the Hall in the late 1600s to early 1700s after John Hopwood married Elizabeth of Speke (whose marriage was commemorated on a plaque in the Oak Parlor). John and Elizabeth decided it was time to improve the Hall, and so they added several rooms, including a banquet room. This was a towering, square-shaped room, where, once upon a time, the family would have hosted grand, formal dinners. The room stopped me in my tracks—it was obvious it had been built to impress, and even with all the dust and debris lying around, it remained dazzling. There were the remains of complex plasterwork patterns on the walls and floor-to-ceiling bay windows filled with tiny leaded glass panes at one end. Below the mantel of the fireplace were colorful tiles featuring tropical birds, bamboo, and water lilies—exotic features that many people at that time would have yet to see in real life.

"The tiles would have been a way for the Hopwood family to show off to guests that they were well traveled," Bob said.

"Kind of like their version of Instagram?" I offered.

Leaving the Banquet Room, we entered the Library, an impressive wood-paneled room that dated back to 1755. In its prime, the Library would have once been home to a collection of leatherbound books and comfortable chairs for reading, but now it was plagued with the dry rot Bob had noted in his email to me when I was still in LA. Thankfully, the Library's two large, half-hexagon-shaped, tall window bays had been preserved. These would have made excellent reading alcoves offering maximum daylight, crucial to be able to see the pages before electricity was invented.

Then we stepped into the Morning Room.

"This would have been one of the grandest rooms in the house, built in the late 1830s in the Georgian style," Bob told us. "The windows face due east to make the most of the morning sun, which explains the name. This is where the Hopwood family would have had their breakfast or entertained guests before lunch."

"Wow, I bet they had some great Sunday Funday mimosa brunches in here," I said under my breath.

I hadn't been able to see this room on our first visit, but even with half the floorboards pulled up, it was stunning. Painted in shades of pink and green with elegant plasterwork on the walls, it had an elaborate decorative ceiling and massive windows looking out over where the gardens would have been.

The shoes Bob had found under the floorboards had already been taken to a museum to be dated, but I spotted the gas mask sitting on the enormous wooden fireplace on one side of the room. We went over and Bob let me try it on. I pulled the odd-smelling rubber strap over my head and stared out through its goggles, trying to picture this place in wartime. Bob reminded me that by 1939, when war broke out in Europe, the Hopwood family had already long since left.

"Back then, the Hall was requisitioned by the Lancashire Cotton Corporation as a base of operations to oversee making uniforms for the war effort. All these rooms you see today would have been filled with workers rushing about, trying to keep up with the demands of the war."

The Morning Room, Hopwood Hall Estate, 2013 *Dave Broga*

Next to the fireplace, Bob pointed out an old Victorian bell that the family used to ring to summon the servants.

"Now, imagine life in the late 1800s, when the Hopwood family were still living here," Bob said. "Let's say you wanted a piece of toast and jam. You would ring that bell, and then an army of servants would scurry around making it for you. The Hall was completely self-sufficient in those days. The flour for the bread was made from wheat grown on the estate and ground in the Hopwood mill. The butter was churned in the dairy from cows that grazed in the Hopwood meadow. The jam was made by the cook from strawberries grown in the kitchen gardens. The bread was toasted over an open fire by one of the kitchen maids, and then a butler would bring it up with pots of jam and butter on a silver platter. It took dozens of people to make you that slice of toast."

I asked if we could go and see the servants' quarters next, but Bob shook his head sadly.

"That wing of the house is collapsing. It's too dangerous to go into, even for me. No one's been in there for years."

The Victorian bell that chimed in the now-defunct servants' quarters. The gas mask from World War II. A uniform factory. A pair of cloth shoes to ward off witches. Gorgeous Georgian-period architecture. All these eras and remnants of the past in a single room . . .

I wondered aloud about what else Bob might find under the Hall's floorboards in the future.

"Well, if I'm lucky, I'll stumble on the buried treasure," he grinned. "Apparently, one of your Hopwood ancestors, Robert Hopwood, went mad sometime around the 1850s. He started to get dressed up for imaginary train journeys and claimed he could see an army of soldiers outside his window. Other times, he'd get undressed in the Library, thinking it was his bedroom. You can imagine what the Victorian ladies thought of that! Legend has it that he hid a big bag of gold coins somewhere in the house."

"Really?!" I replied. "Let's find it! We could use it to pay to fix the place up!"

"Don't get too excited," Bob warned, shaking his head. "I've been working here for years, and nothing's turned up yet. The only thing that the myth of the coins has done is to inspire a bunch of teenagers to break in during the night and do a lot of damage trying to pull up the floorboards to find the gold. That old story has done more harm to this house than good."

After a day of sweeping and learning about the Hall, I returned to my hotel more invested in its revival than ever. The next day, I went right back to join Bob at work, eager to refine my sweeping skills. The side benefit of all this time spent at the Hall was that I was also getting to know my new friend. I discovered that Bob had grown up in the area, one of seven brothers who were all in the construction industry. Prior generations of his family had worked at Hopwood Hall, so his ancestors would have known mine. He met and married his wife, Nidia, a vibrant dark-haired woman with a passion for books and museums, over thirty years ago, and they had two children, now grown. Bob had his own heritage restoration company which specialized in bringing old buildings back to life, and as his beloved father had recently passed away from Alzheimer's, this left him with more time to devote to the Hall's rescue.

Anyone who knew Bob knew that he was the Hall's biggest champion. Not only that, with enough money and resources, Bob had the necessary heritage skills to help bring it back to its former glory.

"I'm not getting any younger, you know," Bob confided in me, grumbling as he climbed down from a ladder about the pains in his knees. "I hope this hotel project gets a move on. There aren't many of us left who understand how to take care of an old building like this one. If things take too long, I might keel over and be forced to pass my skills on to you, and we both know what a disaster that would be."

I knew Bob was joking, but there was also a biting truth to his comments. That afternoon, he explained to me that skills like his can't be learned from a book—you need someone to teach you in person. Bob's biggest fear was that a new generation would have no interest in learning how to take care of old houses, and so everything he knew would die out with him.

"It's an art, you know," he told me, shaking his head. "How to work with old slate roofs, how to make bricks by hand. Funny things like making mortar using goat's hair, which is the way it would have been done hundreds of years ago."

While the idea of grabbing a goat to get ahold of some of its hair did sound like extra work to me, I fully understood what Bob was saying. If he couldn't find someone to teach, all his knowledge would be lost. Just like the Hall.

Bob taught me a lot during that time, but one of the biggest things I took away was that saving Hopwood Hall wasn't just about historic preservation. If the hotel project went ahead, it would bring much-needed jobs to the Middleton area.

"At one point, hundreds of years ago, the majority of people in Middleton worked at the Hall in some capacity or another," Bob reminded me. "There was a whole world of *Upstairs, Downstairs* inside the Hall. It was like its own little industry. They made everything here: the butter, the bread, the cheeses. There was even a brewery on site, where they would brew the Hopwood ale."

But after World War I, the house closed, and the whole area went into steep decline. Factories were shuttered. Jobs went elsewhere. These days, Rochdale and the surrounding towns were considered some of the most economically depressed in all of England.

"The hotel isn't just going to save the Hall, Hopwood," Bob pointed out. "It's going to help transform this area for everyone."

Bob assured me that everyone around town felt the same way: The new plans to rescue the Hall and turn it into a hotel gave people hope. If the Hall could be brought back, maybe it would be able to bring the town along with it.

I was more determined than ever to play my part. The problem was, I seemed to be hindering as much as I was helping. One afternoon, as I continued my sweeping duties, I bent down with my dustpan to collect several bent old nails that were laying on the floor. They were dark, rusty, and about an inch wide—much thicker than a normal nail—and I went to throw them away in my black plastic trash bag.

"What are you doing?!" Bob exclaimed as he carefully plucked them out of the dustpan. "These nails were hand-forged in the sixteenth century! We may be able to straighten them out and reuse them!"

I thought about explaining to him that in America, we throw away practically everything—that we would never dream of saving crooked old nails! But I was pretty sure this would give Bob a chance to make another one of his jokes about dumb Americans, so instead I feigned shock.

"What? There are *nails* in there?!" I said. "My eyesight must already be failing me because I was sure those were dead grasshoppers!"

From that day forward, I learned to never throw anything away without checking with Bob first.

The following Friday, as per Geoff's instructions, I caught the bus into Rochdale to meet with the hotel developer and Bev from the council, feeling hopeful that maybe soon enough, Bob would be able to get to work full-time restoring the Hall. To my delight, the bus was a red double-decker, and after I paid my fare, I went to climb the steps to the upper level, almost falling backward as the bus lurched forward. Once safely ensconced in my seat, though, it was worth it. I had a bird's-eye view. Before long, the bus crested a small hill, and there was Rochdale's eclectic mix of historic buildings set next to twentieth-century structures coming into view.

Geoff had explained to me that, like Middleton, Rochdale was struggling. Work had declined as factories closed, and it felt to some people as if the town had been forgotten. I've always been someone who roots for the underdog, and if there's an area in England that's an underdog, it's Rochdale.

"At one point in the fifteenth century, things were very different," Geoff pointed out. "Rochdale was one of the most influential towns in England, and thanks to its thriving wool trade, some of the wealthiest people in the county lived here. With the development of manufacturing in the nineteenth century, the city switched from wool to cotton, but life in the factories was no bed of roses, and the workers soon decided to organize."

As a result, I learned, Rochdale's biggest claim to fame was its Society of Equitable Pioneers.

"This was a group of workers who banded together to create their own co-op on a street named Toad Lane," Geoff explained, "and thereby kick-starting the modern cooperative movement in 1844."

I loved that the city was responsible for channeling communal spirit into enterprise. Maybe we could bring some of that energy to this new hotel project and help get the whole area back on track. Now that I knew I was genetically connected, I had begun to root for the place in the same way I would if it were my hometown.

I hopped off the bus and turned the corner, looking for my destination. My meeting was taking place at the town hall, which Geoff told me was the most beautiful building in the city. I stared up at a towering structure that looked more like a church than a municipal building, with enormous stained-glass windows, gargoyles, ornate spires, gilded statues, and a tall clock tower to rival Big Ben's. Apparently, Queen Elizabeth had once visited the town hall, and in preparation the townspeople had built her a private toilet, fit for a queen, in case she needed to relieve herself. Unfortunately, she never did. During World War II, Adolf Hitler was said to have given special orders to his forces not to bomb Rochdale's town hall because he had plans to disassemble it and rebuild it in Germany as soon as he successfully invaded England. Fortunately, he never did.

Inside, the town hall was a bit of a rabbit warren, but I found my way to Bev's office, where I flipped through a magazine as I waited.

"Would you like a brew?" said her well-dressed secretary.

It took me a moment to realize she was talking about tea rather than a beer.

Suddenly Bev emerged from her office.

"Hopwood! How are you? Please do come in. This is Oliver Simmons," she said as she motioned toward a very dignified man in a suit with a full head of black hair slicked to one side.

As it turned out, Oliver Simmons did not mess around.

"Hopwood, I want you to be involved in the hotel proposal as a spokesperson," he said in a very proper British accent. "Research shows that restoration projects like Hopwood Hall are much more successful when a family member is involved. I would love for you to be that family member."

I wasn't sure about being a spokesperson, but it quickly became evident that Oliver was an incredible *sales*person. He explained that my participation would be easy: They would wheel me out at certain events as a Hopwood representative. In exchange, I would be kept in the loop and have a voice on the project.

"Part of your role will be to ensure that the restoration is being done with the blessing of your family and the community," he insisted.

The thought occurred to me that maybe in my role as spokesperson I would also be able to give Geoff and Bob a say in what happened next for the Hall.

Within an hour, not only had I agreed to help Oliver with his hotel project, but he also convinced me to return to the UK in the spring to run a half marathon with his running group in Anglesey, Wales. I had never run a half marathon in my life. Oliver seemed exactly like the person needed to help save Hopwood Hall.

Later that day, I met Geoff and Bob at the pub to give them the update. Not just any pub, but the dimly lit Olde Boar's Head opposite St. Leonard's church, "arguably England's oldest original pub dating to 1622," as Geoff described. Walking inside, I thought I'd stumbled into a set from a Harry Potter movie. The walls were crooked, and the low ceilings were crisscrossed with dark, hulking wooden beams. In fact, I was so busy taking it all in that I immediately thumped my forehead on one of them. Obviously, people had been much shorter in the 1600s, as you'd have to be less than five and a half feet to clear the ceiling. The place smelled like the past, in a good way, and the charm of being there made up for my throbbing skull. After buying us three pints of warm English beer at the bar, I went to sit down with my new friends.

I was excited to tell them the news, but Geoff, in classic Geoff fashion, was determined to give me a captivating history lesson first.

"Do you see that outline of a trapdoor?" he said, pointing to a rectangular imprint that was barely visible beneath the rug next to our table. "Legend has it that the trapdoor led to the entrance of a hidden tunnel that supposedly went under the road to St. Leonard's church. Some say there was a branch of tunnels that also connected directly to Hopwood Hall!"

Although these speculations had yet to be proven, the Olde Boar's Head was clearly a place my ancestors frequented in days of yore.

Bob informed me that the lopsided walls were made of medieval goat-hair plaster, slapped between the roughly cut oak beams in a haphazard way that made me think the builders must have been in a hurry to get the place built so they could sit down and have a pint. Or maybe a better explanation was that they were having pints while they worked! Either way, I had to assume that such crude surroundings were handmade by people who would probably run in terror if a time machine had been able to magically transport them to a place like Jonny's favorite bar, Bootsy Bellows on Sunset.

Over our beers, I told Geoff and Bob all about my meeting with Oliver Simmons. They seemed overjoyed—even Bob was smiling. Both men cared deeply about Hopwood Hall and agreed that, given its unstable condition, a hotel conversion was going to be the best and last chance at salvation.

"We're running out of time," Bob reminded me. "The council is only able to pay me to go in one day a month, but that's never going to be enough to stop a historic building like Hopwood Hall from ending up as a pile of dust. If this hotel project doesn't work out, we can say goodbye to the Hall forever."

Bob's threats always made my heart race, but the good news was that if the hotel project went ahead, he'd be able to lead the team restoring the Hall.

I flew back to LA delighted with my trip and convinced that the Hall was in very safe hands.

CHAPTER 8

NEIGHBORS AND MURDERS

Although I was happy to be back in my own bed, and Jay forgave me for missing the meeting with him, there wasn't a whole lot of good news awaiting me in Hollywood. We didn't get the McDonald's job, which didn't exactly surprise me, but another "pass" made me question whether I still had what it took to land work in LA. I imagined Jay was probably wondering how on earth I would be able to get an A-list movie off the ground if I couldn't even make my way in McDonaldland.

I was wondering the same.

Of course, now that I was back, Jonny wanted to know if I would join him at the latest bar he was frequenting off Hollywood Boulevard. After giving my name at the door, I made my way past the velvet rope and found him in the VIP section on a long, low, leather banquette with red beaded lights dangling above. Within minutes of arriving, he had ordered a bottle of vodka, and in the blink of an eye a half dozen scantily clad waitstaff holding gigantic lit sparklers marched out from behind the bar holding the bottle aloft, as if it were the cub from *The Lion King*. Ice, glasses, mixers of cranberry juice, pineapple, you name it—all came to Jonny's table.

How could I even explain to Bob and Geoff and the other locals at the Olde Boar's Head that this was standard in Hollywood? That you couldn't even order a bottle of vodka without an entire production? At least, not if you were Jonny. Before we knew it, throngs of modelesque strangers flocked around us to make conversation and hopefully be offered a drink. This was what we called "Jonny style."

In the weeks to come, I increasingly found myself thinking about what people in Middleton would make of my strange LA universe. Would Bob and Geoff think I was crazy if they found out I was prepared to spend forty-five minutes in traffic in my top-down Jeep to go just a few miles? To valet my car at a restaurant that was clogged with paparazzi because Kim Kardashian (or perhaps just someone who looked like her) was inside? I no longer only saw my life through my own eyes, but through theirs.

A couple of months later, I was due back in Rochdale for a planning meeting about the hotel. Things were moving full steam ahead, designs for the renovation were being drawn up, and my role as "resident family member" was taking shape: I would have a room at the hotel for my private use in return for helping to publicize the Hall and its history. As far as I was concerned, this was a total win-win. I couldn't wait to help spread the word about my newly discovered "ancestral pile," as Oliver Simmons kept referring to it, and was elated that such a large-scale rescue operation was already underway.

As I landed in Manchester for the meeting the following day, my phone rang. It was Jay.

"Hopwood, I got you a meet and greet with the Sony people tomorrow at five," he told me. I could hear the excitement and energy in his voice. "They're looking for a big battle pic, so maybe you could float your Flodden Field idea. Let's start strategizing—this could be a huge deal for you!"

"Um, Jay," I hedged, hoping I wouldn't have to let on that I was actually out of the country. "We're going to have to reschedule. I have something tomorrow . . ."

"Cancel it!" he insisted. "What's more important than this?"

Reluctantly, I had to confess I was on the tarmac in England. Jay's head nearly exploded.

"How do you expect to get work if I have to turn down meetings because you're always unavailable? People are going to start to think you've secretly died or something!"

With all the jet lag, I was beginning to wonder about it myself. But I knew what Jay was saying was true: In Hollywood, you must be available at a moment's notice, whether it's for a meeting or a social event. It's just the nature of the game. If you disappear, even for a week or two, you might as well cease to exist.

Jay was working hard for me, and I wasn't delivering. Why hadn't I been able to put together a Flodden Field pitch after he first mentioned it? Jay always follows up, so I couldn't say I didn't see this coming.

What Jay probably didn't know was that the survival of the Hall, the town, and its people were at stake, and I was feeling a growing responsibility to play my part.

I apologized to my friend and devoted manager and told him that as soon as I returned, I would recommit myself to being available all day, every day. Then I dragged my suitcase off the plane and went to find a black cab. This time, the driver seemed to know where he was going, and we arrived at the Norton Grange Hotel within no time.

The planning meeting the following day was a success, and I was glad I had been there to continue to show my support for the project. It felt like everything was lining up: the council, local politicians, the money people, the support of the community. There was only one problem. Toward the end of the meeting, I overheard Oliver Simmons muttering under his breath to one of his deputies, something about a man with the unforgettable name of Phineas Shellburn, and how he hoped that "Shellburn won't stand in our way."

That evening, I went to meet Geoff at the Hopwood Arms pub, eager to ask him if he knew anything about Shellburn.

The Hopwood pub is another favorite Middleton "local." It was part of the original estate, sitting on the edge of the grounds and owned by the Hopwood family. This was the place where all staff that worked at the Hall ventured to blow off some steam back in the day. Almost every time I stopped by the Hopwood pub, I was prepared for someone to point and shout, "Look! Hopwood's in the Hopwood!" This was often then followed by the bartender sending over a pint from someone who was curious about my connection to the estate, and I would find myself chatting with new friends.

Tonight was no exception. After Geoff and I joked with a few jovial customers, we sat down at a table in the corner. I told him the latest and asked him if he knew anything about this Shellburn character.

Geoff, being Geoff, filled me in.

"I was wondering when his name might come up," Geoff said, suddenly speaking in hushed tones. "The problem is, Hopwood, your family fell out with the Shellburns, your neighbors over the ridge, in the sixteenth century. It was serious. And they haven't forgotten. These feuds run deep."

"What did my ancestors do?" I wondered aloud. "Did they play basketball late at night, or let their dog bark too loud?"

Geoff looked me square in the eye and said, "No, they committed *murder.*"

I quickly learned my ancestor Ralph Hopwood was a bad neighbor. One morning, he saw a man trespassing on his property and drew his longbow.

"Back then, everyone knew not to unexpectedly cross onto someone's land since it could be interpreted as a threat," Geoff explained. "An interloper might be someone who wanted to steal the sheep. Or poison the well. Or set fire to the grain mill."

And so, Ralph loaded an arrow into his bow and fired it off. Ralph Hopwood was related to the same Middleton archers who had helped defeat Scotland. He knew how to shoot to kill.

"Before he knew it, that arrow hit the intruder straight through the chest. He later died in his wife's arms. The problem was that the interloper was Phineas Shellburn's great-great-great-great-great-great grandfather, also named Phineas Shellburn, aka your neighbor."

Five hundred years later, the same Shellburn family still lived over the hill—and they hadn't forgotten the events of the 1500s. Murder was murder.

Geoff explained that the fallout of this age-old feud continued. I learned that the Hopwood Hall Estate used to sit on about five thousand acres, but over the years, pieces of the land had been slowly developed. At some point in the 1990s, when the college was founded on part of the land, a few neighboring parcels were sold off to none other than our neighbor Phineas Shellburn. One of those parcels happened to cross over the original entrance to the Hall, but, as there weren't any family members to object, the sale went ahead—even though this meant that independent access to the Hall was now restricted and subject to permission from the Shellburn family. This had been disastrous for the Hall, cutting it off from the outside world and probably contributing to its decline.

Geoff was worried.

"Shellburn seems to want nothing more than for Hopwood Hall to be lost forever," he said, shaking his head sadly. "Seems like he's not cooperating with Oliver and the hotel developers."

The next night, I received a late phone call from Oliver.

"Hopwood, I need your help," he said. He was calling about the Shellburn problem, as I had started to refer to it.

I immediately shut my laptop and walked outside into the night air at the Norton Grange.

"The good news is that some inroads have been made with community pressure and lobbying from local politicians requesting Shellburn to sell back the piece of land so that we can once again easily access the Hall. The bad news is that we're hitting a brick wall. He's stopped responding to our calls."

I could detect an uncertain tone in the usually ultraconfident Oliver's voice that I hadn't heard before.

Beyond the parking lot, with the night moon, I could see the edge of the original estate lands. It was quiet and peaceful, except for Oliver's worried voice echoing through my cell phone. When someone who's not normally panicked seems panicked, it's unnerving. It reminded me of another late-night call I had received years before in LA, from a producer who was freaked out because a star had dropped out of our film project, and it was falling apart. These issues happen on every project, and they're par for the course: An actor suddenly changes his or her mind, or a financier decides to back out, or there is suddenly an identical competing film project that is going to be released ahead of your film or TV release date. The news is never good on those types of calls, and you knew it had the potential to stop a project dead in its tracks.

But this time, the stakes seemed much higher. It felt like someone was purposefully blocking the momentum of a project that was going to benefit both the Hall and the entire community. My conversation with Oliver lasted for over an hour as we tried to come up with solutions.

Could Shellburn really stand in the way of the hotel project? I tried to understand my neighbor's point of view—how he could have so much animosity based on something that happened hundreds of years ago to people we'd never met. It felt like bizarre Hatfield-and-McCoy territory, and it seemed surreal to somehow be caught up in it. Even though Hopwood Hall had been sitting vacant for three decades, wasting away from Manchester rain and its best friend, dry rot? Surely there had to be something I could do to smooth things over with my disgruntled neighbor.

CHAPTER 9

TIME MARCHES ON

*I*n the small town in Michigan where I grew up, if a building that was erected in 1899 is still standing, we more than likely would hire a marching band, bus in the schoolkids, and have the mayor commemorate it by hanging a bronze plaque during a dedication ceremony. Cotton candy and elephant ear trucks may even show up. Certainly one, if not two, local news stations would be there to film the celebration.

Which is why it seemed unfathomable to me that anyone could sit back and watch a building from *the 1400s* slowly deteriorate. Even worse, that it seemed like he *wanted* it to deteriorate.

Oliver and I agreed that perhaps I could humanize the salvation of the Hall by putting a present-day face on it.

"I mean, if I can help Shellburn realize the ridiculousness of

holding a five-hundred-year grudge, then maybe he'll consider rescuing the local heritage for the betterment of the community!" I
exclaimed, suddenly filled with momentary confidence.

Fortunately, I happened to have a pen in my pocket, and Oliver
dictated Shellburn's phone number to me as I scrawled it on my
wrist. Because Shellburn was a farmer by trade, Oliver suggested
I try to reach him at six thirty in the morning.

"Isn't that a bit of a risk?" I questioned. "If we're trying to win
this guy over and he *isn't* an early riser, I think calling him at six
thirty A.M. will probably blow the whole plan."

"I have very good intel that if we want to reach him, that is the
time to do it," Oliver reassured me.

I couldn't sleep that night. I tossed and turned at the Norton
Grange. This time, I was the first and only person in line for the
breakfast buffet when it opened at six A.M.

I was so amped up that I must've startled the hostess out of her
skin as she walked up to seat me.

"Ya alright?!" I blurted.

". . . Yes, you?" she said as she sheepishly glanced at me out of the
corner of her eye, leading me to my table.

I picked at the food. I guzzled a few cups of tea and looked at my
phone. 6:29 A.M. I took a deep breath and dialed the number Oliver
had given me.

After three rings, a man with a deep, gruff local accent answered
the phone.

"Mr. Shellburn?" I asked nervously.

"We're milkin' the cows, what do you want?" he replied.

I hastily introduced myself. I wasn't planning to bring up the feud
between our families unless he did. I wanted to stick to business.

But first I thought I better say something about the weather because I had learned that is the way most Brits seemed to like to start a conversation.

"Looks like it's going to be a nice day . . ." I fumbled.

"It's pitch-black. What do you want?"

I stammered.

"My name is Hopwood DePree," I told him. "I'm from America, and . . ."

"I know who you are," Shellburn fired back.

In the background, I could suddenly hear what sounded like a milking machine being clicked on. Although to be honest, I have absolutely *no* idea what a milking machine might sound like.

"Look, I don't want to waste your time here," I continued. "I'm just hoping we can work something out that is going to benefit the entire community."

"Yes?" he asked.

"I'm wondering how you're feeling about that small triangle of land you own that crosses the old entrance route to Hopwood Hall." I was trying my best to suppress the nervous quiver in my voice.

"How do I feel about it?" Shellburn paused a little bit too long. "I don't feel anything. I bought the land. It's mine. That's it."

"Well, if you did feel like selling it back to us," I replied. "It would mean so much to me, the hotel people, and everyone in the area, to be honest."

"I tell you what," Shellburn conceded. "I'll think about it. How do you *feel* about that?"

Before I could answer him, he hung up with an abrupt *click*. Or maybe it was the milking machine again. Either way, it felt like I had made a small step forward.

I called Oliver and got his voicemail, so I left a message updating him on the small advancement.

Then I headed straight back to my room and went promptly to bed, exhausted. I don't know if it was the anticipation of the phone call or the sleepless night, but I slept for almost five hours, waking close to noon.

As I opened my door to remove the Do Not Disturb sign from the handle, the housekeeper popped her head around the corner. "Hopwood, you didn't miss breakfast, did you?!"

Clearly this would've been a fate worse than death. I assured her that I had been up since six A.M.

I pulled myself together. I was due for lunch at Geoff and Lyn's house, so I decided to walk over to get some exercise—trips to the gym not really being an easy option in Middleton. I'd recently purchased a new pocket umbrella, which was now as essential as my phone, wallet, and keys. I headed out.

After walking in the freezing rain, it felt blissful to be ushered into the warm and comfortable Wellens home.

Sitting on the kitchen counter was a wonderful display of cheeses on a wooden cutting board. My stomach was growling, so I immediately headed over to it, slicing a piece of cheese and slapping it on a cracker. With my mouth full, I quickly realized I must have done something wrong when I saw Lyn's face. She kindly explained that the English eat cheese *after* a meal, not before! We laughed at my social faux pas, since it was now clear that, in the United States, this would've been like walking into someone's home and immediately helping oneself to a slice of the dessert on the counter before eating dinner.

While we ate, I told Geoff about my conversation with Shellburn. He sighed and told me he wasn't surprised.

"The Shellburns started out as farmers five centuries ago," he explained. "Over time, they amassed a notable amount of success and wealth. Shellburn even invested significantly in Germany. He's got a second home there and a third one in the south of France."

The problem was, Geoff filled me in, my neighbor had recently suffered a stroke, and it changed him drastically as a person.

"Shellburn used to be a friendly and amiable sort, the kind of person who was at every community event and town meeting. But now he's become withdrawn. You rarely see him around town anymore, and when you do, he barely says a word. These days, he walks with a cane." Maybe that was why he was disconnected from the area, aloof, and without local community spirit.

After we finished our meal, Geoff decided to look in his archives for an original map of the area so we could see the particular triangle of land that was causing us so much trouble. While he was out of the room, Lyn mentioned she had seen an uptick in her husband's spirits since I'd gotten more involved in the Hall.

"Meeting you has been good for him, Hopwood," she explained. "Geoff's in his seventies now. All his life he's worked as an undertaker—he's very much aware that the clock is ticking, and no one lives forever."

Lyn told me that now I was in the picture, Geoff felt like there might be someone to inherit everything he knew about the Hall and local history.

I felt honored and humbled. Seventy thousand photographs, seventy-plus years of local knowledge packed into his highly intelligent brain—how on earth could I even be considered a candidate for such a responsibility?

Just then, Geoff came rushing back into the living room covered in dust.

"Well, I didn't find the map . . . but I found this!" he said as he produced an old bottle of port from behind his back.

"This was a gift given to me at the hospital when Lyn had our first daughter, Kara!" he continued.

"Oh, Geoff! Where on earth did you find that?" Lyn said laughing at his spry behavior.

"Right where I left it! I've been looking for it for forty-two years. Blimey. Shall we see how it tastes?"

"Geoff, it's one o'clock in the afternoon!" Lyn reminded him.

"Lyn, we're retired. Now we can do things like this," he said convincingly.

They both turned to look at me.

"What do you think, Hopwood?" Geoff lifted the bottle and raised an eyebrow.

Of course, I couldn't say no. I loved how Geoff and Lyn were always prepared to seize the moment. They knew they were getting older and that their time was limited, and they didn't want to waste a minute.

We chatted the afternoon away, and I ended up staying for dinner too. Lyn cooked her homemade fish pie, and we all sat down to the candlelit table by the fireplace in their comfy kitchen. At some point the conversation turned to my dad.

"How did he die?" Lyn asked. "Sorry if I am being too bold. I am just used to asking these questions at the funeral home."

"It's okay," I replied. "Talking about it helps in some way. It was a heart attack. He was seventy-five, but still . . . it was a shock."

"Well, I hope that when my time comes, it's swift and painless," she said as she gently smiled at Geoff. "He's almost the same age as what your father was when he died. I just can't imagine being here without him."

Geoff reached over and squeezed her hand.

"Honestly, I don't know how your mother holds it together so well," Lyn said, the candles on the table casting a warm glow on her face. "If it were me, I think I'd still be in pieces. I do hope I get to go first!"

That evening was the first time I recognized that being around the undertaker and his wife was changing me, helping me to see things from a different perspective. They had lived with death and history on a daily basis, and this had blessed them with the unique understanding of how minuscule our existence is in the grand scheme of things. It was such a different perspective from the one I was used to in Hollywood, where everything revolves around who returns your phone calls, what project you're working on, what parties you're invited to, and how you rank socially. I also was very aware that I was suddenly becoming very close to people whom I would never otherwise have had the chance to meet if it hadn't been for Hopwood Hall.

Over the next eighteen months, I went back and forth between LA and Middleton, attending meetings about the hotel development, trying to do whatever I could to help push things forward. My phone call with Phineas Shellburn led to a promise of him meeting with Oliver Simmons and myself to discuss the sale of the land next time I was in England. It seemed like progress was about to be made, but then we hit another brick wall: Phineas Shellburn suffered a complication with his heart and had to be rushed to the hospital for an operation and recovery.

As urgent as the Hall was, we all realized Shellburn's life and health took priority. We'd have to wait.

Without Shellburn selling us the land, the whole project might fall apart. Meanwhile, Shellburn seemed to be genuinely struggling with his health, unable to think about anything but getting better.

The meeting was put off, seemingly indefinitely. We tried to forge ahead regardless, but as time went on, I could tell everyone was getting nervous.

When it took Oliver over a week to return one of my calls, I knew deep down that the project wasn't going to happen.

I made one last trip back to England to try to help pick up the pieces, but the meeting did not go well. As I approached the Norton Grange Hotel on my way back from Rochdale, my phone buzzed. It was Oliver Simmons, and it was not good news.

"Hopwood, I am done," Oliver said quite forcefully into the other side of the phone. "My partners have just walked, so I am moving on. Honestly, this whole Shellburn thing is sucking the life out of me. Sorry, I know you care about the Hall, but our project has just crashed and burned."

CHAPTER 10

THE DECISION

I'd briefly thought about asking Oliver to reconsider, but if my time in Hollywood has taught me anything, it's that there's no point arguing with the person who holds the purse strings when they've decided to pull them shut. Trying to persuade them to change their mind usually ends in weeks (or months) of wasted time with the same result. I hung up the phone and walked sadly back to Norton Grange. I thought about the Hall and what would happen to it now. I thought about Oliver and his bottom line, about Bob and Geoff and what they were going to think when they found out that the project wasn't going ahead. All anyone had told me for the past two years was that a hotel was the last chance for the hall's survival. The consensus was "If this doesn't happen, it's not going to happen." Was Oliver right? Was this really the end of the road?

The next day, I grabbed my brolly—as I now knew to call my umbrella—and headed to the Hall, where I was due to meet Bob to work on helping to unload some new scaffolding. As I approached, Bob had a very somber look on his face.

"Nothing like a bit of hard labor to take your mind off bad news, eh?" Bob pointed out.

I nodded, but deep down I knew that wasn't going to be true. Regardless, we got to work. The scaffolding was disassembled and stacked in a heap of pieces in the back of his silver work van. Bob explained that, typically, scaffolding is rented for a short amount of time, but that at Hopwood Hall, where so many parts of the building were in danger of collapse, there would *always* be a need for scaffolding, and so he had found that it was cheaper to purchase it whenever he found a good deal rather than incur the expense of the council having to rent it indefinitely.

In LA, I would regularly go to the gym to use 35-pound dumbbells, but for some reason when lifting a 35-pound piece of scaffolding, I felt as if I were on Jupiter, where things weigh twice as much as on Earth, as if my arms were about to snap off.

One by one we carried the pieces in, through the carriage entrance, up a few stairs from the Guards' Room into the Reception Hall, past the "By Degrees" fireplace, and partway down the long corridor of the Gallery, where we could later assemble the pieces to help prop a section of the ceiling that Bob noticed had recently dropped by an inch.

How on earth Bob could notice that a section of ceiling had settled an inch in this ginormous house was beyond my comprehension. But he had an uncanny talent for it.

He showed me his system.

"Once I notice even the slightest movement," he said, "I hang a long string from the ceiling using bolts as weights and then marked the height of the bolt against a board with a pencil so I can see if the ceiling is moving any farther. Then I can call the council with regular updates."

It reminded me a bit of how my sister Dana measured Jetsen's growing height on a wall chart with a pencil, phoning everyone in the family to report if Jetsen had grown a half inch. Except in this case, it was the opposite—Jetsen was slowly growing *up*, whereas the ceiling was slowly coming *down*. The more it moved, the closer it was to falling completely.

After all the scaffolding was piled up in the Gallery Corridor, I took a rest on the floor, my head in my hands. I was hoping the endorphins from the exertion of hauling might have helped, but looking around me, seeing the sagging ceiling only made me feel worse.

"Need a brew?" Bob said as he opened his thermos and poured himself a hot tea. This time I knew better than to think he was offering me a beer—although with all the stress and uncertainty I probably would've taken him up on it if he had.

"Geoff's on his way over," Bob said as he looked down at the steam rising out of his mug. "Bad news always travels fast."

After Geoff arrived, we stood in a huddle and tried to strategize.

"Just because Oliver Simmons is no longer interested in the Hall doesn't mean that the dry rot is going to magically disappear," Bob said. "Half the ceiling in the long corridor is falling down. There's only so many times I can prop it up before it's going to collapse completely."

Geoff was doing his best to put a positive spin on the situation, but even he seemed depressed.

"Maybe Oliver's right," he said. "Maybe it just wasn't meant to be.

Thanks for coming, Hopwood—your trips really lift our spirits—but it looks like we're in an impossible situation here."

I did my best to inject some good old American optimism into the late afternoon. "Where there's a will, there's a way"—that kind of thing. But Geoff and Bob stared at me over their cups of tea. They seemed unconvinced. I was too.

"I'm due to fly back in a couple of days," I told them. "But in the meantime, I can be here and help you as much as I can, Bob."

Not for the first time, the Hall's caretaker looked at me skeptically.

"To be honest, Hopwood, your 'help' often just slows me down," he said, sadly.

I knew he didn't mean to be rude but rather was stating the facts. We were in an even more desperate fight against the clock than ever, and my talent for sweeping up and struggling to lift things wasn't going to be the solution to the problem.

As it turned out, it was not the end of the line. There was another twist in store for the Hall—and for me.

The following morning, I got a phone call from Vernon Norris, the leader of the local council.

"Hopwood," Vernon explained. "I have a proposition for you."

I told him I was intrigued. Rochdale Council was the official owner of the Hall—it had taken possession of it after the monks who used to live there moved out. According to Geoff, Vernon had also been in office when the council assumed ownership thirty years ago. Back then, the Hall was still in decent condition, and Vernon hadn't been happy that it had been attacked by vandals, causing it to fall into disrepair since—it was a protected building, after all.

Rochdale Borough was an economically challenged area, and the late-night hunt for treasure at Hopwood Hall was a popular one with local thieves. There were also rumors of the Hall being haunted, so breaking in was a common dare among alcohol-fueled teens. Once the damage was done, the challenge to repair the Hall was partly lack of available funds—but also limited time and professional resources. Aside from Geoff and Bob, very few people had contacted the council to campaign on behalf of the Hall.

As a politician, Vernon was beholden to his constituents, and locals had other important priorities, such as police, fire, and health services, that took precedence over rescuing a six-hundred-year-old wreck of a home that was uninhabited and would require a huge and undetermined injection of cash.

"I am having surgery on Tuesday," Vernon went on. "Could you meet me there?"

"You're having surgery?" I responded, concerned.

I had no idea that, in the UK, *surgery* means the time an elected official puts aside to meet with his or her constituents. I assumed that Vernon was having an operation. I'd met him on a couple of occasions in the past, and he once mentioned having his appendix out recently. I thought perhaps there were complications, and he was going back into hospital.

"Could I meet you before . . . or after your surgery?" I held my breath. I'm a bit squeamish.

"Well, if you can't meet me during my surgery, then I suppose we could have a late lunch after."

"Yes! Let's do that instead! I like that idea."

"All right, meet me after my surgery at 3 p.m., and then we'll go to lunch."

"Okay . . . should I come to the hospital?" I wondered.

"No, we do it at the library!" he replied.

By now, I was completely flummoxed.

It turned out that wasn't the end of the day's confusions. I decided that while I was in Rochdale meeting Vernon, I would take the opportunity to get myself some warmer clothes. The Hall did not have any heating, and the ancient stone walls seemed to make the subzero temperature inside feel even colder. After about an hour of helping Bob, I was usually trembling, my lips turning blue, and considering going *outside* to warm up.

There was one big department store in town that would have some thick sweaters for sale. I found the store and hurried inside, picking up a pair of hefty socks I spotted on my way in. I saw a few salespeople behind the counter, so I made my way over to ask where I might find their selection of sweaters.

The salesgirl looked at me rather oddly, then blurted, *"Jumpers* are on the top floor!"

I was baffled at her response. I had no idea that a *jumper* is what people in England call a sweater. The only time I've ever heard that word was on American TV cop dramas when a suicidal person was on the edge of the roof of a building about to leap to their death.

Everyone in the store seemed to be acting normally. How could there be jumpers on the top floor, and no one was doing anything?

I was so stunned at her calm behavior that I stood there in shock. Then I realized she had actually said *jumpers*, with an *s*.

"H-how many are there?!" I asked. "How many jumpers are on the top floor?"

She shrugged. "Dozens," she replied nonchalantly.

"There are DOZENS of jumpers on the top floor?! Is it a protest or something?" I looked between her and her male counterpart, who was systematically folding clothes in the corner.

They both looked confused. "No sir, they're just up there . . . hanging," he said.

"*Hanging?*"

I spotted an escalator in the corner. Perhaps it was the inner Boy Scout in me, but I knew I needed to help.

I tossed the pair of socks on the counter and rushed to the escalator, taking two stairs up at a time. Hopefully I could make it up there in time to talk some sense into the "jumpers" and save some lives.

Of course, as I reached the top floor, I saw racks and racks of sweaters beneath a huge sign that said: JUMPERS—2 FOR £50.

At that point, I was thinking about jumping myself, but I didn't want to be late for Vernon at his surgery. After paying for my new "jumper" and socks, I made my way to the nearby library. I hoped Vernon was doing okay.

I was relieved to find him in good health and meeting his constituents at a table among the shelves of books.

We headed to lunch at what seemed like the fanciest restaurant in Rochdale, with crystal chandeliers, white linen tablecloths, and large glass windows that overlooked the lush green lawn beyond. Vernon was a bespectacled older gentleman in a full business suit, looking very professional.

After we ordered our rag puddings—ground beef and onions in suet pastry, apparently a local delicacy—Vernon got straight to business.

"Hopwood," he told me. "As you know, the hotel plans have dissolved. The Hall is not going to survive unless someone steps in and does something. You seem to have fallen in love with the place. What would you think about stepping up and taking over? I bet you could come up with some creative ways to breathe life back into the Hall. The Hopwoods have been missing for almost a hundred years. It's your ancestral home. It needs someone like you to think out-of-the-box to make it happen."

I told Vernon I was happy to help, but leading the whole project was a different matter. There were lots of elements to consider.

"With all due respect, what makes you think I could take on a renovation project like this?" I said. "I have very little experience doing anything like this. In fact, the last home improvement task I took on ended up with me in tears in a Home Depot parking lot."

"I've done my research online," he replied. "I know you've produced film, telly, and festivals. Aren't your skills—managing a lot of people and moving parts—exactly what this rescue could use?"

He did have a point. The strange patchwork of skills I had acquired over my twenty-five years in the entertainment business was diverse. Home improvements seemed daunting, but thanks to my time producing, I was comfortable handling people and could break down a larger vision into smaller, achievable jobs without having a minor meltdown.

"But who's going to pay for everything now that the hotel people have backed out?" I asked. Watching movies get produced—or not—in Hollywood, I knew coming up with the millions of pounds needed to restore the Hall would be no easy feat, especially with a house that many people might consider a money pit.

"The important thing is that there are grants available to help," Vernon reassured me. He went on to explain that Britain's National Lottery gives out hundreds of millions of pounds every year to help rescue important historical buildings like Hopwood Hall. "With your enthusiasm and drive, they would likely want to help you."

"But . . . I still have a life in LA," I insisted. "And what about my career?"

"You don't have to move here," Vernon persisted. "You can oversee it from overseas, as it were. Perhaps an occasional visit, as you are already doing."

I stared at my glass of water as the waiter filled it. I knew that a main rule of real estate dealings was never to get emotionally connected to property . . . but here I was, emotionally connected.

I also knew what my grandfather, Pap, would have said: "Doing something is better than doing nothing."

Then there was my dad's favorite saying ringing in my ears: *If you don't like the way something is going, then change it.*

I found I was nodding yes.

Vernon's eyes widened. He smiled reassuringly.

"Could you write me a letter?" he asked. "Tell me why you are passionate about the Hall, why you care so much. And how you have the ideas and excitement to save it. If you can do that, I know there are a lot of people out there who would like to see a Hopwood back in that Hall."

I headed back to the bus stop, rode the fifteen-minute journey back to the Norton Grange, went up to my room, and fell onto the bed. I turned on music videos and ordered a bottle of wine and a dish of ice cream from room service. Even though at lunch I'd sat there nodding away, I knew I still had some deep soul searching to do. These two items seemed like the best aids to get there.

Was it crazy to think I could run this project? Taking it over would be a huge amount of responsibility. Yes, in many ways, it would be a lot like producing a movie. But on the other hand, it would likely be more like producing *ten* movies back-to-back. And on the *other* other hand, maybe taking on this responsibility was exactly what I needed. I didn't have kids, I had the time, and perhaps this midlife madcap adventure was presenting itself for a reason. One of the most rewarding but challenging projects I had tackled in my past was producing the annual Waterfront Film Festival near where I was raised in West Michigan. I had founded it with my two sisters and a couple of friends, and we had grown the festival from being nonexistent to attracting over twenty thousand people each year for the four-day event. Maybe Vernon was right that my skills could transfer over, helping take the Hall rescue over the finish line. I scratched my head.

The one person I knew I could call was my mom. Her love of the Hopwood family history was unmatched by anyone.

Perhaps at my age, constantly relying on my mother for her advice made me somewhat of a mama's boy, but since my dad's death I increasingly cherished our relationship and also felt more protective of her. I knew from painful life experience that at any moment, she too could be taken from me forever.

"What does your heart tell you to do?" she asked softly but matter-of-factly in a way that only a mother could.

"I'm not sure," I said. "But if everything happens for a reason, then there has to be a reason I'm here."

"Well, think positively and relax," she said. I could faintly hear the news on the television in the background. "I'm sure the right answer will come to you."

I hung up and thought of her sitting there listening to the news alone without my father. *She must be lonely*, I thought. I felt a tug that I should be there in Michigan with her, not chasing some insane restoration project. I should be married and giving her grandchildren to focus on! But then I thought of my father, how his life had been ripped away from him without a moment's notice, and how it made me sense the ticking of my own clock. Maybe I needed to take these kinds of risks while I was still young enough to do it. I took a deep breath.

There was a knock at my door, and I opened it to find a smiling older woman delivering my ice cream and wine. Apparently, my order had tipped her off, because she seemed to have an insight into my soul.

"You know, the hotel has a lovely hot tub and sauna," she told me as I signed the receipt.

I laughed. "Do I look that stressed?"

"It's open until nine," she said with a friendly wink as she started down the hall.

It seemed like good advice. I took a sip of wine before tying myself into a robe and heading down to the tub, in a newer annex connected to the hotel. The room had a roll-up door that opened to overlook the edge of the original estate.

I sat in the tub by myself. The sun was just setting over the ridge, and it cast a beautiful orange glow on the surrounding landscape and through the windows of the small room. On the side of the hot tub was a large spigot that poured hot water back into the tub like a waterfall. I stood underneath it for a few moments. The water was powerful, and as it cascaded down my back, I outstretched my arm. Suddenly the water, with all its force, was racing down my arms and looked as though it was shooting out of my hands. It was an incredible, powerful feeling. As I raised my arms, water sprayed back into the hot tub, which was now drenched with orange light from the setting sun. I felt like I was playing the part of some kind of bizarre superhero—"Hot Tub Man," or something. As if all the experiences I had in life had led to this very moment. I looked out at the land of my ancestors. I knew everything was going to be okay. I was exactly where I needed to be. I thought about what my mother had said, about my father and Pap. The path forward suddenly became clear.

Back in my room, with wet hair and in the comfortable warm robe, I opened my laptop.

The words started to flow as I began to write the letter.

The title of the email was "Plan to Save Hopwood Hall from Ruin."

CHAPTER 11

OPERATION SAVE HOPWOOD HALL

$\mathcal{T}$he cabinet at the council approved your letter," said Vernon Norris, leader of the council. I could practically hear his smile beaming through the phone.

I almost dropped my skinny vanilla ice-blended. I was at the Coffee Bean in Hollywood near the corner of Sunset and Vine. I immediately shut my laptop and walked outside to avoid the background noise of frothing lattes and people purposely talking too loudly about their next movie so that everyone within earshot would know about it.

Standing outside in the warm breeze, I looked up at the palm trees swaying above.

Vernon quickly continued with the business at hand. "I have instructed our legal department to begin drafting an agreement between you and us that will allow you plenty of time to flesh out your plan to save the Hall."

In my letter I had suggested that I work in collaboration with the council to put together a combination of private investments with charitable donations and grants to stabilize Hopwood Hall, thereby preserving it for future generations.

"Do you have a solicitor?" he asked.

". . . A what?" I stammered.

"A solicitor," he said again. "Well, you Americans call it a lawyer. Do you have one? You may need one in England to help close the deal."

I hadn't even thought about getting a lawyer.

"Yes, I do," I said without a beat.

Half the job of producing is saying yes and then figuring out the details of how to make it happen later. Pacing in front of the Coffee Bean, I realized I was suddenly in full producer mode.

"Great. Bev and our legal department will be in touch in due course to help arrange," Vernon said as he hung up the phone.

And just like that, Operation Save Hopwood Hall was launched.

"That sounds expensive," said Jay later that afternoon as he perused the menu at Villa Blanca in Beverly Hills. "I have no doubt that if you put your mind to it, you'll be able to save it, but have you thought about what you would do with it when it's done? Would you live there?"

"I'm not totally sure," I said as I eyed the $26 chicken burger listed on the menu. It was exactly what I was hungry for, but I had to face my new reality of international phone calls, flights, and now "solicitors." I opted for the $14 soup instead.

A waiter appeared with a basket of warm bread, lowering it toward our table.

"Oh, we're not going to need that," Jay announced. "Too many carbs." He ran his hand over his abs.

The waiter nodded knowingly and walked away. I watched as our fresh, steaming bread disappeared back into the kitchen. I tried to imagine Bob's reaction if someone sent his breadbasket away.

"I'd like to make it a place where people can come and visit," I told Jay, my stomach grumbling. "Where guests feel comfortable. And inspired. Like I did the first time I went there."

"Like a hotel?" Jay asked, a bit dumbfounded. "Are you sure you really want to ditch your career to get into the hotel business?"

"Not a hotel. More like a . . . retreat," I said. "An arts retreat that becomes a gathering place for the community and for people from all over the world. Someplace where filmmakers, writers, performers, and other artists can meet and make art. Get away from their real lives for a bit and feel creative. The idea that Lord Byron went to Hopwood Hall and felt inspired to write his most famous poem while wandering around the woods makes me realize there is something special about the place. I felt the same way. Maybe others would want to go there and experience their own . . . awakening."

Jay stared at me. I wondered if he thought I was crazy.

"Kind of like an ayahuasca retreat . . . but without the ayahuasca," he joked.

I laughed, even though I wasn't completely sure what ayahuasca was. But describing what I had in mind as a "retreat" made a lot of sense. Geoff had told me that in times gone by, stately homes like Hopwood Hall would have been run almost like resorts or hotels, places where guests would visit for weeks on end, with a large staff running the place to make sure everyone was welcomed, fed, and accommodated. I wanted to bring some of those glory days back, even if people nowadays were more likely to arrive with rolling suitcases rather than steamer trunks.

"I love the concept," Jay said. "I bet a lot of our actor and screenwriter clients would be tripping over themselves to stay at a place like that to write, get centered, and come up with their next projects. Just like Lord Byron!"

I was shocked. Jay was always optimistic and supportive of my ideas, but I wasn't sure if he would be on this one.

Even Jonny agreed.

"Bro, that would be cool," he said as he scanned the toned and tanned crowd at Bootsy's. "You could even have DJs there at night! You know, to entertain the artists."

Was I on to something? The more I thought about it, the more the idea seemed to gel.

I knew it would be many years before this vision could be realized, but at least it was a plan. A trajectory and a goal. For now, my focus needed to remain on the task in front of me: Stabilize the Hall before it was lost forever.

The project quickly consumed all my waking hours. I was talking with Geoff and Bob on the phone, googling, finding out all I could about large-scale restorations of this kind. Even at night as I slept, I had dreams about Hopwood Hall.

Suddenly springing awake in the early morning, I had a strikingly clear thought: that the security gate to the Hall had been left open. I couldn't explain it. I got out of bed at 2:13 A.M. and wrote an email to Bob.

"Can you check the gate at the Hall? I woke up from a bizarre dream that someone left it open."

I went back to bed for a few hours. When I got up again, I had an email back.

"The Hopwood ghosts must be talking to you in your sleep," Bob wrote. "It was open! There was a structural survey done late yesterday and they forgot to lock it."

My first reaction to the email was to feel a bit creeped out. But the longer I thought about it, the more reassured it made me feel. Maybe I wasn't pulling all the strings.

Within a few weeks I was back at the Hall and working with Bob and Geoff every day. It felt good to be in the middle of the action again, even if there were immediate problems.

The reason the council had recently ordered the structural survey was to determine the safety of the building and if it might collapse. Because the council owned the Hall, we had to go through all kinds of approvals as governmental bodies typically require.

"Be patient," Bev Percival would say. "In England, whenever you are dealing with historic buildings and government permissions, it has to be a thorough process, one that can take much longer than any of us would like."

Meanwhile, Bob's sagging ceiling measuring system was telling us the Gallery was about as stable as a snowman. Unfortunately, repairing the ceiling fully didn't seem like an option given the high expense—the council simply didn't have the money.

"Why can't we go in and just stick some strong two-by-fours under the ceiling?" I asked Bob, trying to sound like I knew what I was talking about.

Bob explained the repairs were complex. Once you started you couldn't stop, and using the wrong materials had the potential to cause even more damage. As the council had learned from prior experience, what appeared to be a "simple" £2,482 propping job very quickly turned into a £10,711 one with the discovery of unknown factors after the work got started. And these were all temporary fixes, with the money not going toward anything long-term.

Bob mentioned that a bit more of our own propping materials might help. "All you Americans are rich," he said, half kidding. "Why don't you just hire a company to drop off another load of scaffolding?"

Compared to the costs of historical preservation, suddenly a $26 Beverly Hills chicken burger seemed reasonable.

I considered fronting the money for more scaffolding to at least save the ceiling. But although the council was struggling to pay for it themselves, they were also unable to allow me to pay for anything.

"Legally, it puts the council in a precarious situation," said Bev Percival. "We are very appreciative of all your help, but it could cause issues if we allow a private individual to pay for repairs before we have a formal legal agreement in place."

To be honest, I was very relieved, but I also couldn't sit back and watch the Hall crumble. I had to do something. I began looking into the grants that Vernon had mentioned.

As I did some digging, I learned there had been several attempts in the past to apply for grants to save the Hall, but they had all been denied due to the lack of a clear direction for the long term, in addition to the access issue that was the deal breaker for the hotel project. There are so many historical buildings in England in need of repair that most charitable preservation groups will only issue funds to help if it truly seems like the building will eventually be up and running—where it can "wipe its own boots" and survive without relying on grants forever. We needed a crystalized plan with someone to lead it.

I now knew this fell on my shoulders. Bob estimated it was

going to cost about ten million pounds (a little over $13 million in US dollars) to fully renovate the Hall, and then half a million pounds (around $600,000) a year for upkeep. Obviously, very few people on earth could foot this bill themselves. I was going to need help, and lots of it. Especially now that I'd given up my career and all prospects of any job on the horizon!

Fortunately, I had some experience in fundraising for both commercial film projects and charitable community efforts, so it didn't intimidate me entirely. I knew it would be a lot of work, but it could be done if the stars aligned. The council was able to come through with some additional funds and committed to help as much as they could. Bob was able to convince the owners of a local construction site to give us their beat-up old scaffolding in exchange for him consulting with them on a historical section of their project. This would go a long way for more ceiling propping. They also threw in some scrap boards and lumber that we could use for temporary holding efforts, such as closing off dangerous rooms or boarding up windows. People donating surplus supplies was one way we could cut the budget and take another baby step toward the rescue. I went with Bob in his van to retrieve donated materials from the construction site and later from other residents, who contacted us when they found leftover items that could be used. Somehow, between us, the community, and the council, the ceiling was saved from collapse, at least for now.

CHAPTER 12

INVITATION TO
A CASTLE

I've got something to show you," Geoff said one day. We were having lunch at the pub when he pulled out what looked like another vintage book from his collection. "Look at this."

It turned out that Geoff had tracked down an original auction catalog from 1923, the year that all the original furniture was sold from Hopwood Hall.

"You remember Edward and Robert?" he asked.

I did. They were the heirs to Hopwood Hall who had been killed in World War I.

"The poor parents held on at the Hall as best they could until 1921, when they finally decided to move to London. They still struggled for a few years with the decision of what to do with their home, but as their health began to deteriorate, the chattels were all auctioned off in 1923."

"The chattels?" I asked.

"That's what we call the furniture, the family portraits, the crockery, everything that went along with the house," Geoff said patiently.

I carefully opened the yellowed catalog, landing on a page showcasing the most beautiful, ornate wooden four-poster bed. The bed sat on a platform, with two hand-carved columns at one end and a wooden canopy overhead.

"Wow." I was breathless. "This was in the Hall?"

"Yes indeed," he replied. "In fact, that is the 'Lord Byron bed' where he stayed when he visited."

I put my hand on my forehead. I was in awe.

"Where is it?" I asked.

"Beats me!" Geoff said with a laugh. "But there are ways of finding out."

I looked up at him, intrigued.

"In this country, we are very diligent about tracking the provenance of antique and expensive chattels, where auctioneers and furniture houses, buyers and sellers, all keep track of the origin and history of pieces as they are bought and sold and move from one place to the next. There are even 'furniture detectives' you can hire to help you."

I focused on the old, grainy black-and-white photo of the bed, thinking how incredible it would be to find it. I couldn't help but feel like a little kid, excited for an amazing adventure.

I realized I was getting ahead of myself, looking at furniture while the Hall was still falling down, but if my years of producing projects had taught me anything, it was that you have to plant seeds early in order to give them time to grow.

"You know, there are some marvelous auction houses just an hour or so north of here that handle many of the items in the North

The famous "Lord Byron bed," as nicknamed by the ladies of the house,
Hopwood Hall Estate, 1850s *C. Stuart MacDonald "A History of
Hopwood Hall," Waldegrave Ltd.*

West of England. If you find yourself at a loose end one day, you
could take the train up there and do some poking around. Who
knows what you might find? I'd offer to take you, but Lyn has for-
bidden me to go without her because she knows I'll return home
with a boot full of books!"

Geoff gave me the address of an auction house in the next

county over, Yorkshire. The following Saturday, it became apparent that trying to get there by myself might be more challenging than expected, beginning with the simple task of purchasing a train ticket.

Walking up to the automatic ticket machine on the local train platform, I realized there was no roof covering it. *How does someone hold an umbrella and buy a train ticket all at the same time?* I wondered. I tried to balance the umbrella on my shoulder and hold it with my chin as I pulled out my credit card. Perhaps we are spoiled, but in LA it seems like we have a roof over everything. Because if you get wet, you could probably sue somebody.

I noticed a few people looking at me oddly, so I put my umbrella to the side and stood there in the rain, sliding my card into the machine. *This is going to be a bad hair day,* I thought. But now that I have a "solicitor," I wondered if I might have a legal case.

The first button to select on the screen was Peak or Off-Peak.

Hmm. I would guess a Saturday would be off-peak, but I wasn't sure and didn't want to buy the wrong ticket. There were signs posted everywhere saying "Customers with an invalid ticket will be fined and/or jailed," but nothing that explained the concept of peak or off-peak.

I turned toward a woman waiting in line behind me.

"Hi, can you tell me when is peak and when is off-peak?" I asked.

She stared at me for a moment. I think she may have thought I was trying to pick her up. Then, in a strong English accent, she very matter-of-factly said: "Peak is around teatime."

Suddenly, I could hear the train approaching. Followed by the machine starting to beep.

"Hurry up, mate," said a tattooed man waiting behind her. "Train's coming!"

I was frozen. *BEEP, BEEP, BEEP.* The machine blinked at me. I turned back to the woman.

"And when is teatime?" I asked.

The tattooed man exploded. "What kind of bloody game is this, ya wanker? Get your ticket and move on!"

Panicked, I pushed Off-Peak and hoped for the best, quickly gathering my umbrella as the train pulled up. I purposely walked several train cars away so that I wouldn't ever have to see those people again.

As the train wound through the beautiful green hillsides, with sheep, thatched-roof houses, and stone walls whizzing by, the sun began to emerge from behind the clouds. I was drying out and feeling better. Curious, I googled *What is teatime in England?* and quickly found out that, in the North, "teatime" isn't referring to the drink but rather a meal, and is basically the equivalent of America's dinnertime. A lesson I wouldn't soon forget. All this thinking about it made me hungry, so I bought a sandwich and settled in for the hour-and-forty-minute journey.

A few hours later, I was at one of the biggest auction houses in the North of England, called Tennants Auctioneers, in Leyburn. Tennants had been around for over forty years, was highly regarded, and had even been visited by members of the Royal Family. The auction house handled most of the items that would go up for auction in North West England, so this seemed like the right place to start if I was going to be my own furniture detective.

I was also hoping to meet some employees to make a connection so that if they happened to come across a piece that had a provenance connected to Hopwood Hall, they would know to call me.

The staff there was a very friendly bunch, and I soon found myself chatting directly with the owner, Mr. Tennant.

"Yes, of course we can help you find the furniture," he said. "It should be very traceable for a place like Hopwood Hall. In fact, I recall we had a few pieces of yours come through here a few months ago."

"Was it a bed?" I asked hopefully.

"Not a bed. I believe there were a few chairs and a portrait of one of your ancestors. I wish we had met back then . . . But certainly if anything else comes our way, we can let you know," he offered.

He gave me a tour of their massive two-story showroom and warehouse. I didn't want to be rude by asking about costs or peering at the minimum-bid price tags, but the few tags I did see were not for the faint-hearted.

As the tour was winding up, Mr. Tennant turned to me. "You should meet one of our best clients," he said. "His name is Dr. Rolph. He's an American. He's been restoring his castle for decades. Forty years ago, he was just like you; he even looked a bit like you back then, six-foot-two and blond. I bet you two would have a lot in common. I'll give him a ring and see if he would be willing to have a chat with you."

He disappeared into his office. A few minutes later, he returned to say that Dr. Rolph had agreed to meet me, and he wanted me to call his home number as soon as we were finished.

I stepped outside into the cool air in front of Tennant's and dialed the number. I have to admit I was a bit nervous.

"I've just had something come up, and I need to run out in about fifteen minutes," Dr. Rolph said after he greeted me on the phone. "Could I call you back on my cell phone?"

"Yes, of course," I replied, his American accent immediately putting me at ease.

"The only problem is that I'm in the kitchen, and my phone is charging in my bedroom," he continued. "It's going to take me about ten minutes to walk there."

Ten minutes to walk from his kitchen to his bedroom? *Wow, his castle must be huge,* I thought.

Fifteen minutes later my phone rang. "Sorry, it took me a bit longer than usual," Dr. Rolph said. "I try to avoid taking the elevator, but it's quite a distance and I'm getting older, so all the stairs slow me down."

Before I knew it, Dr. Rolph had invited me to Allerton Castle to visit.

"Would you like to join me for tea today?" he asked.

"Sure," I said. "Is that at dinnertime?"

Dr. Rolph chuckled. "No, that's in Manchester. I mean afternoon tea. I'll see you then?" he asked.

"Sorry, I'm not sure what time that means," I confessed.

Dr. Rolph laughed again. "Yes, I remember all the confusion about that from when I first moved here. It varies on which region of the country you are in. Afternoon tea is about four o'clock."

Finally, someone who speaks my language! I thought.

Later that day, my taxi entered Allerton's grand driveway, passing through beautiful green parkland for about a mile before I spotted the mammoth Gothic castle in the distance. I gasped. Allerton looked several times larger than the size of Hopwood Hall, built from dark gray stone, with soaring towers and spires and topped with billowing flags. Even from a distance, you could tell that the place was pristine—no trees growing from the rooftops or dumpsters overflowing with debris outside.

I climbed out of the taxi and walked up to the enormous double doors. I didn't see a doorbell. It seemed more like a place where there would be a rope hanging that would ring a massive bell in a tower. I was a bit baffled. *How do you even knock on this door?* I thought.

Just then, a tall, elegant man with silvery blond hair appeared through the glass panes in the door, descending some steps and opening the giant door with ease. He looked like one of those older models in a Tommy Hilfiger ad.

This was Dr. Rolph. He welcomed me, and I stepped inside. I was immediately taken with his perfectly upright posture, impressive for someone who was eighty years old.

"You're very punctual, right on time," Dr. Rolph said kindly, looking at his watch.

"Yes," I said with a smile, proud I had ticked that box.

He laughed. "In England, you should never be on time for a social occasion," he explained, clearly taking on the role of teacher with me. "In fact, if someone invites you to their home, you should be seven minutes late. You're an American so I can tell you this, but it's an unwritten rule among the British aristocracy. Don't worry, I learned the same lesson at about your age too."

Dr. Rolph closed the door behind us, and I followed him up five wide, red-carpeted stairs flanked by two life-sized statues of Dalmatians. We passed through two more huge ornate wooden doors on our way to the main foyer. Here my host pointed out that all the gigantic mahogany doors in the castle were perfectly balanced and measured so that, even though they weighed at least a ton each, they could be closed by a child.

I couldn't believe the size of the place. I was standing in the largest foyer I had ever seen in someone's private home: seven stories high with windows, arches, a sweeping staircase, portraits every-where. My mouth was agape.

"I've spent the past forty years restoring this place," Dr. Rolph told me. "I've handpicked every antique oil painting on the wall, every table and chair and stick of furniture, to bring the castle back to its original glory. I was searching for a purpose in my life when I found it at Allerton. Restoring this castle has become my life's work."

I wanted to know more about how an American like Dr. Rolph had ended up here in Yorkshire, and he was happy to oblige.

I learned that he had studied business at Harvard Business School and made his first fortune as an executive at the Tandy Corporation. Back then, Tandy was one of the first companies to see the future in home electronics, growing Radio Shack to a household name in the 1970s. Dr. Rolph parlayed his success into numerous other investments that all seemed to turn to gold. By his late thirties, he bought an estate in Fort Lauderdale with its own showroom for displaying the car collection that he had also begun acquiring. He bought a 121-foot, fully crewed yacht and had it docked in New York City so that he had somewhere to stay when visiting.

"I was on a tour of England in the Yorkshire countryside in 1983," Dr. Rolph recounted. "I was test-driving an antique roadster that I was considering adding to my car collection, when I happened upon Allerton Castle and stopped to investigate. It was abandoned, in bad shape, and for sale. I never bought the roadster, but I made an offer on Allerton that afternoon."

It became his pride and joy. He learned all about its history—that there had been a structure here since the eleventh century, but in the 1800s, the eighteenth Baron Staunton, who owned the place, knocked a portion of it down and commissioned a Victorian Gothic castle to be built. Dr. Rolph was entranced. Eventually, he sold off his cars, boats, and Florida estate and retired full-time to living at the castle.

I told him all about Hopwood Hall—my discovery that the castle my grandfather had told me stories about actually existed, and how I had come to Yorkshire to search for some of the house's original furniture.

Dr. Rolph nodded.

"Like you, I wanted to find some of the original pieces that belonged here at Allerton," he told me. "Unfortunately, that's sometimes impossible, so I also began acquiring pieces that are in keeping with the time period and style.

"And this is my baby," he said as he led me into the music room, running his hand over a large wooden curio-type box with glass windows that revealed a beautiful violin inside, with all sorts of metal rods surrounding it.

"It's an automatic violin playing machine that I am told was originally built for Queen Victoria just before she died," he said as he flicked a switch on the side, initiating a loud buzzing noise that sounded like the machine was warming up.

"She loved the violin, and I understand she had two of these built, in case one broke," Dr. Rolph continued. "The other one recently sold at auction for a large sum of money. I didn't pay anywhere near what they sold theirs for, so it was a good investment."

The machine suddenly clicked loudly and then began to play the most magnificent and haunting classical song. I looked up at the ornate ceiling, hand painted with frescoes of cherubs playing harps and flutes. It was surreal to think I was standing there listening to the same music as Queen Victoria.

"When I pass away, I'm leaving the castle and all these pieces to my foundation," Dr. Rolph said. "So that the castle can stay open, and people can come and visit to enjoy it like I have. It's my legacy."

That afternoon, Dr. Rolph showed me secret passageways, grand staircases, moving bookcases, and hidden apartments. He led me through many dozens of the castle's hundreds of rooms—at two hundred thousand square feet, the castle seemed endless. I saw gardens and bedrooms and wings and sections that he hadn't even started renovating yet. What I thought was going to be a quick afternoon tea turned into a four-hour experience of a lifetime.

On the lower level, in the expansive old servants' quarters with endless hallways, Dr. Rolph showed me the system of what appeared to be over a hundred servants' bells that the "upstairs" family could ring downstairs to summon a butler or chambermaid.

"And this is my workshop," he said as he opened a door to a large room. Various chandeliers hung low over a big workbench, waiting to be refurbished. A statue with a broken head sat in the corner; a huge, half-polished copper cup sat on another bench near the window with rubbing compound, rags, and brushes lying next to it. The walls were lined with shelves containing materials, paint, wire, tools—hundreds of items stacked from floor to ceiling. This is where Dr. Rolph had painstakingly restored most of the treasures throughout the castle by himself. All those years of caring for his car collection had taught him some incredible restoration skills. My barely improving DIY talents didn't even come close.

I was already amazed and impressed—but then, as we left the workshop and walked back along the hallway leading to it, I noticed the framed newspaper articles hanging on the walls. "Castle Burns," "Allerton Castle Goes Up in Flames," "Stately Home Gutted," the headlines read, alongside photos of the castle ablaze.

I looked at Dr. Rolph in shock.

"Ah," Dr. Rolph said, noticing my stunned expression. "The fire."

He proceeded to tell me that about ten years ago, just after he had completed restoring the estate, one of his staff called the fire department after someone had smelled smoke. The fire department came out and checked but couldn't find anything, so they left, thinking everything was fine. Unfortunately, their ladders didn't go high enough to reach the top of the chimneys, so unbeknownst to anyone, a fire was burning in a bird's nest at the very top—that then spread to the rafters. Suddenly the roof of the castle was engulfed. A third of the house burned down that terrible night.

"Once I had come this far, I couldn't give up because of a fire," Dr. Rolph said. "I knew when I bought this castle that a project like this would never be over and would be a lifetime commitment, so I rolled up my sleeves, and we got back to work. Instead of thinking that a third of the castle was destroyed, I preferred to remind myself that we had two-thirds still in great shape."

Talking to him made me feel like my "crazy" mission to rescue Hopwood Hall wasn't so crazy after all. In fact, at only fifty thousand square feet, Dr. Rolph would probably consider Hopwood Hall a small project!

If he had the energy to take on rebuilding Allerton in his midseventies, then I should certainly be able to do what I have to in my forties, I thought.

Dr. Rolph must have read my mind, because he looked at me and said with a laugh: "If I can do it, you can do it. And I've done it twice."

Spending time with him felt like talking to the Ghost of Christmas Future. Perhaps for Dr. Rolph, it felt as if I was the Ghost of Christmas Past.

It was getting late, so he offered to drop me at the local train station in his sleek black Range Rover so that I could catch a train back to Manchester. On the ride there, he said that if I wanted, he would be a mentor to me, introducing me to other people who could help with the restoration of Hopwood Hall.

"Dr. Rolph, thank you," I replied. "I'm just at the beginning of this journey in many ways—I can't tell you what that would mean to me."

"Well, the first thing you need to do is to put in an application to join Historic Houses," he said definitively. This was a group Dr. Rolph belonged to, an association representing the owners of many of Britain's largest historic private residences.

"It's incredibly helpful to have a network of people you can call upon for knowledge, advice, and understanding. These big houses are an overwhelming responsibility, so it's good to be able to talk to others who are struggling with the same issues, a bit like a support group. After all, we're all just temporary guardians of these places."

"Sure. I would love to," I said. "If you think they would allow me to join."

"Well, I can't make any promises, but if you can submit an application online, I will certainly give my recommendation to the president, who is a friend, and the board to approve your acceptance."

We pulled into the station, and I thanked him again as I climbed out.

I boarded the train with my off-peak return ticket and fell into my seat. Most people around me were drifting off to sleep, but I couldn't. I was exhausted from a long day, but also elated at where the unexpected adventure had taken me. I loved how being in England made me feel—I had no idea of what to expect day-to-day.

When a train attendant came through with a refreshment cart,

I ordered a mini bottle of wine and opened my laptop as the train shot through the darkened countryside. My life in Los Angeles felt a million miles away. I logged onto the Historic Houses website and filled out the application. I thought long and hard about my answers, as if I were applying to an Ivy League college.

An hour and a half later, as the train pulled up to my stop, I took a deep breath and hit Submit.

CHAPTER 13

MEETING THE ARISTOCRATS

*W*ould now be a good time to sell my house?" I asked, a bit surprised to hear myself saying those words.

I was back in LA, and Jonny and his friend Corey, a former male model turned Realtor, had come over for drinks. When Jonny invited me to go out with them, I suggested we meet at my house, I think secretly in hopes of asking Corey this very question. As he walked from the dining room into the kitchen of my Hollywood Hills Spanish bungalow, I could see he was now clearly appraising the place.

"Yes, it would be a great time," he replied, running his finger over a missing chip of paint in the kitchen. "This area is really hot right now. Why? Would you consider selling it?"

I looked at my white linen dining chairs from Pottery Barn, my vintage 1940s Wedgwood stove, and then down at the kitchen floor, where Marilyn Monroe had probably once laid a bowl filled with Meow Mix.

"I suppose everything is for sale, right?" I responded.

Jonny's eyes widened as he stood behind Corey's shoulder.

"It should be," he said. "In fact, I know of a client who happens to be looking for a place exactly like this. She's willing to pay a lot for a turnkey situation, where she can just show up with her bags and everything is included—furniture, plants, right down to your toaster and silverware."

"The chattels?" I asked.

"The *what*?" he asked, looking at me as if I had descended from another planet.

I was half joking and had no idea this casual conversation was suddenly going to develop into me having an offer to buy my beloved, *historic* home for an amount that could set a new record for a modest house in my neighborhood. Even though I'd been the one to broach the idea of selling my house with Corey, I hadn't imagined it would lead to someone wanting to buy it right away. I grappled with the decision. It was a big deal, and I only had seventy-two hours to make it, as the woman who wanted to buy the place needed to move fast and was considering other options.

Will selling my house mean I've given up on Hollywood? I asked myself. *What will people think?*

Deep down, I knew I had been spending a huge amount of time and money traveling back and forth to England. With my absentee record and distracted state, I hadn't been able to land a gig with a paycheck in quite some time. I was spending my savings on my English passion project, and a sudden injection of cash would allow me to continue my volunteer mission of rescuing the Hall.

Like everyone in Hollywood, I had occasionally daydreamed about packing up and leaving the rat race, but it always seemed impossible. Probably kind of like trying to break free from a cult. How would I be able to explain it to people without them writing me off? And selling my house and all my things in a typical way seemed overwhelming—a long, drawn-out extraction. So the idea of someone knocking on my front door and offering to pay for me to just walk away seemed like the universe signposting a clear direction. Suddenly the future seemed so bright, I had to put on my shades.

I decided to sleep on it.

"What would Dr. Rolph do?" I asked myself as I awoke the following morning. The answer was obvious.

"You're doing *what*?" Jay gasped into the phone. "Are you sure you've thought this through?"

"I think I have to jump on it," I said. "It feels like the right thing to do."

And just like that, I signed the papers and sold my house. I was going to be homeless in two weeks' time.

My initial plan was to stay temporarily in Michigan, closer to my family, before finding a small place to rent in LA so I had a base when I needed to come back for meetings.

The day of the house sale, I got cold feet. I woke up panicking.

I had lived in LA for almost twenty years. If I sold my house, would I still be able to call the city home? Where was "home," anyway? LA? Michigan? Or some small town in England that I had never known existed until a couple of years ago?

I phoned Jay.

"I must be having a midlife crisis, because I think I'm making irrational decisions. Do you think I could still get out of this?"

He laughed. "Even if you are having one, you have to ride it out. Something's telling you to go, so go. You can always stay with me when you come back."

It felt reassuring to have Jay in my corner, and knowing the code to his front door helped my fears subside.

I loaded my clothes and a few belongings into my Jeep and drove cross-country to my hometown of Holland, Michigan. On the way, I called some of my high school friends to let them know I would see them soon.

A few days later, I was parked at an Arby's in Oklahoma, eating a chicken gyro, no sauce, when my phone buzzed on my dashboard.

> *Dear Hopwood,*
>
> *Thank you very much for your application.*
>
> *I am glad to say that it was reported to the meeting of the Historic Houses Council held yesterday and so it has been unanimously approved.*
>
> *You will shortly be hearing from us in formal confirmation of your membership.*
>
> *Best wishes,*
>
> *Peter Sinclair*
>
> *Director of Operations*
>
> *Historic Houses*

I nearly choked on my gyro. I couldn't help but think how ridiculous it would be if I was found dead in the Arby's parking lot with an email open on my phone inviting me to join Historic Houses.

It had been several months since I'd sent off my application. As I hadn't heard anything, I assumed I had probably been rejected. After all, I was just a two-bit Yank without a proper title or affiliation.

I quickly responded with "Thank you! I'm thrilled!" and then fired off an email to Dr. Rolph to share the news and tell him how much I appreciated all his help.

"Fantastic," Dr. Rolph responded. "You are on your way, Hopwood."

A few weeks later, Geoff rang with an update on the Hall: "It has recently been noticed that due to windstorms over the years, an old cast-iron drainage pipe has rattled away from an exterior brick wall, causing another leak," Geoff informed me. "But this time the water was getting in through the wall rather than the roof, which had in turn caused an interior support beam for a window to crack in half, putting an entire two-story wall in jeopardy of further collapse."

Bob had been so busy trying to stop more damage from happening that he didn't have time to let me know.

I could tell it pained Geoff to be the messenger of misfortune. He quickly moved on to a brighter topic.

"Also, a letter arrived addressed to Hopwood DePree, Esquire, in care of Hopwood Hall," he said. "It's in a beautiful, thick, gold-leafed envelope and looks like some type of invitation. Would you like for me to open it and scan it to you?"

"Sure," I said. "But what's an esquire? Does that mean they think I'm a lawyer? I hope not, because I'm not."

"No, no," Geoff said reassuringly. "When British men are invited to important places, such as Buckingham Palace, they receive their invitations with 'esquire' behind their names as a title of respect. Typically, the term 'esquire' is reserved only for British men. Foreign nationals would instead receive it as 'mister.' So whomever sent this to you has clearly already adopted you as an honorary Brit."

It turned out that the invitation was for a Historic Houses reception being held in a few months at Lord's Cricket Ground in London.

As Geoff explained, "Lord's," as it is commonly referred to, is the most famous cricket ground in the world. It has an exclusive private members club with thousands of people on the waiting list for decades, and a lifetime membership that costs well over £30,000.

As soon as Geoff sent me a copy of the invite, I RSVP'd yes. The date of the event was November 23, 2016, just before Thanksgiving. I was going to miss spending it with my family for the first time in my life.

"Going to England for your first Thanksgiving will be just like what the Pilgrims did—but in reverse!" joked my mother. "I'm sure it will feel like a sacrifice, and we'll miss you, but we can always Skype with you on the day. The important thing is that you take the opportunities that will help you achieve your goals for the Hall—even if a lot of my friends do think my son is a bit crazy," she laughed.

I knew it was going to be completely surreal celebrating on my own, especially in a place where no one observes the holiday. On the other hand, perhaps it would do me good to shake the tree and try something totally different in a new culture. I looked up to Dr. Rolph, and he seemed like a guide on the road of life. Since he had waved me this way, could I really skip it?

I landed in London on Tuesday, in time for the event on Wednesday. I had no idea what to expect as I approached the ornate, orangish-brick Victorian building on St. John's Wood Road in London known as the Lord's Pavilion. Dr. Rolph had been thinking of attending, but decided a few days before it was probably best not to make the four-hour trip at his age.

"You'll be better off on your own," he said. "If I was there, I'd be a crutch. Go and shake hands and smile. Just don't make the mistake of showing up on time."

So off I went, knowing I was going to be walking into a room where I probably wouldn't know anyone. In my mind, I was somehow picturing a group of elderly people, sitting around, sipping on tea and chocolate bourbon biscuits (as close as the English get to Oreo cookies). As soon as I walked through the door to Lord's and up the stairs to the reception area, I realized I had underestimated the nature of the event. Immediately, a bow-tied waiter approached and handed me a glass of champagne.

I tried to absorb the opulent atmosphere, wandering around awkwardly for a few minutes before an elegantly dressed woman came up to me to say hello. She was also a member of Historic Houses and happened to be one of the organizers of the event. She offered to take me around and introduce me to people, leading me toward big double doors that were the entrance to the grand reception room, known as the long room. Before we went in, she turned to me with a sly smile and said, "Are you ready to be thrown to the wolves?"

I gulped and we went in.

Everywhere I looked there were more impeccably dressed gentlemen and ladies, sipping on champagne and enthusiastically conversing with one another. Portraits of famous cricketers, dating back to the 1700s, lined walls that were decorated with intricate moldings, and several huge chandeliers hung from high above, alongside two stories of large windows overlooking the cricket field.

My new friend led me around the room. Over the next hour, I met people with so many noble titles I lost track: Sir XYZ, Lord and Lady 123. My head was spinning. In Hollywood, I would at least have *some* idea of who I was talking to. But here, it was a room of complete strangers and a culture I knew nothing about.

"Have you met Geordie and Fiona?" When I replied that I hadn't, my friend introduced me to an attractive, sophisticated look- ing couple who were laughing as they were chatting.

Geordie and Fiona were incredibly welcoming as we said brief hellos. As we continued to move through the room, my guide whis- pered in my ear, informing me that Geordie was in fact a godson to the Queen and that together with his wife, Fiona, they were also known as Lord and Lady Carnarvon, the owners of Highclere Castle, aka the real-life Downton Abbey.

A few minutes later I was introduced to a man in a superbly nice suit who I soon learned was none other than Julian Fellowes, the creator of *Downton Abbey*, as well as his lovely wife, Emma, who was wearing a stunning gold head wrap that made her a standout in the room. They own Stafford House, a grand stone manor in Dorset, on the south coast of England, a little over two hours' drive from central London.

Julian (who is also a lord) seemed surprised to hear I had come all the way from LA to help save Hopwood Hall.

"And how is that going for you?" he asked, with raised eyebrows.

"We're just getting started. But I'm hoping for the best!" I said as confidently as I could.

"Well, first start with the roof, make sure it is dry inside and then go from there," he offered.

You might assume these English aristocrats would steer clear of an upstart outsider American, but in fact, the opposite was true. Everyone I met made me feel especially welcome, and before I knew it, I had a phone full of telephone numbers and email addresses, as well as invitations to visit many of their houses to gain advice. Any preconceived ideas or insecurities I had before meeting the aristocrats were now gone. Because I was a member, and because we had a shared love of old houses and history in common, I felt like I belonged.

Returning to my hotel that night, I was on a high. By an unlikely chain of events that had started in the auction house in Yorkshire, I had somehow stumbled into an entire subculture of stately home-owners with a vast array of expertise about how to restore, renovate, and maintain old houses. I returned to Middleton feeling like I had just returned from the beach. It was Thanksgiving Day, which is just a regular ol' Thursday in England, so I went back to work at the Hall, buoyed by the enthusiasm and know-how of the Historic Houses crowd.

Of course, I told Bob about my newfound friends.

"Make sure to keep your feet on the ground," he grumbled. "We've got some real work to do here, so we don't need you floating off, thinking you're royalty or anything."

Bob's side-mouthed comments often took the wind out of my sails, but I knew this was probably his roundabout way of saying he had missed me being at the Hall. Perhaps I was finally learning how to decipher Bob's Manchester humor: that when he insulted me or rained on my excitement, it was really a sign of friendship.

On the whole, I felt like we were beginning to reach a better level of understanding of each other. While Bob focused on the day-to-day physical repairs, I fell into a rhythm of doing whatever I could to support the overall project and keep it running. Even though we both would be there for each other in a moment's notice to assist, most of the time we knew the best thing we could do to keep the project going was to work to our strengths without slowing the other one down. An unlikely duo, Bob would tirelessly work on repairing a cracked window beam that had the potential to cause an entire wall to collapse, while I pushed for the political and fiscal support needed to keep the entire project from collapse.

Not long after, I received another elaborate invitation in the mail to a second Historic Houses event. I was relieved to take this as a sign that I hadn't unwittingly embarrassed myself or offended anyone, never to be invited again.

This party was to be hosted by the Earl and Countess of Derby at Knowsley Hall, their eighteenth-century home just outside Liverpool. Knowsley was a bit less than an hour's drive from Middleton. I enthusiastically RSVP'd.

In the United States, the idea of driving forty-five minutes and getting a hotel to stay the night would seem ridiculous, but in England this is what many people do, as forty-five minutes is considered "quite a distance." I rented a car and booked a hotel nearby.

It wasn't until a couple of hours before the party that I dug out the invitation to look up the address and actually read the small print. The event was black-tie. Suffice to say I had not brought a tuxedo with me from LA to stomp around the Hall in a hard hat with Bob. I scrambled. It was way too late to rent one. I dug through the limited wardrobe I had brought with me before calling Geoff. From all his years at the funeral home, we were able to piece together a black jacket, black pants, a black tie, a white shirt, even black socks and black leather shoes. The pants were the "one size fits most" kind that people rent for weddings: They had little clasps on each side that allowed you to adjust the waistband.

I took a critical look at myself in the mirror. Not ideal, but it would do. Hopefully the party would be dimly lit, people would be drinking, and from a distance it would look like I was wearing a well-tailored tuxedo.

Now that I was suited up, I hopped into my rental car and made the short—or perhaps quite long, depending on whether you're English or American—drive. After settling into my hotel, I jumped in a taxi to head to Knowsley, making small talk with the driver after he told me he lived just around the corner from my hotel.

"So, did you grow up here?" I asked.

"Oh—no, sir!" he exclaimed, his mood turning, suddenly almost seeming offended.

I was taken a bit aback by his vehement response.

"Sorry," I said, thinking perhaps I had mistaken an Australian accent for an English one, and that perhaps he was a foreigner like me. "So where did you grow up?" I asked sheepishly, trying to smooth the situation.

"In Croxteth. Four miles from here," he clarified.

Given that I was five thousand miles from home, I was a bit baffled that he would nearly bite my head off for mistaking his birthplace from the next village over.

"Oh, wow. What brought you so far from home?" I found myself asking.

"My ex-wife," he confided. "Worst mistake of my life. She moved me away from all my family. All my friends."

I couldn't help but think, *Aren't you a taxi driver?!* Assuming your car can go sixty miles an hour, couldn't you be back home at your birthplace in four minutes? And isn't there always the off chance that somebody might get into your taxi and ask to be taken to Croxteth?

Of course, I didn't say that, and instead remained politely silent, looking out the window at the passing greenery. But I couldn't help but wonder: If he did happen to get a taxi fare back to Croxteth, would he call his mother with tears of joy to say, "Mum, I'm coming home!"?

I chuckled at the thought of homecoming bands, confetti, and "Welcome Home" banners strung over the street as his taxi entered the village, but then I quickly snapped out of my imaginary fantasy world and into a real fantasy world as the driver pulled up to two fifteen-foot-tall black iron gates.

The driver stopped the car so that I could lean out the back-seat window to ring the buzzer. A very deep, distinguished voice answered. I announced who I was and a moment later the ornate gates swung open. Impressive.

We drove through spectacular green parkland for what felt like miles. Probably half the distance to Croxteth. There were sheep milling about, fishing lakes, and at one point the driver had to slow down to let some lavishly feathered pheasants cross our path.

The driver continued to be chatty and was full of local knowledge—surprising, considering he wasn't from there.

"These grounds were designed by the famous eighteenth-century garden designer Capability Brown," he explained helpfully. "They're some of the finest in England."

I tried to imagine how many cabdrivers in LA knew their garden design history quite as well as this guy.

Outside the car windows, I could see immaculately mowed lawns and trees clipped neatly into boxes. It was truly spectacular.

Then suddenly, there in the distance, we could see Knowsley. The house was vast—a perfectly preserved, stately redbrick home with rows upon rows of splendid, white-framed windows.

The taxi driver let out a laugh. "What a house, eh? It gets my attention every time!"

As we came down the long approach, he swung the taxi right up in front.

"I've never been inside," he said, "but if it's good enough for the

Queen to visit, then I'm sure it will be good enough for you. Just mind your table manners!"

I paid him, thanked him for his advice, and wished him luck in hopefully one day making it back home.

Ahead of me were the imposing stairs, flanked by two stone eagles, that led up to Knowsley's shiny, black-painted front door. I could hear music, glasses clinking, and people laughing coming from inside.

I took a deep breath. If I ever felt a wave of social anxiety, this was it. Up the stairs I went and rang the bell. A man with a long, pale face and dark hair wearing white gloves opened the door and welcomed me in.

"Good evening, sir," he said.

"Hello!" I said, probably way too loud and enthusiastic for my own good, stretching out my hand to shake his. "I'm Hopwood. What's your name?"

He seemed taken aback.

". . . I am Wilton, sir," he said, politely shaking my hand.

Suddenly I realized that Wilton was probably the butler and not a family member, and that perhaps I wasn't supposed to shake his hand? I wasn't sure.

I stepped inside.

The large foyer was beautifully decorated, and everyone was dressed to the nines, the women in gowns, the men in penguin suits with white ties. On the walls were oil portraits of thoroughbred horses, their flanks glossy and their manes luxuriant. It occurred to me that I was in the home of Earl and Countess of Derby and that maybe we use the word *derby* for horse races because of this family.

A server offered me champagne, which seemed to be the drink of preference at Historic Houses events. Then, right at that moment I lifted the glass to my lips, the unthinkable happened. The adjustable clasp holding my pants up broke. I clutched them at my waist, praying that no one had noticed. Was there a way to hold my glass of champagne while also keeping my arm pressed against my waistband to avert disaster? There was. Thinking on my feet, I managed to find Wilton and ask him for the directions to the bathroom. After walking down a long hallway decorated with more portraits of horses, I finally made it to the safety of a bathroom. I shut the door behind me with relief and surveyed the damage. The clasp was broken beyond repair. The only solution was to roll up the top of the waistband so it would stay in place a little better. Pants somewhat secured, although noticeably shorter, I went back out, hoping for the best.

Despite my compromised attire, I managed to have a very nice time at the party. I circulated the room, hoping that one person would introduce me to the next, which they invariably did. At one point, I was introduced to Ralph Assheton, a tall, slim, friendly man with hair slightly graying at his temples. When I mentioned Hopwood Hall, his eyes lit up.

"I am very familiar with Hopwood Hall!" he exclaimed. "My family is originally from that area."

And then it struck me: Assheton is the last name of Lord and Lady Clitheroe. It turned out Ralph was their son. We were all related! I excitedly explained I had met his father and mother a few years before at a dedication of the Flodden window.

"You should come and visit us sometime at Downham Hall. My wife, Olivia, is a writer, so I am sure she would be very keen to meet you."

Ralph took me around to meet many of the people in the room. Everyone was incredibly welcoming.

At 7 p.m., Wilton rang a bell and announced that we were all to be seated for dinner.

As we walked into what was known as the state dining room, I felt my heart skip a beat. The dining room was probably forty feet high in the raised center to allow for windows to let light in, with a beamed ceiling and intricate carvings and moldings. About ten tables, with ten chairs each, were set to look like someone's storybook wedding reception within the stunning turquoise walls, covered in gold-framed family portraits of all the previous Earls of Derby dating to the 1500s. Ralph explained that although the current house dated from the 1700s, there had been a structure on this site since the 1400s.

"William Shakespeare is said to have been close with the family, as they were significant patrons of his work," he said in a hushed voice.

The eyes of the Earl and Countess's forebears stared down upon us as we chatted, and dinner was brought in by a bevy of staff.

The delectable food was complemented by endless pairings of exquisite wine, better than in any LA restaurant I had ever been to. Before dessert—and the cheeses!—the Earl of Derby stood up and gave a short speech, hoping we all had enjoyed our meal and that he was honored to play host to a group such as ours, with its commitment to preserving the historic properties of Great Britain. As the candles burned low and I was wrapping up my conversation with the guests next to me, I felt a hand grasp firmly on my shoulder and a man's voice saying, "I would like to hear more about this gentleman."

I turned around to see the Earl of Derby standing there, smiling. I quickly stood up and shook his hand, thanking him for his hospitality and saying a silent prayer that my pants wouldn't suddenly give way and hit the floor.

"Hi, I am Teddy," he said grandly. "I understand from Ralph

Assheton that you have relocated here from Los Angeles to renovate Hopwood Hall?"

"That's the goal," I said. "That's why I've recently joined Historic Houses. To learn as much as I can."

"It is wonderful to have a family member involved. Often, we are the only people insane enough to take on these rescue projects," he laughed. "Please know, Knowsley didn't look like this thirty years ago. Like many of these houses, Knowsley had been taken over by the government in World War II and then was used as a police headquarters for another decade. It was completely institutionalized and, quite frankly, a mess when my wife, Cazzy, and I inherited it."

"Well, that's very encouraging," I replied. "Because it's absolutely beautiful now."

"I will be in touch," Teddy said. "Perhaps we can be of help."

We spoke for a while, and I learned that I had been correct in assuming that the family was associated with horse racing. One of Teddy's ancestors, the twelfth Earl of Derby, otherwise known as Lord Stanley, had founded the original Derby horse race. This is what horse races such as the Kentucky Derby are named for (although in England it is pronounced to sound like "Darby"). Not only that, another ancestor, the sixteenth Earl of Derby—also Lord Stanley—was appointed governor general of Canada and gave the nation the championship trophy for the National Hockey League, known thereafter as the Stanley Cup. My head was spinning from all these new associations and facts.

As the night wound down, I was making my way back toward the foyer to make my exit for my taxi pickup when a very stylish blond woman, wearing a black dress fit for a Hollywood red carpet, walked over toward me.

"Hello, I am Cazzy," she said. "Teddy told me about you."

I quickly realized she was the Countess of Derby.

"We want to help you. Do you know anyone in England? Do you have any friends?"

I laughed. "A few, but not many."

"Well, we will be your friends. I helped renovate Knowsley, so I have an idea what you will be going through. We had to buy enough fabric to fill a warehouse just to make the curtains. I can suggest where to find good prices. It is a lot of work, but it will be worth it in the end. If you need any advice at all, just let us know."

CHAPTER 14

ATTACK ON THE HALL

"Hopwood, wake up!"

It was Bob calling me at 7:30 A.M. while I was still in my bed at the Norton Grange in Middleton, his voice slightly quivering on the other end of the phone. I had never heard him sound like this before.

I sat up, half-awake, trying to comprehend exactly what he was saying. The sun was just rising, the darkened hotel room illuminated by my glowing phone.

"Vandals broke in and made a mess of the Hall!" he went on. "The police are in there now."

Earlier that morning when Bob entered the courtyard, his flashlight reflected at him from the ground, glinting off shards of broken glass. He immediately knew something was wrong.

"Did someone leave the gate unlocked?" I asked, trying to recollect if it somehow could've been me.

154

"No, they climbed the security fence. One of them must've slipped and sliced themselves at the top because there's blood everywhere. I realize you need your beauty sleep, but you need to get over here as soon as you can."

I didn't need to hear any more. I threw on my clothes and phoned for a taxi. Today I would be skipping the buffet.

My heart was thumping on the ride over, and I could feel the adrenaline coursing through my veins. I had been praying that this was a problem of the past. Over the thirty years that the Hall had been vacant, intruders had broken into it on a regular basis—but this was the first time it had happened on my watch. Oftentimes, Bob would recount horror stories for me: discovering a brick smashed through a grand, circa 1700s beveled-glass mirror above the marble fireplace in the Banquet Room, or the time an ancient wood-carved angel statue was snapped off of a wall carving in the Oak Parlor, leaving behind only its ankles and feet.

I knew this was going to happen at some point. Because of the local legend that one of my Hopwood ancestors had gone mad and hidden gold coins under the floorboards, vandals often broke into the house hoping to find the buried treasure—to no avail. The threatening spiked-razor fence made it incredibly dangerous for offenders to gain access, but I suppose once inside they viewed Hopwood Hall as the ultimate playground. Many snuck in simply to destroy rather than steal. Perhaps the excitement of their "sport" was boosted by the possibility of getting caught, or taking one misstep and falling through a floor, or entering the wrong room only to end it all underneath a collapsed ceiling. Or maybe they were so intoxicated that none of those hazards ever even crossed their mind.

Every time I thought about it, it made me sick to think of a proud fifteenth-century woodworker putting the final touches on his prized angel, only to know that six hundred years later some hoodlum would snap it off as if it were a dead branch on a tree. Or all the colorful life events that had once been reflected in the smashed mirror—perhaps people dining and dancing in their powdered wigs, buckled shoes, and billowing gowns as the orchestra played behind them, Frédéric Chopin playing the piano or Lord Byron reciting a poem, faces flickering in the glass that now, thanks to senseless acts of vandalism, was nothing more than mere shards on the floor.

As my taxi pulled up to the Hall, I shuddered at the troubling images flooding my mind as I tried not to think about what I might find inside.

Bob met me at the gates looking white as a ghost, his normal humor gone.

"It's not good," he exhaled. "And I've only seen the first three rooms. The police asked me to wait out here. Hopefully they'll be able to find their way back out."

As we stood there patiently, I noticed the morning light cast a shadow through the security fence, making the Hall look striped with bars, like it was trapped in a prison and yearning to be free.

The crisp morning air whirled around us, and we didn't exchange another word as we waited. It was an anxious but speechless type of silence that reminded me a bit of how I'd felt standing in the waiting room of the hospital, holding on for the doctor to come out to give my family a prognosis following my dad's heart attack.

I had a pit in my stomach.

Finally, the police emerged from the arched stone carriage entrance, walking over to us near the security gate. One of them jotting in his notebook.

"How bad is the damage?" I asked tepidly.

"In a building like this, it's hard to tell," he responded, not meaning to make light of the situation. "You'll need to have a look yourself and let us know."

"But be warned," said his partner, who was standing behind him. "I've been to crime scenes from stabbings, and this one has about the same amount of blood."

Bob and I looked at each other, knowing it was probably going to be up to us to clean it up.

"The good news is, I think we were able to get a good DNA sample," the officer continued. "We'll have the lab run it to see if there's a match. If there is, we may be able to make an arrest."

With the police officers departing in their cruiser, Bob and I hesitantly made our way into the courtyard. I gasped. By Bob's quick calculation, at least thirty original leaded-glass windows were now smashed. Some of the broken individual glass squares were still attached to the mangled lead support, which meant they hung limply out of their frames, as if they once had life but were now dead.

Tears welled up in my eyes. It seemed Bob was in a similar state as we looked away from each other. He picked up a broom and began to sweep the destroyed remnants of a happier history long gone by.

"So, if they climbed the security fence, it still doesn't explain how they got into the courtyard," I said, trying to make sense of it all.

"Most of these windows are smashed from the inside," Bob said, looking down at the clinking fragments as he swept. "That's why the glass is out here. I suspect they must've gone in through one of the windows on the far side. We'll be able to tell once we find the trail of blood."

After a few more moments in silence, Bob laid the broom against the redbrick wall and looked me squarely in the eyes.

"Are you ready to go in and see what else they did?"

157

I knew I was going to have to face the situation sooner or later, so I nodded, although I knew in my heart I was not at all ready for what came next. On the floor ahead of us were splashes of blood. We followed the trail into the Morning Room. This part of the Hall had been built in the 1800s and had huge windows that faced east to capture the morning sun.

My focus immediately went to the elegant engravings on the wood door that led into the Library. The door was fractured in two, splinters everywhere. It looked like someone had kicked it open, a chunk of the door with the knob still attached cracked off and lying on the floor.

"These are some of the earliest English Gothic revival carvings in the country," Bob said in disgust as he stooped down to pick up a small etched wooden rose detail that had dropped in the dirt below removed floorboards. "We'll need to get out the sieve and see if we can find any other missing pieces."

We continued to follow the splashes of dark blood on the floor of the Library.

"Oh no!" Bob shouted as he entered the Oak Parlor, freezing in his tracks. I hurried to his side, although I was dreading what I was about to witness.

As I rounded the corner, I saw what looked like a pile of trash on the floor. Above it was a glaring vacant spot on the wall where a piece of oak paneling had been forcefully yanked from its centuries-old anchor. Now it laid in a heap, smashed to bits. That particular panel was one of the jewels of the Oak Parlor—the wooden-chiseled ceremonial marriage plaque commemorating a wedding of one of the Hopwoods to Elizabeth of Speke, another prominent family in the area. Among the broken pieces, I could see a few numbers that had been inscribed into the wood: 6–8–1.

Bob knelt and gingerly sorted through the wreckage, pulling out the numbers and placing them next to each other on the floor to read "1689," the year of the carving.

We carefully picked up the remains and gently placed them into cotton cloths and bubble wrap to be held for safekeeping until we could hopefully one day have them repaired, storing them in a locked area where Bob kept some of his tools.

Then we continued to follow the bloody path deep into the Hall, where we found the vandals' point of entry: a cut-wire security mesh placed over a second-floor window that had been smashed in a previous attack. From there we could literally follow the footsteps of the intruders, or at least the one who had been severely injured.

"I doubt the police went in this far," Bob said as we made our way up the stairs.

"How could the intruders continue on if they were cut so bad?" I asked incredulously.

"It was dark, and if they were under the influence, as most of these thugs are, then they may not have realized the severity of the gash," Bob explained, shining the flashlight on the hearty blood trail leading down a shadowy corridor.

"Look!" he suddenly hollered, illuminating the word "HELP" written in fresh blood on the wall.

"This is *creepy*," I muttered, thinking whoever wrote that must've really been flying high on something.

We passed more broken windows and then came to a section of the Hall that was too unsafe to enter.

"Do you think they went that way?" I asked.

"It looks like the blood keeps going," Bob said, worried. "If they went back there, then it's likely they fell through the floor. Maybe they're injured somewhere in there. Or dead. It's not safe for us to walk any farther. Let's go downstairs and see if we can trace their footsteps from underneath."

Due to all the prior invasions, Bob kept the Hall locked up like a fortress. There hadn't been any funding for security cameras or alarms, so Bob tried to outsmart anyone who might try to get in. Certain areas were blocked off, with deterrents in place everywhere. To break in was not easy, but to break *out* was probably just as difficult. I'm not even sure if Indiana Jones could've done it unscathed. Hopwood Hall, like a lot of old houses, is a bit of a maze. Trespassers may shatter a window thinking it's an easy exit, only to then find themselves trapped within the confines of the soaring four walls of the courtyard. They would then have to break in again—either through another window or back through the sharp pieces of glass of the exit window. It would be dark, cold, and dangerous. Finding their original entry point in the black labyrinth of the Hall, with all its pitfalls and deathtraps, would not be easy—especially if you were under the influence, hemorrhaging blood, scared, and confused.

It was hard to have any sympathy for the fools who caused all this damage, but it was also hard not to, seeing the amount of blood loss.

"I found it!" Bob exclaimed from another room where we would rarely go because it was so perilous. "Over here—it looks like they fell through the floor!"

Sure enough, looking up, the rotten floorboards had given way, revealing a gaping hole where a body must've plunged through. Below was a heap of debris, splintered wood, and nails in the spot where they would've landed.

"Ouch," I said, seeing blood on several of the thick rusty nails.

"I'm surprised they survived that," said Bob. "They may very well still be somewhere nearby. I bet they could only crawl after a drop like that."

Bob shone his light down another expansive corridor that looked too hazardous to follow.

"Look at this," I said as the flashlight on my phone lit up what looked like bloody scrape marks. "What do you think this is?"

"It looks like drag marks. Maybe they were trying to drag a body out of here?"

Just then, we heard what sounded like a moan.

"I think someone is still in here," Bob said.

"Should we call the police to come back?" I asked.

"I don't think we have time. If they're still here they probably desperately need help," Bob replied as he headed off in the direction of the noise.

I quickly followed, not wanting to be left alone.

"It sounds like it's coming from down there," Bob said as he motioned to the mossy old brick stairs leading down into the cellar.

"You think we have to go down there?" I asked.

"I fell off the ladder yesterday and hurt my knee, so I can't make it. You go check it out."

"Me? Alone?! This feels like a scene from a horror movie!" I responded.

"You'll be fine," Bob said, in the most comforting voice he could muster. "I guarantee they aren't going to be in any shape to jump out at you. At least, I hope. I'll be right here. Just yell if you get into any trouble."

A few minutes later, I found myself doing the unthinkable as I made my way down into the dank, cavernous brick cellar. The cellar was the place where, prior to refrigeration, the family would have stored much of their food to keep it cool. It was hundreds of years old, with arched brick ceilings and an underground stream that ran through it to keep it perfectly chilled at three degrees Celsius. Centuries later, it still worked. I shivered as I entered its walls. Any childhood interest I ever had in exploring dungeons or caves suddenly disappeared. I couldn't help but wonder if this was also a place where people would've been laid to rest underneath the stone floor. I said a prayer that I wouldn't soon be one of them.

"If you trip over anything, it's probably a three-hundred-year-old petrified pig carcass from one of their hog roasts," Bob shouted after me.

I knew he was joking, but it still made me wince.

I followed the winding, twisting hallways, branching off into individual brick chambers along the way. In one corner, there were rusted meat hooks still hanging from the ceiling, and the smell that confirmed they had definitely been used—perhaps for the aforementioned hogs. In another room there were broken bottles and corks strewn on the floor. This would have been where the family kept their wine on large stone shelves built into the walls. If I had been with Jonny at a club in LA, this probably could've been cleaned up with bleach and aromatherapy to be a popular VIP area, fitted out with leather couches and a DJ table, but in this moment all I could think about were the giant patches of white fungus growing overhead like some creature from the deep.

My heart was pounding, but despite my best efforts to locate a body, dead or otherwise, it looked like the cellar was empty, at least of human carcasses. I exhaled, realizing that I had probably been holding my breath for a full fifteen minutes.

I ducked through the sticky cobwebs and made my way back up

the stairs to the main floor where Bob was supposed to be intently waiting for me, as he promised he would. I found him across the hallway in the Morning Room sieving the dirt to find the missing smithereens of the door.

"I thought you were waiting for me in case I needed help!" I was properly shocked he would ditch me.

"Calm down, I could hear you from here. Besides, I'd already checked the cellar myself this morning—I knew there was no one down there," he said, smiling slyly. "I just wanted you to understand the type of things you will need to do to save this place. It's not going to just be picking out curtains and paint. Being brave enough to walk into your nightmares is one of them. If you're to become 'Hopwood of Hopwood Hall,' then you need to be ready to handle the massive responsibility."

"So . . . what are you saying, sending me into the cellar alone was like a fraternity pledging exercise?"

Bob looked down.

"Are you hazing me, Bob?!" I asked with a laugh.

"Hazing you? I'm not sure what that means," he responded, chuckling. "But on bad days like this, we need to do something to lighten the mood. Even if it is at your expense."

Bob was right. His prank did lift our moods, and we both got to work focusing on the task at hand rather than wallowing in the upset of the attack. I helped Bob sieve the dirt, and we found several smaller hand-whittled flowers to be reattached to the door when we could eventually have it repaired.

"It can be fixed, but just know this is tens of thousands of pounds worth of damage," he told me. "It's such a waste, when that money could've been used to save other areas of the Hall."

The day finally ended and we left together, locking the security gates behind us.

Bob offered to drop me back at my hotel, so we both clambered into his silver van, pushing aside various repair materials and tools sitting on the worn front seat. We made small talk on the drive, but I could tell there was something bothering Bob.

As we pulled up to my hotel, his tone suddenly became more serious.

"I didn't want to bring this up today, but . . ." he began.

I could tell this wasn't going to be good.

"I just don't know if I can do this anymore," Bob said firmly, putting his hands on the steering wheel. "I'm getting old, and it's hard enough to try to save the Hall, never mind having all this unexpected chaos in my life. I just stopped in this morning for a quick check, and it ended up taking up my whole day. I had to cancel my other job to deal with the situation. Not to mention if someone had still been in there, drugged-up thieves could've easily jumped me. My wife thinks the peanuts I get paid to do this isn't worth it and doesn't want me doing it anymore."

To make matters worse, Bob went on to say that his contract was going up for renewal, and the council was concerned it didn't have the funds to pay him anymore.

"If that happens, it's a matter of survival that I'll need to find other work to support my family," he concluded.

I told him I fully understood and that we'd somehow figure something out. I shook his hand and thanked him profusely before climbing out of the van. He gave two short blasts of his horn as he pulled away and down the hill away from the hotel.

Dirty, sore, and freezing, I made my way back into the Norton Grange to take a hot shower and order room service, which was proving to be the best therapy for easing England's damp cold that seemed to permeate my bones. What would happen to the Hall without Bob? Without its trusty caretaker, what chance did we have of saving it?

Emerging in a white robe from the steamy bathroom, I noticed the message light blinking on my phone.

It was a voicemail from the police officer who had promised to call me with an update. Immediately I rang him back.

I had a feeling it wouldn't take long to find the culprits. Middleton is the kind of place that if someone's bicycle disappears overnight, the locals will figure out who is to blame and the bike will be returned unharmed, no questions asked, before 6 P.M. the following day.

In this instance, it turned out that there had been an anonymous emergency phone call last night to summon an ambulance near the Hall. The rescue workers were shocked to find an unconscious teenager dumped on the curb of the main street at the foot of the road that leads toward the Hall. He had a severely sliced arm and was lying in a pool of blood, apparently abandoned by his friends.

"Not surprisingly," the officer continued. "We ran his blood, and the DNA matches."

As much as I originally wanted to strangle the vandals if we found them, I suddenly had ambitious thoughts of perhaps seeing if there would be a way to rehabilitate this young person—maybe we could invite him to the Hall and teach him about its history. Or he could help us with the renovation as a kind of community service and we could educate him to understand the importance of heritage. Perhaps he would come away from it as a new person, never to vandalize again. But the officer quickly informed me that English law doesn't allow the identity of young offenders to be revealed, so it would remain a mystery.

"Are you saying he'll be back out on the street without any punishment and can try to break in again?" I asked.

"'Fraid so," said the officer. "But I doubt he will be back out on the streets. Right now, the doctors think he'll probably lose his arm, and maybe worse. Also, it seems on his way back over your 'scrotum shredder,' he may have accidentally experienced a bit of that pain too, so I'm guessing there might not be any future generations of his offspring to be troubling you either, if you get what I mean."

Ouch.

The whole incident left me rattled. By complete chance the break-in had happened while I was in England, which meant I was able to be on-site within minutes to help pick up the pieces. But what about next time?

I was beginning to realize that helping take care of the Hall long-distance just wouldn't work. I couldn't properly oversee this project phoning it in from five thousand miles away. The writing was on the wall. Literally. The Hall and Bob desperately needed my bloody "HELP."

Meanwhile, the agreement the council had been establishing with my "solicitor" was finally ready for signatures, and the council cabinet approved, giving me the exclusive right to accept responsibility for the Hall. The deal gave me five years to come up with a workable plan to prove I could save my ancestral home and create a sustainable model for running the place. Members of the council needed to be assured that it would be safe to fully release the obligation of protecting the Hall for generations to come to me. The arrangements also allowed for me to move into the Hall as soon as it was safe and accessible to do so. Having someone living on site with a 24/7 presence would be a huge help for the security issues. When I was able to demonstrate the plan for the future, the Hall would be fully transferred into my care.

At that moment, a switch clicked in my brain, and I suddenly began to think of the Hall as a new life partner with her own persona.

It was as if the Hall and I had been dating, and now it was time for me to make it official and put a ring on her finger. Or perhaps it was more like adopting a child—except that a child would be grown in eighteen years, and Hopwood Hall was a six-hundred-year-old child who would only age but never grow up and would need my constant care and attention, as well as access to my dwindling pocketbook.

In July 2017, I found myself nervously sitting alone with my solicitor in the glass-walled conference room of his firm's swanky offices in Manchester, perched high above St. Peter's Square, about to sign papers accepting the responsibility for the Hall.

It was hard to believe over four years had passed since my original online discovery and how much my life had changed.

My hands were shaking.

"I do just need to make sure you are fully aware that you are on a path to accepting complete responsibility for Hopwood Hall," he said as he placed the thick contract in front of me. "This means that if it is ever proven that you are negligent about its upkeep in any way, you could go to prison."

I gulped. "Prison?"

He nodded, handing me a pen.

I knew that as soon as the ink was dry, this contract was going to dramatically alter my life even further. There weren't going to be any half measures; I was going to have to devote all my time and energy to the Hall. I would have to turn down any offers of work in LA. My old life would be on hold, and what's more, I knew I needed to work fast to save the Hall that was deteriorating so rapidly. There wouldn't be much of her left if I didn't get a move on. Aside from a few weeks around Christmas when England shuts down, there would be no rest for me, no downtime, no vacations. It would be full-on.

As I put pen to paper, I felt sick to my stomach, but it was too late to turn back now.

Once I'd signed on the dotted line, I walked out into the city square, feeling overjoyed, energized, and also a bit overwhelmed.

Over the next month, things moved fast. I put wheels in motion to get a UK visa—a complex process of paperwork, phone calls, advisors, and proof that I was indeed a real person with real intentions, no felony record, or drug or money laundering history, and with a clear upward trajectory that would bring benefits to the people of England. Along the way, I heard numerous stories of seemingly wonderful people who had been rejected for all sorts of reasons. It was a competitive process with limited slots, so I bit my nails, said my prayers, and occasionally dry heaved into the toilet.

"They're having an issue with your visa," my immigration advisor said in a message on my voicemail. "I spoke to one of my contacts over there and quite frankly they're questioning why anyone in their right mind would give up life in LA to move to Northern England to help rescue an old, abandoned house. I realize this isn't funny and we'll probably get through this, but I felt I needed to let you know right away that there may be a problem."

She had left the message at the end of the day on a Friday, so it left me on a cliffhanger for the weekend.

This is ridiculous, I thought. *I'm struggling to do all this, and it might not work out because they think I'm making a poor life choice?*

What's next—are they also going to tell me to stop drinking, do more cardio, and eat flaxseed?!

On Monday morning, my immigration advisor called again. Apparently, the glowing recommendation from Vernon Norris, the leader of the council, had turned things around.

"Whew, that was close," she said. "It looks like we're back in business."

On Tuesday, August 15, 2017, my visa finally came through. Without much time to think or say goodbye to family and friends, I packed my bags, and within two days I was on a flight to England, leaving my old life behind me.

I landed in England on August 18. Later that day, I checked into my room at the Castleton Hotel, not far from the Hall. "Hotel" is a bit of an overstatement. The Castleton was a former private home turned bed-and-breakfast turned rent-a-room-by-the-month house owned by a local couple. I knew this was ideally suited to my needs until I could eventually, hopefully, one day move into the Hall. The Castleton also provided significant cost savings compared to staying at a hotel like the Norton Grange for what could be a potentially endless period. But at the same time, moving into the Castleton meant I was going to be living in a single rented room for the first time since my student days. I had no car, no English bank account, just two suitcases to my name. The thought crossed my mind that this was a lot like leaving home and going to college all over again.

Except that I was forty-seven.

CHAPTER 15

MIDLIFE MELTDOWN

"**W**HAT HAVE I DONE???"

The words were screaming in my brain. I was lying in bed, still jet-lagged, and unable to fall asleep.

It was 3:30 A.M.

I couldn't help but think that my friends in LA were probably just coming in from a day at the beach.

In the darkness, I looked around my new headquarters for the foreseeable future—one medium-sized room—and although it was perfectly comfortable, I couldn't quite get over the fact that it resembled my college dorm room from thirty years earlier. It was just big enough for a double bed, a desk, a chair, a wardrobe, and a dresser. The main difference was that this place came equipped with an electric teapot known around these parts as a kettle. A hotel room in England without an electric kettle would be as unheard of as a room without lights. Thick brown decorative curtains covered a wide picture window to keep the cold night chill from creeping in. I could hear the howling wind unrelentingly whipping outside, and if there was any hope at all of possibly drifting off to sleep, it was dashed by a tree branch that would sporadically knock against my second-story window as if to say, "Wake up, Hopwood! Welcome back to your dorm room!"

Most people my age would've probably attempted to reclaim their youth by simply buying a sports car, or perhaps dating someone fifteen years younger. Not me—for some reason, *my* midlife meltdown entailed going so far back in time that I was now going to relive the past of my ancestors!

The reality of my situation had begun to sink in. I was thousands of miles away from my real home, which I had sold. I knew only a handful of people. I had taken on a massive project with no end in sight. I had turned my back on my life and career in Los Angeles. The fact that I was basically staying in a rented room only added to the feeling that I regressed back to some kind of overgrown adolescent.

As I tossed and turned, I decided what I really needed were sleeping pills. If I were in LA, I could drive over to the nearest twenty-four-hour pharmacy and get whatever I needed. But England was going to be trickier. I'd learned the hard way that on this side of "the pond," most stores closed by 5:30 P.M. The only places I knew that were open in the middle of the night were the gas stations—and the nearest one to the Castleton was the Hopwood Service Station. Surely, they must have some NyQuil—or whatever it was called over here. So I got up, threw on some clothes, and crept downstairs, grabbing an umbrella and letting myself out the front door.

Outside, it was pitch-black, pouring with rain, and freezing, even in August. I shuddered under my umbrella. I didn't have a car, so I walked along the side of the road until the gas station came into view, glowing like an oasis in the desert.

At this hour, it was exterior counter service only, so I walked up to the window and banged on the glass to get the attention of the clerk who was lucky enough to be dozing peacefully in a chair behind the counter.

"Hi!" I shouted, waving at him as if I was trying to get the attention of some type of zoo animal. "I'm looking for something to help me sleep."

"You what?" he stammered, clearly startled.

"Some sleeping pills! I need some sleeping pills!"

He looked shocked and perhaps a bit terrified, as if I was asking him to sell me heroin.

Perhaps I was imagining it, but it almost appeared as if he was slowly reaching to push the silent alarm button under the counter. Maybe he thought he was about to be robbed by a tall blond American.

I was desperate for some shut-eye and didn't know what to do, so I pulled out my ID and pressed it to the window.

"My name is Hopwood. I'm guessing my ancestors once owned this land that your gas station sits on, since it's named Hopwood too. Or perhaps you and I are somehow related. The point is, I'm hoping you can help me get some sleeping pills?"

He studied my ID, then suddenly relaxed and smiled.

"Mate, I've heard about you. You're the bloke from LA that's here to save the Hall. Wish I could help ya mate, but 'fraid 'round here you'd have to get what you're looking for from a chemist."

After a bit of back and forth, it became clear that over-the-counter sleeping pills were not a thing easily available in England.

"I've got aspirin," he told me. "Want to try that?"

I decided against it, politely declining and saying farewell. It was now 4:30 A.M. and raining even harder. I was cold to the core. I had been in Middleton for less than twenty-four hours and I'd already had enough of being a "fish out of water"—even though I was soaking wet from the rain.

I trudged back to my dorm room in the darkness, hair drenched and freezing at the ends, pondering the decisions that had brought me to this point in my life.

The next morning, after falling into a fitful sleep around dawn, I decided to make the best of things. I got up and dressed for breakfast, prepared by Michelle and Mark, the friendly couple who owned the Castleton Hotel. Michelle, a radiant, smiling blonde, ran the front of the house and had perfected the art of welcoming guests. Mark, bald and strong and a talented chef, was often seen working in the kitchen or going up and down ladders doing maintenance. Now in their fifties, Michelle and Mark had met twenty years ago in a pub just up the street on game night and had been inseparable ever since, eventually deciding to open a bed-and-breakfast. A few years ago, they decided to slow down their lives a bit and relieve themselves of the day-to-day pressures of running a B&B and restaurant, so they opened the rooms to longer-term guests looking to stay for a month or more.

The Castleton was quaint and welcoming and the perfect place for me to hang my hat during my self-imposed life transition. Positioned on a beautiful corner lot surrounded by trees and gardens in the front and a neighborhood bowling green behind, it had once been a large private residence, built in grand redbrick during the Victorian era in the 1800s. Faded gold lettering announcing CASTLETON HOTEL ran along the exterior for all to see. Inside, the homey English interior was decorated in burnt orange and brown tones. There were antique brass light fixtures, woven ornate carpets, and inviting fireplaces, with a large central wooden stairway in the center of the home, topped by a massive stained-glass window shedding daylight from the ceiling above. There were nine bedrooms upstairs in the main house, and the carriage house behind it had been converted into another five bedrooms. Mark and Michelle ran this business as a family affair, building themselves a private apartment in the third-floor attic where they lived with their young son.

On my first day as a long-term Castleton inhabitant, Michelle welcomed me with a sunny "good morning" and proceeded to introduce me to my fellow residents. Staying at Castleton were Mitch, a good-looking professional cricket player from New Zealand, with his petite girlfriend, Terri; Keith, a boisterous tattooed guy with a big laugh who had recently broken up with his wife; and Mary from Ireland, a white-haired, bespectacled woman in her nineties living in a room down the hall from her sixty-five-year-old son, Jimmy, who looked like an accountant and was an expert at TV quiz shows.

Over the coming months, these people would become fixtures in my daily life, like an extended yet wildly diverse family.

"He's a Yank!" bellowed tattooed Keith, pointing at me as I approached the table.

"Pipe down!" Mary snapped back at him in her Irish accent.

Michelle looked at me apologetically as if she had just thrown me to the wolves.

"But I've never met a Yank before!" Keith loudly explained. "Can I call ya Hank the Yank?"

Mary slapped her hand on the table, shaking the water glasses. "Keith! Stop acting the maggot!"

I don't know if it was Keith's loudness that irritated Mary, as she turned down her hearing aid, or if it was that she found "Yank" to be some sort of inappropriate slur. Probably both. But either way, it was clear that Mary had decided to take me under her wing.

Jimmy calmly touched his mother on the shoulder to reassure her, then looked at me.

"Don't worry 'bout Keith, he always acts like this," Jimmy reasoned. "We've been hoping he would move out and leave us all in peace, but his intelligent wife won't take him back."

"She doesn't know what she's missing!" barked Keith, eating his food. "And if I left here, neither would you!"

"His name is Hopwood," Michelle stated calmly, as if she was addressing a group of disruptive school children. "And he's come from Los Angeles to help save Hopwood Hall."

I held my breath, suddenly having déjà vu of my first day of kindergarten, when all the kids pointed at me and made fun of my name.

There was a beat of silence while everyone at the table sized me up.

Mitch was the first to speak.

"Good to meet ya, mate," he said with a winning smile as he put his arm around Terri.

"That's so amazing," Terri added. "If there is anything we can do to help, just let us know."

Just then, Chef Mark emerged from the kitchen in a splattered apron. "The Man U versus Swansea game is on later today," he announced. "Who's up for some pints?"

And with that, the topic was changed and I was welcomed in, just like one of them, taking my seat at the table.

It's unlike me to turn down a pint of beer, but after breakfast was over, I walked over to the Hall. There was no time to lose. On

September 9, in only three weeks' time, I'd agreed to take part in Heritage Open Days—a massive annual event in Britain orchestrated by the highly respected National Trust, where across the country private historic buildings open their doors for at least a day. While the thought of welcoming the public to Hopwood Hall was more than a little intimidating, I'd put back on my LA producer hat ("commit, and figure the details out later") and agreed to seize the opportunity when Geoff had suggested it to me. Hopwood Hall's doors had been closed for nearly thirty years. Never mind the missing floorboards, falling ceilings, and slippery flagstones—instead I was focused on the idea that this would be a great way to make a splash and generate some excitement about the project by letting the locals know what we were up to.

It had been a little while since I had last been at the Hall, so as I walked up to the gate, I realized my deluded mistake in thinking this place would be ready for visitors any time this decade. Not that she had been in the best condition the last time I'd seen her, but the summer weather of heavy rains followed by warm days and cold nights had completely transformed her exterior. Waist-high weeds sprouted from in between the flagstones. Mud had washed in and lay everywhere like a thick layer of lava. Worms and insects were having a field day. Over the wet summer, Bob had been completely overwhelmed just trying to keep up with the leaks. Not to mention, there was probably still a lot of broken glass, blood, and debris around from the last vandal attack. I could feel my heart begin to race.

WHAT HAVE I DONE?! pounded through my mind yet again.

I didn't own a shovel, or a rake, or anything but my two hands that could possibly help me clean up this mess.

I looked up at the sundial that hung above the front of the house, as if it might provide me with some kind of inspiration—"Time waits for no man" or something like that—but it was so cloudy that the gnomon (the part of the sundial that tells the time, according to Bob) failed to make as much as a hint of a shadow.

I decided to pace around a bit to clear my thoughts. Unfortunately, my pacing led me to perhaps the most distressed area of the entire estate—the servants' wing. One hundred years ago, this three-story structure would have been bustling with an army of twenty-eight staff members—including cooks, maids, butlers, and underbutlers—ready to wait on the family at a moment's notice. Not only did the servants work here, they lived here, in a series of bedrooms on the upper floors. Downstairs were the kitchens, the buttery, and the bakery, a hub of activity at all times of the day. Today, the servants' wing was deserted, a bona fide wreck. Although it didn't look too bad from the outside, Bob told me that the old kitchen room was filled with junk and debris where one of the floors had collapsed. I hadn't been able to see it with my own eyes as it was too dangerous to step inside.

"No one goes in there anymore," Bob had once told me solemnly. "Unless you count the spirits of the servants."

Peering in through the windows, the whole wing looked so forlorn and run-down it was hard to imagine even a ghost wanting to haunt it. Feeling more overwhelmed than ever, I turned back and walked toward the main entrance, trying to think of which rooms *would* be safe enough to host actual people.

Call Bob, I thought. But deep down I knew from our previous conversations, both in person on my last visit and during the phone calls that followed, that he was unable to put in the kind of time he had before. While I was sure he would be there in a pinch if I was desperate, I knew I couldn't possibly burden him. He was busy with other jobs, supporting his family. This open day had been my idea, a foolish snap decision I'd made without thinking of the repercussions.

My father always said when you don't know what to do, make a list.

So I pulled out my phone and began pacing in front of the Hall, writing down everything I could think of that would need to be done to have people come and visit. Obviously, they wouldn't be able to walk through the entire place, but perhaps we could get two or three of the more stabilized rooms and the courtyard cleaned up and ready for a party in three weeks' time?

The Family Chapel, the Guards' Room, the Reception Hall. It was a tall order, but it was at least a goal.

One thing was very clear. I didn't have an army of servants at my disposal, but at the same time, I wasn't going to be able to do it alone.

On my way back to the Castleton, Bob called to see how I was settling into my new home there. Even though I tried to keep from dragging him into my current dilemma, I couldn't help myself.

I explained to him my perhaps mistaken decision to participate in the open day.

Bob being Bob, his first reaction was to laugh. I felt a wave of relief. Sure, it was laughing AT me, but still it was better than yelling at me.

"Don't worry, Hopwood," he said between guffaws. "I'll help, and we'll do our best. With any luck, you won't have to embarrass the entire community by canceling the open house."

As I keyed my way into the Castleton front door and walked into the conservatory, I ran into Mary, who was standing there sorting the mail.

"Are you okay? You look like you haven't eaten since breakfast!"

"Well . . . I guess I haven't," I replied sheepishly.

"Oh, for pity's sake!" she exhaled. "Follow me."

She promptly marched me toward the kitchen and declared she was going to show me how to make beans on toast, an English delicacy that, until now, held no appeal for me.

"If you're going to eat beans," I reasoned, "why would you put them on toast? Do you spread them on like peanut butter and jelly?"

Mary was outraged at my ignorance and gave me a step-by-step lesson, talking me through every part of the process.

"First, we open the bread bag," she said kindly, as if being American was synonymous with having the mental capabilities of a four-year-old.

I decided to do as I was told.

"Next, you take two slices and put them in the toaster . . ."

I obeyed. By the end of my lesson, I knew how to do everything, including opening the can, heating the beans, and pouring them over the toast.

Within a few minutes, Mary had Jimmy summon Michelle from the third floor to come down to the kitchen to clear me my own corner of a shelf in the refrigerator.

"The boy forgot to eat!" I could hear her whispering to Michelle. "We need to make a little space for him so he can keep some milk and such."

It felt good to feel like people cared about me so far from home.

I dutifully ate my plate of food. If truth be told, the beans on toast were actually quite good and satisfying. I wondered how I had gotten through so many years of my life without experiencing this simple pleasure. Mary watched as I ate, making sure I finished every morsel like the surrogate mother she was. She also explained that if I liked a bit of variety, I could get a knife and a block of cheese and slice a piece of the cheese, which I could then lay over top the beans, allowing it to melt.

But no need to get ahead of ourselves. That would be tomorrow's lesson.

CHAPTER 16

IT TAKES A VILLAGE

 he next morning, I was startled awake at 5:30 A.M. by knocking. At first, I thought it was the friendly tree branch, but then realized it was something much louder.

"Hank! Mary's cooked! Your eggs are gettin' cold!"

I sprung up out of bed and opened my door to reveal Keith dressed and ready to head off to his trucking job.

"I'm off," he said. "But I hear you have a lot to do at the Hall. If you need anything delivered, just let me know. We can use my truck." As he turned to walk down the stairs, he looked back up, adding, "God bless ya, Hank. Hank the Yank, all the way from the Hollywood Hills!"

I was surprised by Keith's jovial demeanor—and when I got downstairs, I quickly realized everyone was treating me differently.

It was like a little bird had flown in and told them about my situation at the Hall.

"Hopwood, can I drop you at the estate on my way to the post office?" Michelle asked as she set some freshly baked bread in front of me. I quickly pounced on the "empty carbs"—this time, Jay was five thousand miles away, and there was no threat of him sending it back to the kitchen. I slathered on a healthy dose of real English butter and Michelle's homemade strawberry jam to add to the guilty pleasure.

Michelle continued, "I was talking with Mark last night, and we want to help with your upcoming open house. Would that be possible? We could start later this afternoon."

I was quickly learning that Middleton was the kind of place where if someone needs help, others would come out of the woodwork, especially where Hopwood Hall was concerned. I was just beginning to get a taste of how the "village" mentality worked.

Within a few hours, I was back on site at the Hall, and I didn't feel alone any longer.

Mark and Michelle, Bob and his wife were there too, all of them ready to shovel up the mud. I had desperately needed hands, and now, they were here. And with Al and Geoff making phone calls and contacting friends, we soon assembled an even larger local crew of volunteers. Locals knew locals, and they all wanted to get involved. A teacher from the local elementary school brought her friends, and so did the checker from the nearby grocery store. A florist offered to make floral arrangements. Twin brothers who recently received their security certification stepped forward to help monitor guests. Zena, a supporter with marketing experience, was willing to call the newspapers. Even a signmaker volunteered his skills—the list went on and on.

Hopwood outside the Hopwood House,
Hopwood, Pennsylvania, 1976
Photo: Deanna DePree

Lady Susan Hopwood with her dogs and horse on the lawn at Hopwood Hall Estate,
1880s
Photo: The Middleton Collection, care of Local Studies, Touchstones, Rochdale

Hopwood Hall Estate and the sunken rose garden, circa 1993
Photo: Mrs. Christine Pierce Jones

The Reception Hall fireplace
showcasing one of the Hopwood
family coats of arms, which could
change due to marriages between
other prominent English families
Photo: Fred Leao Prado

Geoff and Hopwood discussing Hopwood Hall and his family lineage

Photo: David Rowlinson

Hopwood discussing plans with members of Rochdale Council and the renovation team

Photo: Fred Leao Prado

A corner of the Banquet Room, 1880s. A portrait hangs of Lady Susan Hopwood, who utilized the space primarily as a drawing room.
Photo: The Middleton Collection, care of Local Studies, Touchstones, Rochdale

The same corner, Hopwood Hall Estate, 2013
Photo: Fred Leao Prado

The Oak Parlor, 1800s
Courtesy of Hopwood Hall Estate

The Oak Parlor at Hopwood Hall Estate, 2013, the oldest known room in the Hall, dating to 1426. In the mid-twentieth century, "improvements" were made to the Hall, including the modern lighting fixtures.
Photo: Fred Leao Prado

The west wing of the Gallery Corridor, a main walkway through Hopwood Hall

Printed with kind permission of the De La Salle Trust, Oxford

The east wing of the Gallery Corridor after the floorboards were removed

Photo: Dave Brogan

The east side of Hopwood Hall, late 1800s. The two-story bay window looks into the Banquet Room.

Photo: The Middleton Collection, care of Local Studies, Touchstones, Rochdale

A similar angle. The ground floor windows look into the Morning Room and the Library.

Photo: Fred Leao Prado

Hopwood DePree celebrating the first Hopwood family Christmas in Hopwood Hall in over 100 years

Photo: Charlotte Graham

I called my sister Dori in the States to tell her the good news. I think it must've been a case of Tom Sawyer convincing everyone to paint the fence for him, because when she heard about the local people volunteering, she was so excited that she looked into airline tickets and found an amazing deal for my entire family to fly over.

Michelle made up some of the extra rooms at the Castleton for my family to stay, and within days, my mother, Dori, Dana, Erik, and Jetsen all arrived and rolled up their sleeves just like the locals.

We quickly fell into a routine at the Castleton, waking up early for a hearty breakfast and then heading to the Hall. As soon as we arrived, we got straight to work alongside the volunteers, removing rubble, washing windows, and clearing away dirt, mud, and other grime. Like any family, we certainly had days when we disagreed on what needed to be done next, but the important thing was that, just like me, my family members felt a strong tug of connection to this place, their ancestral home. Watching them labor to make the Hall presentable for the open day after flying across an ocean to be here, I felt a massive jolt of gratitude—even when my sisters suggested I was taking too long of a tea break.

One afternoon, as the sun crept out from behind yet another rain cloud, my niece Jetsen made a discovery.

"What's that?!" she exclaimed, pointing at a huge rusty gear-shaped piece now visible where some of the mud and weeds had been cleared away in the corner of the courtyard.

"That's a piece of the mechanism from the Hopwood Hall water mill that was built in the 1500s," Bob explained as Jetsen started to walk toward it. "The mill was situated by the stream that runs through the estate. It collapsed a long time ago."

"Be careful! You don't want to have to go get a tetanus shot!" Dana shouted, which immediately stopped Jetsen in her tracks.

"This piece would've been very important to your family," Bob said, undeterred, pulling some more weeds away with a rake. "Grinding wheat into flour was a big source of their income five hundred years ago, and without it, they wouldn't have been able to feed themselves or everyone else who worked on the estate."

I tried not to think too much about the obvious symbolism: that such an integral part of Hopwood history was now a broken chunk laying in the corner, rusting away.

That afternoon, to give Jetsen and the other members of my family a bit of a break from their chores, I decided to take them on a tour of the upper rooms of the house. This would be a chance to show them the actual bedroom where Lord Byron stayed when he visited the family in 1811. It was a room I imagined would be for very special guests when the Hall was finally renovated, and people came here for artistic retreats.

Bob hadn't felt comfortable taking us up the rickety staircase when we first visited, and with good reason—at that point, getting upstairs was a treacherous process. You had to skip the bottom step unless you wanted to fall through the floor and wind up in the cellar. Then, stepping carefully, you needed to make sure not to activate a loose floorboard which might cause you to lose your balance and plunge backward. And, most important, only *one* person could be on the stairway at a time or, again, you might wind up in the cellar.

Since our original tour, Bob had put in some new scaffolding supports, which meant the stairs were much sturdier, and one wrong step would no longer necessarily lead to an unexpected freefall. It was still wise to approach with caution, however.

My family and I picked our way over the stair treads. The dark dogleg wooden staircase was yet another example of the incredible craftsmanship that had gone into building Hopwood Hall. Dating back to the Jacobean era and adorned with hand-carved spindles, the stairway featured smooth banisters that were well worn from so many generations running their hands along them. We ascended past a large leaded glass window with a view out to the courtyard before reaching a small platform, known as a "look-over," at the midway landing. By now, I'd done a bit of a research into the hall's most famous guest, Lord Byron, and was excited to share my discoveries with my family.

"When Lord Byron visited the Hall in 1811, he was a twenty-three-year-old poet, very handsome, with long, curling dark hair and pale features, and so he caused quite a stir among the ladies of the house," I explained. "This look-over is where female members of the family would have stolen a glimpse of any arriving guest, which was helpful, because if a gentleman wasn't to her liking, a young woman could ask the butler to send him packing."

That wasn't the case with Lord Byron. Although Robert Hopwood, the squire of the house, was away at the time, the Hopwood ladies were delighted to host the poet, laying on every comfort and luxury available. Byron was a vegetarian, so the cooks in the kitchen were tasked with feeding him meat-free dishes along with his favorite pickles. This didn't seem to cure Byron of his notorious melancholy, and by the time he left, he was apparently still in a gloomy mood.

"While he stayed here, Byron worked on his long narrative poem 'Childe Harold's Pilgrimage' about a depressive hero, based on Byron himself, who's wandering around the world, trying to cheer himself up," I recounted. "Byron wrote in his bedroom and in the Library downstairs and also wandered around the Hopwood Woods, which may have provided inspiration for a well-known line in the poem: *There is a pleasure in the pathless woods . . .*"

At this point, my sisters both gave me their best side-eye, as if to say, "What has happened to you?"

Upstairs, along multiple corridors—some very long, others very wide—there were doors leading to about twenty bedrooms. Many of these had originally been larger rooms that the monks had subdivided and converted into small cells to accommodate them and their students. Others were much grander in scale but in varying states of disrepair. Like every part of the house, the upstairs area had been added to and altered many times over her six-hundred-plus years of history, giving her the feel of an eclectic maze.

"And this is the Lord Byron Bedroom," I told my family dramatically, ushering them into a room lined with mahogany wood panels and huge exposed curved beams at one end that looked like something from an old ship. "These beams are original, dating to the 1420s."

The bedroom was enormous—about 30 × 30 feet with high ceilings, but still medium-sized compared to some of the others in the house—with impressive dark-wood beams at the far end and delicate wooden carvings on the fireplace, including one of King John, who ruled in the 1200s. Completely empty of furniture or anything but dust, cobwebs, and maybe the occasional rodent, it may have been hard for my relatives to see the potential. Eager to spark their imaginations—and inspired by Geoff's ability to conjure up history wherever he went—I told them I wanted them to travel back in time to 1811 when Lord Byron had first visited.

"Imagine you're Lord Byron," I instructed. "You've just finished a long walk in the woods, where you've been waiting for inspiration to strike for your latest poem. You come back to the house, and you recline on your enormous, built-in, four-poster wooden bed, letting poetic sentences drift in and out of your mind. Hung from your intricately carved bed are rich, deeply colored drapes that match the curtains framing the diamond leaded windows, lending the room a cozy, sumptuous feel."

Hopefully my imaginative rendering would help my family to forget about the cracks in the glass windows and the giant holes in the floorboards. Never mind the skeleton of a squirrel I'd just spotted in the corner. It was a trick I found myself doing more and more often when I was at the house: I shut my eyes and imagined what things used to be like. Doing so gave me a vision for the future and helped stave off what I had come to think of as the old house blues—those moments when the scale of the renovation felt so overwhelming that I just wanted to give up and go home and never again have to deal with emptying another bucket after a rainstorm.

I guided them into the adjacent space, with a fireplace to one side sporting a huge lion's face that looked more like a monkey carved in the middle above the mantel. "In the smaller room, off the bedroom here, there would have been a nearby table on which a pitcher and jug would be placed. One of the chambermaid's duties was to bring hot water from the kitchen to fill the pitcher. Imagine Lord Byron washing up after a hard day's work of writing poetry. Then, if nature called, he could relieve himself in the chamber pot."

"Is the chamber pot where Lord Byron would've pooped?" Jetsen asked with a giggle.

"I suppose so," I chuckled. "And to think all that important 'history' happened right here in this very room!"

It was while I was showing my family around the upstairs bedrooms that I realized I already knew how to make the open day more enjoyable for everyone. I just had to try to help them close their eyes and imagine.

Finally, the day of the open house dawned. Zena managed to

help get the regional BBC station to do a segment on how we were opening Hopwood Hall's doors for the first time in thirty years, and so in addition to the hundred visitors the council had approved us for, we had another five hundred people on the waiting list. Clearly there was plenty of interest in the Hall. A light gray fog hovered in the morning air as the sun failed to make an appearance through the clouds. People began arriving around 10 A.M. Bob and I were there in our hard hats and "high-vis" vests to greet them. We gave every guest similar safety gear too, warning them they were entering a building site and to wear it as a precaution.

After having honed my technique with my family members, I told the guests to picture what it would have been like to arrive at Hopwood Hall in the 1600s.

"You're in your carriage, with your horse and driver," I intoned. "Pulling up in this courtyard, the clattering of the horse's hooves on the cobblestones, and, as you step out, all the members of staff are lined up to greet you!"

I could see people's eyes misting over as they got lost in the wonderful history of it all. Or maybe it was just that the rain was making their glasses fog up.

I then walked everyone into the Guards' Room and the Reception Hall, describing how guests would have been checked for weapons before being welcomed by the Hopwood family. I showed them pieces of artifacts that Bob had collected after they had fallen from the walls and ceilings in the Reception Hall. Everyone seemed absorbed and fascinated. They wanted to know more. They wanted to help.

Later in the day, an elderly man showed up on a mobility scooter and carried a watercolor painting in his hands that his grandmother had painted of the Hall. He said his grandfather had been a chauffeur here in the early 1900s. Another woman attended who said her great-grandfather had been one of the gardeners on staff.

After the last crowd left, Bob and I shut the heavy wooden carriage entrance doors and had a seat with the rest of the volunteers. We were all elated. It felt like through an incredible amount of teamwork we had been able to spark some life back into the Hall. There was suddenly a renewed interest in the rescue project and a whole new network of people willing to get involved. I couldn't help but think perhaps I hadn't made such a giant mistake in moving to England after all.

The only sadness was that the next day my family were due at the airport for their flight back to the United States. As they packed up and loaded into their car to leave, I felt well and truly gutted.

"Good luck with that whole castle thing," my brother-in-law joked as they pulled away.

I laughed, but once their car disappeared beyond the Castleton's brick wall, I have to admit I may have wiped away a tear. I was going to miss them.

Luckily there was more good news on the horizon. The month after I arrived, we learned that we'd been awarded a grant by the Architectural Heritage Fund. Grants were the typical way an enormously expensive heritage project like this might be funded. It was extremely exciting news. The grant was for £10,000 (about $13,000), but more important, the Architectural Heritage Fund was a well established, highly reputable organization. In other words, this wasn't just a much-needed injection of cash; it was giving us the seal of approval, sending a signal to all the other heritage organizations that we were a legit project, worthy of support. The hope was that more grants and funding would follow.

The village of Middleton had pulled together to make the open day happen, but it didn't stop there. Geoff, Bob, myself, and some of the other volunteers decided to form the Friends of Hopwood Hall Estate, a group that would meet regularly to find ways to raise money and put on volunteer events to benefit the Hall. I was proud to be part of their community.

My feelings of belonging didn't last, however. In early November—the Fifth of November, to be precise—I got a lesson in how much further I had to go before I would be considered a true local.

CHAPTER 17

GUNPOWDER, TREASON, AND PLOT

*B*OOOMMM!!!

An explosion ripped through the street below, shaking the glass in my bedroom window. I was in my room at the Castleton, lying in bed, scrolling on my phone.

I jumped up, my heart racing. What was happening?!

A moment before, I had been comfortably relaxing. Now my phone was on the floor outside the bathroom. I had been so startled, I accidentally threw it across the room!

I cautiously made my way to the window, shielding myself behind the edge of the wall in anticipation of another possible blast. Crouching down, I carefully peeked out from behind the curtain to see what was happening in the road below. It was only about 5 P.M. but already dark.

Smoke drifted across the moonlit sky like a war zone. There was nothing but silence.

A moment later, a car alarm began shrieking out, disrupting the eerie stillness.

Suddenly, three more huge bombs, even bigger than the first, erupted behind the house in the direction of the bowling green, which I couldn't see.

BOOM, BOOM, BOOM!!!

I yanked the curtain shut and hit the floor.

My palms were sweating, and my heart was thumping in my chest. I was in a total panic.

I crawled to my bedroom door and pulled it open, calling out to see if anyone else was around in the Castleton.

"IS ANYONE HERE?!" I shouted. "THERE'S SOME KIND OF ATTACK OUTSIDE!"

The hallway was dark. No one was home. Not even Mary! What was going on?

BOOM, BOOM, BOOM, BOOM, BOOM!!!

Five more detonations echoed from outside. It sounded like the situation was escalating and getting nearer with more explosions louder and closer together.

Here I was, thrust into the middle of a nightmare. Terrified, I wasn't sure what to do. I'd never been in a situation like this before.

I pushed the door shut and clambered toward the bathroom, picking up my phone. My first thought was to call 911, but when I went to dial it occurred to me that England must have a totally different number for emergencies. Was it 991? 119? Or 99?

Wait . . . I thought. *Isn't a 99 what Brits call an ice cream with a cookie stuck in it? Ahhh! It's all too confusing!*

With trembling hands, I quickly called Bob instead.

"Bob?!" I pleaded, relieved to hear his voice on the other end of the line.

"Hopwood?" he replied. "Ya alright?"

"No! I'm not all right!"

He sounded like he was at some kind of party.

"Bob, are you hearing this? There are explosions right outside my window. What is going on?!"

On the other end of the line, I knew it must be bad, because it sounded like Bob was . . . crying? I was horrified. What was happening?!

Then I realized, no, in fact, he was laughing at me again. Frankly, I didn't think there was much that was funny about the situation.

"They didn't tell you?"

"NO!" I replied. "Tell me what?!"

"Hopwood, *we're being invaded*!" he bellowed, howling with laughter.

Clearly the joke was on me. I slowly drew open the curtains to expose several larger explosions, but this time seeing the red and blue glittering aftereffects of fireworks.

Eventually, Bob was able to explain to me that it was actually the Fifth of November, otherwise known as Bonfire Night—a national English holiday on a par with the Fourth of July.

"It's an annual tradition, Hopwood," he said, in between his hysterics. "Everyone lets off fireworks in their back gardens . . . Even a two-year-old knows about Bonfire Night."

I had no idea! No wonder everyone was out—they were celebrating! Even Mary! How had I missed this major cultural detail?

Eventually, Bob calmed down and contained his hilarity enough to relay that the Fifth of November commemorates an event that took place in the early 1600s.

"What happened was, a Catholic called Guy Fawkes and his co-conspirators were about to blow up the House of Lords and assassinate Protestant King James I," Bob told me. "He didn't manage to get away with it, but for some reason, we let off fireworks every year to celebrate his complete and utter failure."

"Wait, isn't Guy Fawkes the guy who visited Hopwood Hall?" I asked.

He was.

I'd heard Bob and Geoff mention Guy Fawkes several times, but they must have just assumed I knew who he was—and I hadn't thought to ask them for more information.

I decided I needed to buff up on my English history. I opened a bottle of wine and spent the rest of the evening googling and reading about Guy Fawkes and Bonfire Night. Normally it would've been impossible to be at home studying among bombs bursting in air, but tonight I was desperate to no longer feel like an idiot.

Guy Fawkes and his coconspirators were Catholics, and they were not happy about the Protestant king, James I. As a result, they had been planning to blow up the king to put a Catholic monarch on the throne.

A few days later, I followed up with Geoff, certain that he would be able to fill me in a bit more. We were at the Hall and were taking a break from emptying the buckets.

"So what's the deal with Guy Fawkes visiting Hopwood Hall?" I said casually, as he poured boiling water from the kettle into his teacup. I hoped that Bob hadn't told Geoff about my Bonfire Night ignorance.

"Well," Geoff began in his best professor's voice. "It all started back in 1527, when King Henry VIII wanted to get a divorce from his wife, Catherine of Aragon, as she had failed to give him a male heir. He asked the Pope, but the Pope wouldn't let him. And so, Henry broke away from the Catholic Church to form the Protestant Church of England, during a period that we call the Reformation. After that, it became dangerous to be a Catholic, with many gentry having their lands confiscated and privileges removed.

"Despite the risk, the Hopwoods remained devoted Catholics," Geoff went on. "During the reign of Elizabeth I—who was Henry VIII's daughter—a map was drawn up that showed the houses of English gentry who were Catholics or of 'dubious loyalty to the Church of England.' Someone placed a cross next to Hopwood Hall. So they must have been Catholics at that time."

It seemed surreal to be hearing about the history of my ancestors and the Reformation in England in the 1500s while sitting in the same location at the Hall where so much of it actually took place. It made me feel like a drop in the ocean of time.

"Would you like one of Lyn's homemade biscuits?" Geoff offered.

I declined at first, but when I looked inside the small tin he had brought along, I could see a stack of freshly baked cookies drizzled with melted chocolate. As I had to keep reminding myself, in England, a "biscuit" was not something one would eat with gravy.

Geoff noticed my piqued interest, so he slid the tin toward me.

He explained that the record wasn't exactly clear on what happened next, but sometime in the 1500s, Edmund Hopwood, the squire of the time, seems to have switched teams, becoming a Protestant. He became so zealous that people started calling him Edmund the Puritan and he gained a reputation as a "witch hunter"—someone who tracked down Catholics and those suspected of witchcraft, putting them on trial.

It was Edmund's second son, also named Edmund, who returned to the family's original faith, because in the very early 1600s, Edmund Jr. is listed as taking Catholic orders.

"This younger Edmund may have been the reason Guy Fawkes felt safe to visit Hopwood Hall," Geoff continued. "The year was 1605, and legend has it that Fawkes went on a tour of Northern England in search of supporters to finance his attack on King James I, which brought him to Hopwood Hall."

"Sort of like an olden days Kickstarter campaign?" I questioned.

Either my comment was foolish, or he didn't hear me, but Geoff continued.

"In fact, they would have likely met in this very room," Geoff said as we wandered into the Oak Parlor. I clutched my warm mug of tea and looked around at all the carved wood faces staring back at me. To think of the centuries of history that they had witnessed was mind-boggling.

"It would have been a secret meeting," Geoff continued. "For Edmund Jr. to have someone like Fawkes at the Hall was incredibly risky. And of course, Edmund would have not known why Fawkes was seeking funds until the two actually sat down together. It's not the type of information Fawkes would have sent ahead of time in a letter."

"So what did Edmund do?" I asked, a tad afraid to hear the answer.

"Well, being a proper Englishman, he probably offered him tea and a biscuit."

I laughed. I felt like a curious child being teased by his father.

"But about the gunpowder plot?"

"Edmund turned him down—told him he didn't want to contribute. He sent him on his way. Perhaps he felt the mission was too dangerous, or too malicious or perhaps because he feared retaliation by his Puritan father, who lived until 1612. But one thing we know for sure is that the Hopwoods were not involved in the plot."

I let out a sigh of relief.

"It's a lucky thing too, because after Fawkes was discovered with twenty kegs of gunpowder under the British parliament, he was arrested, tortured, and sentenced to death . . . Although before that could happen, he apparently fell off the scaffold and broke his neck and died! But if Edmund Jr. had been involved, it's likely he too would have met some type of similar fate, and you wouldn't be standing here today because you would never have been born."

It was hard to wrap my mind around the fact that my entire existence was somehow connected to a holiday that I had no knowledge of just a few days before.

"Although he never got to detonate his supplies, this is why everyone celebrates the anniversary of his attempt by letting off fireworks," Geoff concluded.

I thanked Geoff for the helpful lesson and wondered, not for the first time, how I would've navigated life in England without him—there was so much history to grapple with here, and a cursory understanding of it was essential. I was lucky to have someone as knowledgeable as Geoff willing to help coach me beyond my ignorance. Things were now making more sense, and it was fascinating to continue to grasp all the incredible history that happened prior to the Golden Age of Hollywood.

I was walking a bit taller on my way back to the Castleton and decided to pop into the Hopwood service station to say hello to my new friend the clerk, and to see if he happened to sell loaves of bread and cans of beans. Tonight, I felt due for a celebration, and I was sure Mary would be thrilled if I surprised her by making dinner for everyone with my new British cooking skills. Certainly, she was sure to be doubly impressed if I had the ability to also locate a store, purchase the correct groceries, and then carry them home all by myself.

"Hey, Hopwood! How's your week been?" the clerk chimed as I walked into the store.

"All good!" I replied, noticing that he was looking at me rather oddly.

"How was your night on the Fifth?" he snickered.

Clearly word had traveled that I had been guilty of being a clueless American.

"We couldn't stop laughing when we heard about how scared you were of Bonfire Night!"

He must have seen my face drop, because he quickly added: "Don't feel bad, mate. My dog gets scared and runs in circles when she hears fireworks." Then he burst into uncontrollable laughter. "I bet you did the same thing, eh? Did you hide under the bed too?"

I could barely contain my embarrassment, so I just laughed along. Meanwhile, I was dying inside from the utter humiliation of being compared to a dog named Dolly.

On my way out of the store, carrying my bread and beans, I decided to play along, pretending to bark like Dolly and running in a little circle before exiting the store. It brought the house down including a few customers who obviously were in on the joke too.

For the next few days, wherever I went in town, I would notice people pointing and whispering to their kids, "That's the Yank who didn't know about the Fifth of November!!" followed by fits of uproarious laughter.

Clearly, Bob had been dining out on the story of my Bonfire Night ignorance, telling everyone within a five-mile radius who would listen that the fireworks had freaked me out. I have now come to accept that it's probably an embarrassing fact of my life that I will never live down.

I often think about Dolly and wonder if she feels the same way too.

CHAPTER 18

ESCAPE TO ROCHDALE

After being publicly shamed thanks to my lack of knowledge about English history, I decided it might be a good idea to buff up on it as much as possible. Ever since I'd moved to England, Geoff had been telling me I needed to pay a visit to a place called Touchstones Rochdale when I had a day off from the Hall. This is where many of the Hopwood family records are stored. After the Bonfire Night debacle, I called Touchstones and spoke with a researcher named Heather, making an appointment for the following week. Perhaps whatever I found at the Touchstones archives would provide some much-needed information—and inspiration—as my mission to restore the Hall continued.

The afternoon of my appointment, I hopped off the bus and went looking for the archives, housed in a building across the street from Rochdale's town hall. I walked up to a large old limestone structure with statues and faces carved into the upper levels and three gables perched on a slate roof. This was the place.

Heather welcomed me inside.

"I've pulled out loads of documents and photographs for you to look at," she explained as she led me into a room lined with shelves of books and archival files, with a table in the middle and a few boxes and books laid out on it. As I sat down, I saw that they were labeled HOPWOOD ARCHIVE.

I wasn't aware that this much material was still around; if I had known, I would have visited sooner. Heather handed me a pair of white cotton gloves to put on while sifting through the materials.

"This is brilliant!" she exclaimed as she carefully handed me a large gilt-edged invite addressed to the Hopwood family to attend George the V's coronation.

I began to read the hand-drawn pen-and-ink personal invitation as I laid it on the table.

"The Coronation of Their Majesties, King George the Fifth and Queen Mary. By command of the King. The Earl Marshal is directed to invite you to be present at the Abbey Church of Westminster on the twenty-second day of June MCMXI."

"MCMXI," Heather said kindly. "That's 1911."

"Wow, I assume that's Westminster Abbey?" I said, taking a closer look. "Where William and Kate got married?"

"Indeed," she nodded. "And look at this."

It was a faded invitation to "Col. and Lady Hopwood" from over one hundred years ago, inviting them to a party at Knowsley Hall, from the Earl and Countess of Derby. In other words, my ancestors had gone to parties with Teddy and Cazzy's ancestors! In fact, I had attended one of their present-day parties on almost the exact same date of the year (this time wearing pants *without* clasps). One hundred and ten years later, I was following in the steps of my fore-bears making friends with the descendants of *their* friends. It was all a bit mind-blowing.

Then she solemnly passed me a yellowing piece of paper.

I quickly realized it was something far less welcome than an invitation to the coronation of a king or a party at Knowsley. It was the telegram sent to Lord and Lady Hopwood after their son's plane was shot down in World War I.

"We regret to inform you that a report on this day has been received from the War Office notifying the death of your son, Robert . . ."

Robert was one of two sons killed in the war, after which time the Hopwood parents, overcome by grief and loss, left the Hall and moved to London.

Holding it in my hands, I felt prickles down my spine, knowing the grief and repercussions this exact piece of paper had caused one hundred years earlier. I tried to imagine how it felt to be the parents who received such a telegram. The devastating nature of it. I thought back to the day after my dad's unexpected heart attack—that moment when I first heard "I'm afraid he's gone," and the after-shocks that continued long after the day of the event.

I found myself staring at the telegram, lost in a moment in time. I had no idea if five minutes had passed or twenty, but I finally snapped back into the present as Heather brought out a file labeled HOPWOOD AMERICAN BRANCH.

I was mesmerized sorting through the documents, which included an old book that went as far in the family line as my great-great-grandmother, Alcinda Hopwood, who had resided in Pennsylvania.

"Alcinda is the reason I'm called Hopwood!" I exclaimed, let-ting Heather know that Alcinda was the last of my American line to carry the Hopwood last name and that when she married, she insisted her grandchild had Hopwood as his middle name so that the name wouldn't die out altogether. "That was my grandfather! And I'm named after him."

I spent the rest of the afternoon surrounded by papers and photos, rummaging about in the past.

"Seeing as you're interested in the American connection, you might want to learn some more about John Bright," Heather pointed out. "I don't think you're related to him, but he was a prominent figure in Rochdale history. He was an abolitionist and a friend of Abraham Lincoln."

It turned out that Bright, who owned a cotton mill in Rochdale during the period of the American Civil War, refused to accept Southern slave-grown cotton, even when there was a cotton famine caused by the war. When Lincoln was assassinated, the president had a few items of sentimental value that he carried with him in his pockets; one of them was a testimonial letter from John Bright, calling for Lincoln to be reelected.

It made me proud to know that the people of Rochdale and Middleton were not afraid to stand up for what they believed in.

One of the most exciting finds at the archives that day were several photographs of Lady Susan Hopwood. Thanks to Geoff, I'd heard of Lady Hopwood's legend, but I had yet to see a photo of her.

Lady Hopwood was born Susan Baskervyle Glegg in 1819 and married Robert Gregg Hopwood, heir to Hopwood Hall. She was known for her love of horses and dogs and was an outspoken anti-vivisectionist long before it was fashionable to oppose operating on animals. Not only that, she was such a good horsewoman she thought nothing of leaping over a nearby canal on horseback. It wasn't until later in her life, however, that she found her true passion.

"In her old age, she became an environmental activist," Heather explained. "This was the era of the late nineteenth century, when the mills and factories of the Industrial Revolution era were spewing out smoke and coal dust from every direction. Lady Hopwood was at the forefront of the fight against pollution: She hired smoke inspectors to investigate and bring prosecutions against mill owners and campaigned for smoke abatement laws, which meant factories had to regulate the amount of exhaust they could emit."

In 1893, Lady Hopwood even held a Smoke Abatement Gala on the Hall grounds that attracted five thousand people. Heather found a copy of Lady Hopwood's obituary to show me that included a description of exactly how she held mill owners to account for polluting the atmosphere.

"She would go out on a tour of smoke inspection in her carriage," Heather read, "drawn by a pair of small ponies, carrying with her a camera, and take photographs of offending chimneys, afterward to be used in court with an effect which taxed all the ingenuity of the defending solicitor to get over . . . The defense could, of course, do no more than sigh and submit to a fine."

"She was like a one-woman nineteenth-century Greenpeace!" I quipped.

"Meanwhile, her son, the squire of the Hall, was trying to lease out portions of the estate to the same mill owners, which must have led to interesting conversations around the dinner table." Heather smiled.

One of the photos showed Lady Hopwood in her horse and carriage with a driver behind her, dressed all in black, surrounded by what looked like five dogs, with a giant fur hat on her head and a rather dramatic black veil pushed over to the side. According to Heather, she had been widowed quite young and, like Queen Victoria, wore black for the rest of her days.

"You can't see it in the photo, but as part of her protest against factory pollution, to make a major public statement, she also often wore a white mask," my archivist friend explained.

Lady Hopwood's faded black-and-white face and eyes stared back at me in a haunting way. I felt a sudden responsibility to live up to the extraordinarily high standards she had set with her own example: to follow your own convictions and to fight for what is right.

I thanked Heather for all her help and gathered up my things, my mind racing with all that I had learned: a prominent family, a lineage cut short by the tragic loss of two sons. The matriarch and her tireless activism on behalf of the environment. An abolitionist

Lady Hopwood and her driver with her beloved dogs in front of the Hopwood Hall carriage entrance, 1880s *Local Studies Centre Touchstone Rochdale, Rochdale Arts & Heritage Center*

with strong ties to America and the president. Somehow, my own small story had gotten caught up in their much more important ones. I climbed aboard the bus, making sure to sit upstairs so I could look out over the city of Rochdale as I left it. Past and present felt linked as they never had been before, and I felt more knitted into this part of the world than ever.

CHAPTER 19

CHRISTMASES PAST

The Brits go all out for Christmas, with decorations going up in September and holiday music blaring in every store starting as early as October, but for some reason I was avoiding thinking about the holiday season.

Perhaps I had been blocking it out because I had been so focused on the Hall.

Or maybe, I was suddenly realizing, it was something much deeper . . .

My father was born on Christmas Day in 1934. The joyful timing was unexpected, and his parents, my grandparents, were so thrilled with the surprise that they debated giving him the first name Noel. My dad loved Christmas for all the obvious reasons, and the importance of the celebrations were heightened because it was also his birthday. When I was young, my family recognized the dual event with huge family gatherings, meals, presents, midnight candlelit church services, going overboard with decorations, caroling in the neighborhood, and delivering surprise gifts to those in need. It was always a magical time in my life.

Even as I got older and moved to Hollywood, the tradition continued. I threw an annual Christmas birthday bash that was legendary among my friends. Large wreaths and stockings would be hung, white lights strung on the trees and overhead, and the table set with both red and white wine crystal glasses. My family would fly in, bringing festive holiday attire, my dad dressing in his signature red suit and red derby hat. Jonny and Jay attended on multiple occasions, with Jonny often asking to borrow my dad's red hat to snap some photos of himself. Jay, on the other hand, was typically dressed in black-tie.

But as time ticked on, our Christmases slowly dwindled in attendance with the deaths of various extended family members. Eventually, the biggest blow was struck, turning my world upside down, when my dad died from a massive heart attack on December 4, 2010. Presents had already been purchased; parties had been planned. The process of returning the gifts that had been wrapped up for him, and opening the ones he had purchased for us, was an emotional rollercoaster. His funeral, a week before Christmas in Michigan, was a testament to the type of life he had lived and one to which I aspired. He was a man who had accepted and encouraged people in all walks of life through his volunteer work. His funeral was attended by everyone from successful businesspeople in the community to single parents on welfare. Members of Congress and actors from Hollywood flew in, and local migrants who worked in the nearby blueberry fields took the bus. The US Marines presented a flag to my mother and trumpeted "Taps" with a 21-gun salute outside the church for my dad's service to the country. The most memorable was a soulful gospel choir from a church in Muskegon, an hour's drive away, arriving in a van on the snowy winter night, to sing their hearts out and pay their respects. Their rendition of "O Holy Night" still haunts me, and to this day, whenever that song comes on the radio, I feel the tears start to stream.

After my dad's fatal heart attack, Christmas took on a connection to the birth *and* the death of my father, so it was filled with both wonderful memories but also a great deal of sadness. I felt that our Christmas traditions had come to a tragic end, and I stopped throwing my annual party as it didn't seem right to continue doing it with our key player now gone forever.

This was going to be my first Christmas in England. Could I really continue to spend the holiday, which is incredibly joyous to so many others, with my own personal blinders on? I suddenly felt a tinge of hope. Something in me was now changing. Or perhaps healing.

It had occurred to me that it might be nice to have a party for the volunteers and other members of the community, to celebrate the season and show them how much I appreciated their hard work on the hall's behalf—and in the hope that it would perhaps revive my Christmas spirit after so many years without a proper celebration. I decided to run the idea of the Christmas party by Geoff. By this time, I'd started going over to Geoff's house about once a week for dinner. Lyn kindly encouraged me to bring along my laundry each time so it could wash while we ate.

When I mentioned Christmas at Hopwood Hall, he smiled.

"You'd be bringing back a grand tradition," he told me as he passed the salad. "The Hopwoods had legendary Christmas parties, dating back centuries, where they would open their home to the whole community. I have an old newspaper article that was a young girl's account of attending a Christmas party at Hopwood Hall in the 1890s. Perhaps you would like to see it?"

I was so eager we skipped dessert and retired into their living room. A few minutes later, Geoff emerged with the yellowed newspaper clipping, sitting down between Lyn and me on the couch facing the fireplace.

According to the article, in Victorian times, Christmas at the Hall was such a big deal that preparations began weeks in advance. Puddings and cakes were made, poultry were fattened up on the farm, and holly was brought in by the gardeners. The servants cleaned and polished the furniture, beds were made up with fresh white linens, and fires were lit in every room, "until the house was warm and cozy ready for the party," as the author of the article described it.

The Hopwoods hired an entire train to bring family members back to Middleton. Neighboring lords and ladies climbed into their carriages and made the short ride to the Hall, where all the staff—including the housekeeper, butler, footmen, and maids in their crisp white caps and aprons—would be waiting in a long line for their arrival. Inside the house, the air was filled with the scent of potpourri in big brass bowls and fires blazing in the fireplaces. The family decorated the Christmas tree and went riding on the grounds. They held skating parties on the lake while hot chestnuts and potatoes were roasted on braziers and lanterns were hung from the trees. Later in the week, all the townspeople were invited to a New Year's concert at the local school where the ladies from the Hall appeared in their long sparkling evening gowns and lords wore their starched shirtfronts and white waistcoats, everyone singing songs around the piano.

"But then it all came to an abrupt end about a hundred years ago with the deaths of the two Hopwood sons in World War I," Geoff told me. "After that, no more Hopwood family Christmases were cel-ebrated in the Hall."

To say I was awed and inspired would have been an understate-ment. After reading the article, I was determined to bring Christmas back to Hopwood Hall. I wasn't sure how I would do it, but we had pulled off Heritage Open Days, after all. Perhaps we could now do something more elaborate for Christmas. Even if it was small to be-gin, it could grow and improve each year.

When I confided in Geoff about the holiday and what it meant to my family because of my dad, he nodded sympathetically.

"A party might be good closure for you," Geoff suggested, once again displaying the amazing bedside manner learned from decades of work as an undertaker.

"Who knows—it may also provide closure for the community," Lyn remarked. "So we can all come full circle after the events of World War I that caused the Hall to go into decline."

"In so many ways, it could be a fresh new beginning and step toward healing for many," Geoff said, nodding to add his approval of the idea.

By the time I returned to my room I was buzzing with excite-ment, so I phoned my mom.

"Mom, I'm bringing back our Christmas traditions, but this time at Hopwood Hall!" I told her while unpacking my large bag of clean laundry, folded by Lyn. "The Hopwood family used to throw their own huge parties there, but it all stopped a hundred years ago. I'm totally convinced I can relaunch it. How fun would it be to bring it back in honor of the Hopwoods, and Dad too?"

"Sounds fantastic. It seems like I'll need to book another flight?" my mother asked with a smile in her voice on the other side of the Atlantic.

I paused and tried to wrap my mind around it. With the holidays right around the corner, time was of the essence. Never mind that there was still rubble falling from the ceilings and the only running water was down the walls. We'd clear up a bit, hang some tinsel on a tree, and serve drinks. It was going to be fabulous!

"I don't know," I said to her, "but I'll look into it and let you know ASAP."

The next morning, I was sitting at my desk, having a cup of tea and making a to-do list, when I received a call from Geoff.

"I hate to be the one to tell you, but there might be one major stumbling block with trying to hold a Christmas party at the Hall," he said in a low voice. "It turns out the college entrance road to the Hall that we used for Open Days will be closed during the Christmas break. So it appears if you want to have the party, you are going to need to get permission from your neighbor Phineas Shellburn."

My heart sank. I knew what Geoff was saying was true. We had been through this before with the hotel project. I guess with my Yankee optimism, I was still hoping the problem might magically go away. At the very least, I wanted to put up a good fight. I first tried calling the college to see if there was any way they could leave their gates open for the party. But due to security and limited staff over the holidays, the answer came back as a final "Unfortunately not possible."

I decided I couldn't put it off any longer. I needed to go and meet with Phineas Shellburn. Perhaps if we were face-to-face, I could try to make amends for my ancestor's misdeeds from five hundred years ago.

Geoff put out the word among his contacts at the local pubs to let him know if anyone spotted Shellburn coming into their establishment.

A few afternoons later, I was sitting back at my desk, plotting out the party, when my phone began vibrating like it was possessed. It was Geoff calling.

"We have a Phineas Shellburn sighting," Geoff said, clearly excited. "Apparently he's just walked into a pub on the outskirts of Rochdale."

I needed to quickly spring into action.

"What should I do?!" I asked.

"I am being told that Shellburn doesn't get out much these days, so if I were you, I would put down my tea, throw on my boots, and get over there before he leaves."

Within a few minutes I was suited up for the biting-cold, windy winter air. It had been wet all day, so water had frozen on tree branches in drips, making them look like glass that could shatter at any moment. I kept repeating to myself that confronting Mr. Shellburn was going to be fine, even though I was dreading the encounter. Geoff told me that when I arrived at the pub I should look for a large, burly man with a long beard and a walking stick.

The whipping wind yanked back the heavy wooden door as I opened it to walk into the pub. A few customers looked up at me, clearly not enjoying my foolish mistake of accidentally letting in an unexpected cold blast.

I scanned the bar and a few tables, but it looked like Mr. Shellburn was no longer there. Just as I was about to turn and leave, I spotted him sitting at the bar around the corner near the billiard table, a large golden retriever lying at his feet.

Shellburn was indeed a burly man with a beard and a scowl that made his eyebrows knit in the middle above his nose. He seemed to be preoccupied watching a game on the television, so this probably wasn't the best time to approach him, but I had to give it a shot. I took a deep breath.

His walking stick was leaning against the bar. I wondered if he might hit me with it.

"Excuse me, Mr. Shellburn . . ."

It took him a beat before he looked at me. I immediately felt like I was talking to my high school principal.

"What do you want?" he muttered.

"First, I want to buy you a pint," I said, giving him a full-beam smile in the hope that it would help distract from how loud and out of place my American accent suddenly sounded in the middle of an English pub. "I know there has been a long feud between our ancestors, and I wanted to make amends."

"With a pint?!" he barked.

"How about a shot of Scottish whisky?" I asked timidly, recalling the bonding success I had experienced at Flodden.

Clearly, he wasn't interested in downing shots. Or at least not with me. Mr. Shellburn started back at the TV.

"Whatever you've come to ask me for, forget it. I'm not interested."

I knew I had to push forward and go for it.

"It's just that . . . Christmas is coming up, and we want to have a party at the Hall. The college will be closed, so I'm hoping you'll allow guests to cross over your property to get to the event?"

"I just said I am not interested," he said sternly. "Now if you'll leave me in peace, I would like to get back to my game."

"Could we pay you?"

"I'M NOT INTERESTED!" he shouted.

His dog sat up and began barking at me.

The customers looked over at me again. I suddenly had the feeling

I had become a nuisance and that I was no longer welcome. Perhaps I was being overly sensitive, but I felt clearly that I was not a local. I had a different accent, and I needed to leave.

I scurried toward the door. English pubs are often very warm or overheated, so stepping outside into the frigid afternoon air literally felt like a slap in the face.

As I headed back to the Hall, my mind was reeling. I felt lightheaded—partly from being embarrassed, and partly from being so angry.

All I had done was ask a perfectly reasonable question of a neighbor. To have been completely rebuffed for no good reason seemed like horrible manners to me. Weren't the English supposed to be more polite than that?

I stumbled into the Hall, stomping over to the Banquet Room, where I was due to have a meeting with Bob later that afternoon about restoring the enormous leaded-glass windows there. As I waited for Bob, I felt crestfallen. The idea of planning a Christmas party had been helping me keep my homesickness at bay. Now I had to call my mom to tell her that she wouldn't need to book a flight. I dialed her number and told her the news. She was sympathetic, but I hung up feeling even worse. Being so far away from home made me miss her *and* my dad even more.

I was sitting on the floor in the corner of the Banquet Room with my head in my hands when my phone buzzed.

I felt a spark of happiness: It was Jay calling from LA. The signal must've gotten through this time thanks to the large windows in the Banquet Room. Maybe a chat with him would cheer me up. He was calling on FaceTime to see what my plans were for the holidays.

"How is it going there?" he said. "You still enjoying the adventure?"

I did my best to happily cover—I didn't have the heart to explain about my neighbor and the now-impossible party.

"It's great," I muttered. I'm sure he could tell I was lying.

"Well, we all miss you. Wish you could be here with us," he said.

Then Jay panned around to show me where he was. He owned a seventy-foot sailboat, where he was throwing a party with my entire crew of close friends. I could see a bright blue sky, sparkling turquoise ocean, sunshine glinting on the waves in the background. Someone had opened a bottle of champagne.

"HAPPY HOLIDAYS, HOPWOOD!!" they all cheered.

Jay also mentioned a potential job in LA in January. "When are you coming back, Hopwood?" he wanted to know.

I told him I wasn't sure.

As my friends celebrated thousands of miles away on the ocean, I looked around the Banquet Room. This would have been the place in the house where grand balls and parties were thrown in years gone by. *Not anymore*, I thought. There were giant gaps in the plasterwork, missing floorboards, and a crumbling fireplace. The vast, twenty-foot-high bay window had cracks in the glass and was smeared with mud and hung with cobwebs.

I began to think about that window and what it would take to restore it. When I'd first come to the Hall, I'd thought of this as one big window. Looking at it now, I realized it was actually composed of forty smaller windows. And then I started looking at each one of those windows. They were made up of individual hand-blown, diagonal panes of glass—almost all of which would need to be repaired, replaced, or restored. So I started counting the tiny panes and doing the math. The forty windows all had over fifty—sometimes over eighty—tiny windowpanes. This meant that, in total, there had to be over 2,710 very small windows that needed repairing to fix the one big window. And that's just one window in one room! And it was up to ME to do it! And I was five thousand miles from home, and I couldn't have Christmas, and it was freezing cold in the Hall without heating while my friends were living it up on a sailboat in blue-sky California.

No wonder the UK visa immigration department doubted my sanity! No wonder people pointed and laughed at me as I walked around town. I was the idiot who had left his life in paradise and taken on the restoration of Hopwood Hall. Not because I had to, but one hundred percent by choice.

CHAPTER 20

WITH A LITTLE HELP FROM MY FRIENDS

A new year dawned, and even though I made a slew of resolutions that mostly revolved around traveling to sunny places and perhaps discovering an exciting new romantic relationship, I remained cold and damp and single.

One morning at the Castleton, I mentioned to Mary that I was so tired I had overslept my alarm and almost missed joining her for breakfast.

"Well, I wouldn't know about that!" she retorted. "I've never used an alarm clock in my life! Instead, I use an old Irish method my grandmother taught me."

It turned out that whenever Mary wanted to wake up early, say at six A.M., she would knock her head against the pillow six times. "It's worked for me for over seventy-five years."

I looked at her askance, but she seemed to be deadly serious. I told her as much as I believed the technique worked for her, I was a heavy sleeper, and it wouldn't work for me.

"You've gotten soft," she said as she buttered her toast. "Probably all those years in LA . . . but don't worry, you're still young enough to get back on track."

She also suggested that I start taking vitamin D.

"Especially someone like you who's used to absorbing it from the sunshine. Otherwise, you'll end up all depressed. Your body needs vitamin D!"

I loved how people from the UK pronounced it as *VIT-amin*. I couldn't help but smile as she stared at me over her spectacles with the look of a worried mother. I assumed she had either noticed my lackluster attitude prior to Christmas or Bob had told the town about my tears in the Banquet Room. Either way, Mary was concerned. She had pointed me in the right direction for beans on toast, so I decided to follow her advice on the vitamin front.

Of course, I didn't dare risk embarrassing myself by asking my clerk friend at the Hopwood service station for vitamin D, in fear that, in England, trying to buy it might be comparable to attempting to score opioids. Instead, I headed to the local chemist, where I was able to obtain a small bottle without feeling like they might yank me into the back room for an emergency intervention.

Despite my newfound addiction to vitamin D, I did have to face a cold, hard fact: There was no heating in the Hall, and so the brick and stone building held onto its subzero temperature like a giant freezer. There were days when I couldn't feel my fingers or toes. I could, however, see my breath.

"You look like the castle dragon in a hard hat," Bob regularly reminded me as I huffed and puffed around, exhaling "smoke." It certainly made me conscious of always carrying mints on the mornings that I preferred coffee over tea, to avoid any of Bob's additional observations about the dragon also having coffee breath.

That January, Bob decided it was time to start repairing the Edgar Wood ceiling in the inglenook. The inglenook is the small room under the low beam, home to the Lord Byron fireplace, that Bob had shown us when I visited on the very first day with my family. Back then, I had been struck by how cozy and appealing the place must have been in such a large and drafty house, and immediately started imagining myself sitting there once it was renovated, in a large armchair, with my feet up, warming myself by the fire. Even so, I couldn't quite believe we were going to tackle this next.

"Wait, are you telling me we're going to start fixing a ceiling before we can even get to the 2,710 damaged windows in the Banquet Room?" I asked incredulously.

"The inglenook ceiling is in immediate danger of collapsing and being lost forever," Bob explained. "So the Banquet Room windows will just have to wait."

Geoff explained that because Edgar Wood, who designed the ceiling, was one of the best-known proponents of the Arts and Crafts movement, the ceiling was of great architectural importance. It was certainly beautifully decorated, with clusters of grape vines and flowers rendered in extraordinary detail. It was also on the verge of collapse. Over the years, the rain had gotten in, and now the ceiling was bulging and cracked, with giant chunks of plaster littering the floor.

I understood the urgency of the ceiling, but it was also hard to wrap my mind around the fact that the massive project of 2,710 windows that might take us months or even years to repair was a project that wasn't even on the to-do list yet!

"How long will the ceiling take?" I asked.

"It's difficult to know until we get into it," Bob replied. "For the full process, it could take months. Why? Do you have something more important to do?"

I realized he was asking a rhetorical question.

The plan was to take down the pieces, then lay them out in order on a table, safeguarding them until the ceiling—and roof—could be properly repaired. As a kid who used to turn over the pieces of a jig-saw puzzle to make assembling it more challenging, this held some appeal for me. We got to work, carefully removing each of the plaster sections and placing them in position on the table.

Thanks to his work in the historical restoration field, Bob was clearly a patient man—*much* more patient than I am. In Hollywood, everyone wants (and often gets) everything now, now, NOW! The work on yet another ceiling looked like it was going to be incredibly tedious and time-consuming, a fact that I made the mistake of mentioning to Bob.

"Hopwood, what you have to realize is this hall took centuries to build into what it once was at its finest. We're not going to see dramatic changes here as quickly as someone walking into a Beverly Hills plastic surgeon."

I wasn't sure if Bob was accusing me of having some "work" done myself or if he was just making a point, but I understood what he was saying.

Bob's banter helped keep the mood light even on the darkest, wettest, and coldest of days. I couldn't help but think that he was beginning to like having me around. At the least, I certainly must've made his workday pass by faster, since if I wasn't there, he wouldn't have anyone to insult. Yes, the work was boring in some ways, but it was strangely compelling as well, and ultimately rewarding, a bit like those jigsaw puzzles I loved when I was younger.

During the long winter, Geoff took it upon himself to drive over to the Hall to give us regular pep talks. Often, he'd tell stories of my Hopwood ancestors, knowing that I loved to learn more about them. Maybe he somehow realized that I was having doubts and that I needed a pick-me-up.

One afternoon, during one of his visits, we took a walk over to the Banquet Room to warm up from "freezing" to "not-so-freezing" and so that I could show Geoff the panes of glass that were the scene of my moment of greatest woe.

"When Lord John and Lady Elizabeth Hopwood lived in the Hall in the early eighteenth century, they were known for the lavish parties they used to throw in this house," Geoff began. "In fact, in this very room."

Despite the bone-chilling cold, I lit up. Geoff obviously knew that I would be pleased to hear I was related to party animals.

"Clearly you didn't fall far from the tree," Geoff said with a wink. "That's why they built this grand room, so that they could fit more people in, and entertain aristocrats such as the Earl and Countess of Derby and many others," Geoff explained. "On nights when they held their formal balls there would have been an orchestra playing, guests and family dancing till the early hours whilst footmen dispensed drinks and the maids served food."

I looked around the expansive room. Ornate moldings, now crumbling. The back of the frame of a huge mirror above the fireplace mantel that had been smashed by vandals. A circular floral pattern on the ceiling, now cracking from water leakage, that was certainly once home to a gigantic, candlelit chandelier.

We both absorbed the sight for a moment, with a bittersweet energy in the air.

Geoff picked up the mood with one of his historical quizzes.

"And can you guess what John and Elizabeth made sure to have at every single party they ever had?"

"Umm, alcohol?" I replied.

Geoff laughed.

"Yes, that, but also . . . wait for it . . . a pineapple," he said.

According to Geoff, in the 1700s, it was the height of fashion to have a pineapple at your party.

"The problem was, because this precious fruit had to be grown in hothouses or imported from far away, a pineapple back then would have cost the equivalent of about £6,000 today."

By now I was getting pretty good at converting pounds to dollars, so I knew that was somewhere in the region of $8,000.

"Pineapples were extremely fashionable, but they were also extremely rare, which meant you had to be fabulously wealthy to afford them. Back then, the pineapple was a status symbol. It told people that you'd hit the big time," Geoff continued. "The good news was that if you couldn't afford to buy a pineapple, you could always rent one at the cost of £600 a night. Per pineapple."

I was shocked.

"You mean the little round yellow slice of pineapple that came with my grade school hot lunch that I always used to throw away was actually worth about a hundred dollars?!" I joked.

Geoff chuckled. "Had you been brought up in the 1700s, you probably would have treated it much differently. It would've been a delicacy. Or you would've been a spoiled brat!"

We started joking around, imagining what it would've been like to be a fly on the wall in the 1700s, hearing the party guests gossiping with one another as word got around Middleton about the upcoming shindig at Hopwood Hall:

"Did you hear the Hopwoods are having another party? This time they're going to have TWO pineapples!"

"Are you certain they won't just try to trick us with a mirror?"

"No, there's definitely going to be two. But I bet they'll probably be *rented*."

"I wonder how hard it would be to return a pineapple and get your full deposit back after *renting* it?" Geoff wondered.

"Sir, half of this pineapple is eaten!" I chimed in.

"No, I'm pretty sure those bites were missing when I rented it," Geoff replied, giggling.

As Geoff and I sat there laughing about pineapples, right on cue, Bob walked in with his lunch box, wearing his heavy work boots and keys jangling. That morning, his wife had packed his lunch in Tupperware—including three slices of pineapple. Actually, there had been four, but Bob had already eaten one. Bob took another one for himself and offered the rest to us.

"Here you go, lads." He grinned. "Tuck in."

Even though it was funny and might sound mundane, I realized this moment was very special. I looked over at my two unlikely friends, whom I never would have otherwise met if it hadn't been for the discovery of Hopwood Hall. Geoff and Bob went way back; meanwhile, I was the new kid in the group who wanted to do whatever he could to show his new buddies that he could fit in if they would let him. Fortunately, they were letting me. The three of us were so different—Geoff with his gentle bedside manner, me with my persistent Yankee optimism, and Bob with his gruff Manchester humor. But even so, we had a lot in common. We all desperately wanted to save the Hall. And the ups and downs of taking care of her were making one thing abundantly clear: If I wanted to keep this project going, I would not only need to draw on the strength of my ancestors—but also the camaraderie of my Middletonian friends.

And there the three of us sat, eating our pineapple, laughing and talking and forgetting our troubles . . . at least for a while.

Before long, it was time to head back to the Castleton. Outside in the crisp air, I popped another vitamin D and chased it with a swig of tea from my thermos. Yes, I was now carrying a thermos, along with wearing work boots and work pants that had slots, straps, and pockets to hold various tools. If my LA friends could see me, I knew they wouldn't believe it. Or they would probably assume I was dressed in character on the set of a movie.

My cell phone began to vibrate. It was the Countess of Derby calling.

"Hopwood, it's Cazzy. Teddy and I are a bit worried about you as we haven't heard from you in some time," she said.

It was a very welcome call even if I could only hold my phone for five minutes without my hand going numb in the freezing wind.

"Sometimes it can be so daunting," I said with a laugh, trying to maintain my American cheerfulness. "How did you handle it when you renovated Knowsley Hall?"

She paused for a moment and then sympathetically said, "Hopwood, it is very important that you stop yourself anytime you begin to compare it to renovating a flat or a normal-sized home. Think of yourself as the director of a museum. To have the patience and practice to know that it may take years, or even a lifetime, but ultimately you are delivering a project that will outlast yourself. Once you embrace that concept, then it will free you . . . and, most important, allow you to enjoy the process."

It was incredibly calming to talk to someone who could

understand the demands of rescuing a historic house and had made it through to the other side.

"Come visit us this weekend," she offered. "We will have food and wine and you can have a nice, long soak in a bath and relax. A weekend away will do wonders."

A few days later, I pulled up to the familiar iron gates of Knowsley Hall and pressed the buzzer.

"Good day, Mr. DePree. We've been expecting you. Please park in front of the house and we will unload your bags," said the familiar-sounding voice on the other end as the gates swung open.

"Wilton? Is that you?" I asked.

There was a momentary pause.

"Yes sir," he said. "See you shortly."

It was an amazing feeling to return to such a beautiful location and feel like a regular. I followed Wilton up the winding staircase and down a long corridor to eventually reach the room where I would be staying.

It was a large, beautifully decorated guest room, the size of some apartments, with a huge four-post canopy bed. Glass bottles of water, sumptuous looking chocolates, a wide selection of English teas, and decanters of fine alcohols were all displayed in the room, eagerly awaiting my arrival. It was like a five-star hotel.

"Wow. Is there a dishwasher in the room too?" I joked.

Wilton gave a polite smile and continued toward the bathroom.

"Lady Derby informed me you would like to have a bath," he said, opening the door and showcasing a large tub, a white robe, slippers, and fluffy towels that looked like they were straight out of a Downy detergent ad. In the corner was a linen box filled with absolutely anything else I could possibly need, toothpaste and various shaving creams and body lotions.

"If you could be dressed and ready at about eight o'clock for cocktails before dinner, it would be appreciated," he said as he exited the room, closing the door and leaving me to myself.

From my time with Dr. Rolph, I knew that "about eight" translated to 8:07 P.M. I was learning.

That gave me four hours to relax.

After a long soak in the bath, I was feeling rejuvenated. I got out of the tub and did something I wouldn't normally do at someone else's house. Yes, at a hotel, but not at a house. I cracked open one of the complimentary body lotions! It was French. I slathered myself from head to toe.

Now smelling like tapioca pudding, I poured myself a small sipping glass of brandy. I was in heaven.

Cazzy was right. This was exactly what I needed. Just before eight, I dressed for dinner. I was thankful that I had left the pants with the broken clasp at home.

At exactly 8:07 P.M., I made it to the bottom of the staircase, just as five couples began arriving through the front door. Another member of the house staff escorted us to a nearby room where the Earl and Countess were entering from an opposite door. Upbeat music was already playing.

"Hopwood, you look rested," Cazzy said as we exchanged two side-to-side cheek kisses. "I am so glad you were able to make it."

As multiple servers scurried around, several bottles of champagne were uncorked, and the party was launched.

Within minutes, I was introduced to the other ten dinner guests who would also be staying the weekend: owners of a bread empire, owners of a jewelry empire, owners of a beer empire, a successful British television producer and his wife, and a young couple who had just inherited one of the largest castles in Scotland.

All the guests were very welcoming and seemed to fully understand the challenges of renovating a historic property.

"Would you like to join us on our pheasant hunt tomorrow morning?" Teddy said as he gave me a friendly handshake when I finally got a chance to say hello to him.

I had heard about pheasant hunts in England, but wasn't totally sure what it entailed, and I was slightly panicked that I wouldn't fit in.

"It is a traditional English event where each year the pheasant population needs to be managed in order to ensure it does not get out of control," Teddy explained. "So we will head out onto the estate tomorrow morning at nine. All birds will be used in our kitchens, sold in the local farm shop, or donated to those in need."

"Sure," I replied. "But I've never been hunting before, so I don't want to slow anyone down or get in anyone's way." Secretly, I was hoping maybe he would let me off the hook as I was already feeling pangs of nerves.

"Do not worry. We will make sure you do not get in anyone's way as we will be shooting up into the sky, not at you," he laughed. "Also, you will not have to actually shoot. You can simply go along and watch like some of the others."

The following morning, Cazzy opened a large closet off one of the side entrances that was chock-full of hunting gear for visitors. It looked like a rack had been wheeled in from an L.L.Bean showroom. Wilton helped me to quickly suit up in knee-high "wellies," a green waterproof wax jacket, and a traditional green plaid English flat cap.

Looking at myself in the floor length mirror, I couldn't help but chuckle at the juxtaposition between the dirtied work clothes I had been wearing a few days prior and this designer hunting outfit. I felt like a bit of a fraud!

I couldn't resist. "Wilton, would you mind snapping a photo of me?" I asked when we got outside, handing my cell phone to him.

We loaded ourselves into a fleet of black Range Rovers and headed out across the sprawling estate in a convoy. Cazzy followed in her own car since she was only planning to join us for part of the shoot.

Teddy loaned me an extra pair of his ear defenders, so I guessed whatever we were doing, it was going to be loud. We traveled in a caravan from the main house out into the woodlands and then to a clearing. They had sent the resident gamekeepers ahead of the party to prepare the site.

I was a bit nervous when the shoot began, what with all the rifles being fired, dogs barking, and rushing off into the woods to return with a pheasant, which the gamekeepers collected.

Around lunchtime, our fleet of Range Rovers wove through the woods toward a quaint cottage in the middle of a clearing with smoke rising out of its chimney. The cottage was quirky and charming, with gingham curtains, and looked like it was out of a storybook. This was our lunch spot.

Teddy explained the cottage had been a present from the people of Canada. They had gifted it to his

Hopwood in traditional English country wear *Courtesy of the author* ancestor, who was one of his predecessors as the Earl of Derby. Wilton and the staff had come down from the main house and prepared a lovely meal and hot drinks.

After lunch, Cazzy offered to drive me to the next meeting place. It worked out perfectly because it would also give us a chance to catch up.

As we drove, I confided in her about how cold it was at Hopwood Hall, the thousands of windows that needed repairing, the inglenook ceiling, the uphill struggle to find funding, and how many months and years I guessed it would be before we got the place into fit shape.

"Most people think that when someone inherits a huge house, they are so lucky," Cazzy pointed out. "But in reality, to take care of a grand estate can feel a bit like someone handing you the keys to a museum and saying, 'Here you go!' It is yours now—it is up to you to take care of it, and you must pay for all the maintenance and upkeep. Yes indeed, like a museum, it has a great value, but it can never be sold. Therefore, we have to embrace our duties as caretakers."

I'm sure that some people who aren't aware of the reality would have a difficult time feeling sympathy for landed aristocrats, but it was becoming clear to me that Teddy and Cazzy's lives brought with them an overwhelming amount of responsibilities—not only caring for their estate but also doing endless hours of volunteer work, helping in the community, and sitting on over one hundred charitable boards each.

"Most people are handed this responsibility and have no choice," Cazzy pointed out. "From a very young age, the firstborn is groomed to take care of the estate and to accept the role of the title. They never have any choice in what they will do—this is just their lot in life. But in your case, you *decided* to take on Hopwood Hall!"

"I know," I laughed. "I used to think it must be frustrating to be the second son who doesn't inherit anything. Now I realize they might be the lucky ones. They get the freedom!"

"Just remember that these houses have been around for centuries," Cazzy said, her voice warm and her words full of wisdom. "Trust in yourself that they will lead you, rather than you leading them."

Then our chat came to an abrupt halt as Cazzy realized she had become distracted by our conversation and we had gotten lost.

She pulled the car over on the gravel road, and we looked around at the twenty-five hundred acres of sprawling green around us.

"I think I see a sheep over there, if that helps?" I said pointing to a small blob of white on the horizon as if it was the North Star.

We began to laugh.

She picked up her cell phone. "Oh no—I do not have any reception. What about you? Do you have a signal?"

Unfortunately, I didn't.

"Hopefully we don't die out here," I joked.

Somehow, I knew that if the Countess of Derby was missing in her own backyard, someone was sure to find us.

A bit farther up the road, we were able to locate a signal, and she phoned for Wilton to come and get us.

"Can you imagine if they never found us and ten years from now, they discovered our skeletons with our cell phones in our hands in a rusted-out old car?" I laughed.

"Stop it. We cannot tell others about this," she said playfully. "They would probably never let me drive a car again!"

We all had another fabulous evening of dinner and drinks. The following morning, I packed up my bags. I knew I needed to get back early so that I could prepare for a busy week of hard work at Hopwood Hall.

On my way out, I said goodbye and thanked everyone for a fantastic weekend. It is an English country house tradition that when an overnight guest is departing the estate, you must sign the guest book. This has been going on for hundreds of years, so a place like Knowsley literally has volumes of guest books stored in its library.

"Hopwood, you may want to take a look at this," Teddy said as he walked over to me with a particularly ornate-looking old guest book with gold edging. "One of our researchers found this, and we thought it might be of interest to you."

He handed me the heavy leatherbound book and pointed to a signature about halfway down the weathered page, under the date 17th October 1881. In faded cursive was inscribed the signature "Lady Hopwood."

I got the chills.

"It looks like your ancestors were guests of my ancestors at Knowsley as well," he said. "You are walking in their same footsteps."

I told Teddy about my visit to Touchstones archives, where the archivist had shown me the invitation to the garden party, also at Knowsley. They must have been good friends.

"We will make a copy and send it to you. Perhaps it will help with your ancestral sleuthing," he said as I stepped out the front door.

As I made my way to my car, I couldn't help but feel like everything was somehow on the right path, even though feeling lost had seemed to be a running theme in my life.

These houses have been around for centuries. Trust in yourself that they will lead you, rather than you leading them. Cazzy's words rang in my head.

Suddenly it felt like getting off course was sometimes the right course, and the small signs along the way would let you know you are headed in the right direction.

I took a deep breath and climbed into the car as Wilton approached.

"Good day, sir. Do you require any further directions?" he asked.

"Maybe just in life," I joked.

He paused for a moment and gave it thought. I could tell he took his job very seriously.

"Well, sir, if the path you are on hasn't led you to plunge off a cliff or encounter wild animals, then you are probably on a good one. The bumps along the way are all just part of the adventure," he said, with a slight smile.

I departed, passing the green pastures, driving through the main road to exit the estate. I felt incredibly lucky to have been invited to experience this side of life. Part of me felt unworthy for having had these fabulous adventures due to the family I had descended from. The other side of me felt daunted with responsibility for the exact same reason.

As Knowsley Hall disappeared in my rearview mirror and the big black iron gates closed behind me, I focused on the road ahead leading back to Hopwood Hall. I soon would be back in my work boots and hard hat, and I was looking forward to the challenge.

CHAPTER 21

NEW DISCOVERIES

"Ahhhh! There's a ghost!"

It was my now seven-year-old niece Jetsen, throwing down my sister's iPhone after she had zoomed in to a random photo of Hopwood Hall. Jetsen and my sister Dana were taking a quick trip to see me during Jetsen's midwinter break, early in the new year of 2018.

I picked up the phone to see what Jetsen was talking about. Dana had taken the photo earlier in the day as we walked around the muddy lane leading to the original entranceway and had quickly snapped it because she liked the distant view through the trees of the Hall majestically perched up on a hill, showcasing the beautiful architecture of the castellations. I looked closely at the image that was blurry from the zooming in. Sure enough, there was a black-and-white figure that seemed to be a woman wearing a long nineteenth-century-type dress with wavy pleats and a large hat on her head. Covering her mouth and nose appeared to be a white face-mask. This was pre-COVID, so in those days very few people were walking around wearing facemasks.

What was going on?

Upon closer look, the woman in the image looked uncannily similar to several of the photos I'd seen in the Touchstones archives. In those pictures, Lady Hopwood was dressed all in black, often surrounded by her five dogs, with a giant fur hat on her head and a rather dramatic black veil. According to the archivist at Touchstones, Lady Hopwood had often worn a white mask over her face as part of her one-woman protest against factory pollution.

I got goosebumps! Had we captured the ghost of Lady Hopwood in a photo?! We never would have even noticed the ghostly figure if it weren't for my niece fooling around with the picture and the incredible zoom capabilities of mobile phones.

I quickly called Geoff and asked if he could meet us for dinner to show him the haunting discovery.

A view of Hopwood Hall from the woodlands *D. DePree*

Note: Unexpected figure is circled. *D. DePree*

Upon closer inspection, the ghostly figure bears a striking resemblance to
Lady Hopwood, who often wore a white mask to protest the Industrial Revolution.
Local Studies Centre Touchstone Rochdale, Rochdale Arts & Heritage Center & D. DePree

Over dinner at the Hopwood pub, Geoff peered at the photo over
his glasses and nodded his head sagely.

"Ah, yes," he intoned. "There have always been rumors that the
Hall was haunted. I suspect we've just received confirmation."

Lady Susan Hopwood, 1850 *Local Studies Centre*
Touchstone Rochdale, Rochdale Arts & Heritage Center

Jetsen's eyes widened.

Geoff went on to explain. For years, people had claimed they had seen a woman walking the long Gallery Corridor at the Hall. Bob's son said he'd experienced a creepy, bluish cold spot pass by him, and there were stories of local workers running from the site and leaving all their tools behind, never to return. Another highly respected man visiting Hopwood Hall said he felt a few sharp taps on his shoulder.

"Lady Hopwood had the corridor built so that she could walk up and down it as exercise without having to get the sun on her face,"

Geoff explained. "In those days, having a tan meant you toiled in the fields, and no respectable aristocratic woman wanted to be mistaken for a peasant."

The photo was taken about twenty-five footsteps from the Gallery!

It seemed that, even in death, my most formidable ancestor continued her protests, haunting the corridors and environs of Hopwood Hall, dressed in her fur hat and white mask.

But why had she made a reappearance now? According to Geoff, she hadn't been seen for some years.

I thought about Lady Hopwood's walks along the corridor, which she'd built to keep her skin looking alabaster. If she was so against having a tan, maybe *I* was the reason she'd come back from the dead. She'd seen my LA bronze, and it had freaked *her* out!

Who is this peasant, walking in my corridor? she'd probably thought to herself.

"It's a spray tan!" I wanted to tell her. "I didn't get it by working in the fields. I paid to go into a booth and have it misted on!"

Geoff had a couple of other theories. It turned out that Lady Hopwood wasn't only anti-pollution, she was strictly anti-alcohol too.

"When a new railroad needed to be built over her land in 1838, she had one condition," Geoff explained. "She requested that no passenger whatsoever would ever drink alcohol during such time that the train passed over Hopwood land."

And back then, it actually worked—people followed the rule!

"Can you believe it?" I asked Jetsen, proceeding to do my best impression of a man in a top hat saying to his elegantly dressed wife, "Oh look, Gertrude, we're about to cross Mrs. Hopwood's land. Please put down your drink. Actually, I think we should dump it out. Out of respect for Mrs. Hopwood."

Maybe Lady Hopwood was upset about my wine consumption, and that explained why she had come back from the dead?

Or maybe it was something else.

"When she became mistress of the house in the mid-1800s, Lady Hopwood decided that the place needed sprucing up," Geoff explained. "She was an avid antique collector and filled the house with Jacobean and Tudor furnishings that were in keeping with the original architecture."

This was extremely exciting information. Not only had Lady Hopwood been someone with drive and tenacity to spare, she was a woman with a strong sense of mission and purpose who also had a penchant for interior decor. I knew that the renovation of the house was going to require me to be just as fearsome as she had been. Was she returning to make sure we got the job done? Or perhaps to inspire us to keep going? Although I was also still committed to turning the Hall into an artists' retreat, with actors, musicians, and filmmakers coming here to work on their projects, maybe we could host environmentalists too. I hoped Lady Hopwood might approve.

Whatever came to pass, I felt sure she was keeping a careful eye on me.

Lady Hopwood's ghost wasn't the only discovery that winter. One freezing, damp morning, Bob and I were working on the ceiling in the inglenook when he called for me to come over.

"Look up there," he said.

Now that the beams of the ceiling were exposed, we could see a gap overhead, above the fireplace. I got out my phone and shone a light into the space; it seemed to extend quite a long way up. Bob got a ladder and climbed up to see what was going on.

"I think it's a priest hole," Bob told me.

"A what?"

"A secret room where Catholic priests could hide out in the 1600s," he explained.

A secret room? I always hoped we'd find something like this!

I positioned the ladder a bit closer so it was directly under the gap, then climbed up to get a better look, still shining my phone into the abyss.

"Wait a minute, there's something else up here," I told Bob. Peering into the beam of phone light, I could see a rectangular shaped object. "Oh my gosh, it looks like a chest!"

A secret room. A hidden chest. This was all my Harrison Ford/ *Raiders of the Lost Ark* childhood dreams come true!

We carefully lowered the heavy chest down so we could take a look at it.

"I think it's a tabernacle," Bob said. Then he added in anticipation of my ignorance, "You know, the box where the priests would have kept the chalice."

Even though I wasn't exactly sure what he was talking about, my Indiana Jones moment was complete.

"Do we need to call somebody?" I asked Bob.

"Like who?" he asked.

"I dunno," I said. "I just thought in a situation like this an ambulance full of archaeologists would show up. To me, this is like finding a dinosaur bone!"

Bob looked at me like I was crazy and directed our attention back to the chest.

It was fairly large, made from a heavy dark wood and intricately carved with patterns in the shape of arches that looked like church windows, with a bit of faded gold gilding visible in places. It had a definite ecclesiastical vibe, even if the whole thing was covered in dust, cobwebs, and mold. Although there wasn't any treasure inside it, as far as I was concerned, the *chest* was the treasure.

I knew I needed to get someone to check it out, and thankfully I knew just the person for the job. Henrietta Graham was a former Christie's appraiser whom I had met through Ralph Assheton, the man who had befriended me at Cazzy and Teddy's Historic Houses party. A few days after the discovery of the tabernacle, I borrowed Bob's car and drove over to meet Henrietta at a nearby antique furniture warehouse, with the chest in the back wrapped in a blanket. I carefully carried the swaddled "baby" through a large roll-up loading dock door and set it onto a sturdy, padded observation table in the middle of the room.

I had always secretly thought it would be fun to go on the TV program *Antiques Roadshow*, where people take their precious family heirlooms to be appraised. The guests on there always seemed like their minds had been blown with their unexpected family discoveries. I wondered how exciting that must feel—so experiencing this felt like a close second.

Henrietta adjusted her spectacles and leaned in to peer at the chest.

"It appears to be seventeenth century," she said, looking at the Gothic-style arches carved on the box's sides and the crenellated decorations around the top. "It's definitely ecclesiastical."

She pointed out the gilding on one side, explaining that originally, it would have been painted and quite bright and pretty.

Like Bob, Henrietta agreed that she thought the chest was likely used to hold religious objects. She said it might be worth as much as £5,000 pounds at auction (about $8,000) but thought it was a much better idea to clean it up and put it on display in the house. I agreed.

"In all my thirty years of appraising, I've never seen anything like it. That's an interesting one," she said.

I returned to the Hall with the tabernacle wrapped up again in its blanket, eager to tell Bob the news. He was equally excited to see me. It turned out that while I had been at the appraiser, he'd managed to track down the original entrance to the priest hole, directly above the inglenook in one of the upstairs corridors.

We went upstairs so I could have a look. Bob showed me a square hole that would have likely been hidden behind the back of a cupboard.

I snuck inside the nook, pushing aside the dust and cobwebs to get a sense of what it must have felt like to hide up here. Inside it was lined with brick and mold. It smelled dank, and it was cold. Cobwebs hung from the ceiling. I couldn't imagine being trapped in here for more than a minute without getting claustrophobic.

I thought back to the days of Guy Fawkes—how the Catholics were persecuted by the Protestants and Hopwood Hall was marked with an *X* on the map of prominent Catholic sympathizers. I imagined Protestant vigilantes searching the house for my Catholic infidel ancestors while they hid up here, trying not to make a noise or risk being caught and potentially thrown in prison—or even executed! Maybe that was why my family members had left this place in the seventeenth century to make the treacherous journey across the Atlantic Ocean to America. Maybe they were fleeing for their lives . . .

Once again, I was struck by how much my ancestors had endured: They had survived wars, plagues, persecution, and even, in Lady Hopwood's case, the challenges of getting factories in the Industrial Revolution to stop polluting the environment. I was beginning to

A sketch of a similarly designed priest hole that appears
to be a normal cupboard *Allan Fea, illustrator*

The back of the cupboard could swing open to create
a secret hiding place. *Allan Fea, illustrator*

believe that there were ghosts of some kind or another dwelling in
every corner of this house. I knew we needed them on our side, root-
ing for us, if Hopwood Hall was going to survive at least another
generation into the future.

. . .

$\mathcal{N}$ot long after we stumbled on the priest hole and the tabernacle, however, Bob made another, much less welcome discovery.

"More dry rot!" he announced to me over the phone.

My heart sank. I knew from prior experience how hard it was to get rid of dry rot once it set in. Caused by damp, the fungus can spread rapidly, destroying any wood it touches by decomposing it and turning it to dust.

"Where this time?" I asked.

"Running along some of the floorboards on the east side of the long corridor," he sighed.

Also known as the Gallery, this was the room built by Lady Hopwood in the 1800s that led to the inglenook and the Lord Byron fireplace. Geoff had shown me pictures of what it looked like in its heyday, so I knew (*a*) what we were aiming for and (*b*) how much further we had to go.

Much like the rest of the house, the Gallery wasn't in the best of shape, but the floorboards looked fine to me, and I questioned whether it was necessary to pull up an entire section of them.

But Bob was adamant: We needed to stop the rot spreading and damaging other parts of the house. For a restoration project, dry rot is like leprosy. The two of us got down on our knees to take a crowbar to the floorboards. Once the compromised boards were pried off, we could air out the whole area and then put any usable boards back, along with replacement boards later when we had the funding to do so.

"Let's start with these over here, because you can see that for some reason someone has already lifted them in the past," Bob said.

"Maybe that's where the treasure is hidden!"

Bob rolled his eyes, slowly prying up the board, shining a light and peeking underneath.

Seconds later, he stopped, his face falling and turning white.

"Uh-oh," he said as he put the board back down and slowly stood. "Not only do we have dry rot, but it looks like there's an asbestos covered pipe down there."

"An asbestos pipe?!" I said incredulously. "How the heck would that get down there in the 1800s?"

"It didn't," he said out of the side of his mouth. "That's why someone had pulled up this section before. There's a minibar with a sink on the other side of this wall that was installed in the 1950s. The monk's contractors must've done it."

I felt like I was in a weird dream. Dry rot? Monks with a mini-bar? Asbestos?!

"So do we need to go to the hospital or something?" I asked.

"No, I didn't disturb it, so we're fine. It's only dangerous once it's in the air and you're exposed. But even then, there's really nothing you can do anyway, other than die a slow painful death in a few years."

He brushed off his hands and walked toward the exit.

"We can't do anything more today. We're going to need some experts."

With a quick phone call, the council dispatched its top asbestos specialists, and a few days later, Bob and I returned to the Hall when it was considered safe again. Well, "safe" from asbestos, but not from other potential deathtraps, such as collapsing ceilings and unstable staircases.

As we walked around the corner, pushing back some plastic sheeting to reveal the corridor, my jaw dropped. It looked so different. The entire floor had been removed, and about three feet below that was simply dirt.

Bob noticed something midway down the corridor and quickly headed over to see what it was—he'd made another one of his discoveries.

"Look at this," he said. Now that the floorboards had been removed, you could see that there was a rough flagstone path beneath them leading toward the end of the corridor. We followed the path, which led to a large square brick pit that would've also been hidden under the old floor.

"What is that, a tomb?" I asked.

"I think it was probably some kind of old firepit. It's deep so maybe it was somewhere you could roast a hog."

I shone my cell phone light on it to see if we could find any markings.

"Perhaps the flagstones were a type of wheelbarrow path where the servants could cart food to and from the outdoor firepit. Who knows how far back it dates?" he questioned.

He walked over and looked out the window into the courtyard like a detective on the trail.

"Before the Gallery, the flagstones would've been in the courtyard," Bob mused. "But they would have been covered up when Lady Hopwood built the Gallery, so they may not be related to the firepit, and they could be from different periods hundreds of years apart. Or maybe they *are* connected, and instead of a firepit it was a horse trough for the carriages, and the wheelbarrow path was used to carry water."

This was what I loved about the house: Every time you peeled back one layer of history—in this case, floorboards from the

1800s—you found another layer underneath, in this case a stone path and a firepit maybe from as early as the 1500s. What I didn't love was the fact that now the floorboards had been removed, the Gallery looked worse than it had before we started. At least before there had been a floor in there. Now there was nothing but dirt and old floor joists.

"It has to get worse before it can get better," Bob said sagely when I complained. I hoped he was right.

CHAPTER 22

LADY T.

*A*s April approached, the landscape around the Hall began to transform. Suddenly, trees that had been bare began to show new green growth. Underfoot, the daffodils were peeking up through formerly frozen ground, leaving spots of yellow everywhere. Sometimes, when I was feeling overwhelmed by everything that we still had to do with the house, I would walk out onto the grounds to try to clear my mind. The problem was, if I spent too long on the grounds, I'd start feeling dizzy at the thought of everything we had to do there and would have to come inside again.

I knew that the gardens here had once been spectacular. Prior to World War I, there were many gardeners on staff, and if you look at photos from that era, you can see immaculate lawns and roses in bloom and manicured paths. There would have been a kitchen garden where the gardeners grew vegetables, fruits, and herbs to feed the family. Geoff had a postcard of the hall's gardens in his collection that showed the herbaceous borders filled with flowers, an expansive rock garden, and an "Italian garden" with elaborate geometric beds and "rooms" made from hedges, with a lily pond featuring a fountain with a statue of a Roman god in the middle of it.

My favorite bit of trivia about the garden, however, was the "ha-ha." According to Geoff, the ha-ha had been a feature of English gardens like these since the 1700s. Basically, a ha-ha is a hidden ditch that's cut into the land at the end of the garden to stop live-stock from getting in, while ensuring an unobstructed view of the landscape beyond. Because you couldn't see the ha-ha until you were right on the edge of it, you might fall into the ditch—hence the name ha-ha. It was basically a pratfall built into the garden design with a joke to go along with it. I loved it.

But that was a hundred years ago. After decades of neglect, the hall's pathways were completely overgrown, the roses had long since stopped flowering, and the ha-ha had disappeared completely. Meanwhile, weeds had taken over the herbaceous borders, and a plant called knotweed that Geoff pointed out to me.

During one of my phone chats with Cazzy, she mentioned that her gardeners were helping her to prepare the gardens at Knowsley for spring.

"What are you doing about your gardens?" Cazzy asked inquis-itively.

"The gardens?" I laughed. I wasn't sure. At all. Personally, I had found it a huge struggle in LA just trying to keep my potted cacti alive. "Well, there really aren't any gardens left unless we can con-sider overgrown weeds a garden," I explained. "And some strange plant called knotweed seems to be everywhere. Wow, what a hearty plant that is. We certainly have plenty of that!"

"Hopwood, knotweed is an invasive species," Cazzy said, concerned. "You need to get a specialist in there right away to deal with it or there could be many more serious issues in the future."

Uh-oh. I didn't realize the severity of the situation. However, one thing I was beginning to learn from my conversations with others from Historic Houses is that grounds are almost as important as the house itself. In America, some people like to garden, but in England, knowing how to garden is an instinctual birthright. I knew I needed to begin to tackle the outdoor area, but unlike my English friends, who seem to have been born with a shovel in hand, I was clueless.

Cazzy declared that I needed to speak to Xa.

It turned out that Xa (pronounced *Zah*) is short for Alexandra Tollemache, otherwise known as Lady Tollemache of Helmingham Hall in Suffolk.

"Xa is a prominent garden designer," Cazzy explained. "Do not worry, I will introduce you. She is the best person to help you."

Before I knew it, I was being included on an email to Xa, who immediately invited me to join her for a private tour of the Chelsea Flower Show in London. As Cazzy helpfully explained, each year, garden designers from all over the world come to Chelsea to create incredible garden displays costing an average of £250,000 each (over $300,000). Some build small cottages and scaled-down castles within their displays; others create babbling brooks and waterfalls. The stakes are high, as winning a gold medal from Chelsea Flower Show can change a designer's career. It's also a major event in the English social calendar, regularly attended by the Queen, who is the patron of the Royal Horticultural Society that runs the show.

Xa was a former Chelsea Flower Show gold medalist and now was serving as a judge. She told me if I wanted to join her to have a look around, I should hop on the train to London the night before, as we had to arrive at 6 A.M. when it opened. This was a huge opportunity and I immediately agreed to go.

"Is it a formal event?" I asked Xa, in hopes I wouldn't have to borrow the tuxedo again.

"Oh, many people at the flower show are dressed quite casually," she replied.

I took the train down to London the day before and checked into a hotel not far from the Royal Hospital, where the flower show takes place. That night, I was so worried I might oversleep that, as a double backup to my cell phone alarm, I decided to try Mary's trick of knocking my head against the pillow to set my internal alarm. I chuckled as I drifted off to sleep, but to my absolute shock, I woke up on my own, moments before the alarm. It worked!

Outside the flower show, I met Xa, who glided toward me with a dignified presence, her light brown hair carefully wisped to the side. She was elegantly dressed in the kind of perfectly tailored skirt suit that most women in the United States would wear to a wedding. Meanwhile, I was wearing a T-shirt and jeans and carrying a sweatshirt. Obviously, my understanding of the word "casual" was more LA-inspired than British.

"Do come with me!" she said invitingly, thankfully without chastising me for my outfit, ushering me through security and into a large fancy tent inside the Royal Hospital. Rather than being a hospital in the usual sense of the word, I learned from Xa that the site is a home for senior citizens who have served in the British military. Founded in the 1700s, it's a vast and beautiful redbrick building that sits on sixty-six acres of land, perfect for a gardening show.

Before I knew it, I found myself in a tent filled with people, all the women as well-turned out as Xa, many of the men in ties and jackets. I pulled my sweatshirt across my chest and hoped for the best.

Within minutes, I had lost sight of Xa as I chatted with various people in the crowd who perhaps thought I was one of the gardeners.

"Oh, there's Birgitte!" a man standing next to me said happily.

And before I knew it, I had the pleasure of being introduced to Her Royal Highness Birgitte, Duchess of Gloucester, wife of the Queen's cousin and full-time working member of the Royal Family. In my jeans. Without a tie.

"The Duchess lives in Kensington Palace," the man said. "She has the loveliest gardens there."

It was all I could do to smile and perform the world's most awkward half bow, half curtsy.

Eventually I found Xa and I spent the next few hours with her, having breakfast and touring the show. The gardens were stunning, every corner of the Royal Hospital grounds filled with incredible displays of flower and foliage. There were rose gardens and tropical gardens, meadows filled with wildflowers and elegant topiary hedges. My new friend pointed out all the different ways the garden designers had created vibrant contrasts of color and texture, using plants and flowers the same way painters use a palette.

I was also amazed at the strict guidelines the Chelsea Flower Show judges imposed. I was introduced to one of Xa's fellow judges, and he explained that as much as he appreciated the talent and skill that went into a large outdoor garden cabana in one of the displays, he'd had to deduct points because he could see pencil marks of where the carpenter measured to cut the wood that were accidentally left on the underside of the roof.

One female garden designer we met that morning had spent the night prior hand-scrubbing individual stones in her man-made babbling brook so that green algae wouldn't be able to accumulate, concerned that it might be considered unsightly by the judges, which would result in a deduction of points.

In a few short hours, I had a new appreciation for gardens and gardeners. Clearly gardening was serious business. And I had no business being part of it!

After we'd finished our tour, Xa made sure I tried the signature drink of the show, a Pimms cocktail with slices of cucumber, which, it turns out, was delicious and refreshing—and surprisingly intoxicating. As I sipped on my Pimms, I asked her about her own home and garden, the magnificent Helmingham Hall in Suffolk.

"The house has been in my husband's family since it was built in 1510," she explained. "In fact, there may have been a structure there since the 1400s."

She showed me a few photos on her phone of a stunning redbrick hall surrounded by an enormous moat, an orchard—and lavish semiformal gardens, including a rose garden and a knot garden (where hedges are precisely trimmed into the shape of woven knots).

"Hopwood Hall doesn't have a knot garden but we do have knot-weed," I joked, as Xa chuckled and continued on.

"When we first moved in," she explained, "our gardens needed extensive work too. I had young children at the time, and I would be out there, working with the gardeners on the herbaceous borders, the kiddies around my ankles. It really was a labor of love for many years, and I am so happy that now thousands of visitors come each year to enjoy them."

By the end of my visit, Xa had offered to be my gardening mentor. She also gave me some important life advice.

"These homes and gardens need children to grow up in them,"

she told me. "They need those little people to slide down the banisters, hide in the walled gardens, and run around the borders, to climb in the trees and become attached to the place. That way, when the children get older, they deeply care about keeping it going. Without that passion, you would be amazed how quickly gardens grow over, and houses turn to ruins."

Later that night at the Castleton, I poured myself a glass of red and thought long and hard about what Xa had said. It had struck a deep chord with me. I knew I eventually wanted children; I felt the clock ticking. I had loved being a part of Jetsen's growing up and my role as her uncle. My sister had been someone who hadn't thought she had wanted children, yet she had one hundred percent embraced and coveted her job as a parent. It seemed like the next step would be to have some kids of my own. But how would I get there? I was still single—although that wasn't entirely true, as I was now married to the Hall. How could I possibly have children with everything else going on? And when? And with whom? There hadn't been much time for a social life outside of working on the Hall. Every now and again I ran into someone who seemed interesting, but I certainly hadn't had the time to develop a relationship or come any closer to finding someone who could start a family with me. A few years back, one of my actor friends in LA who wanted kids but hadn't yet found the right partner had gone ahead and found a surrogate. Twice. He raved about it. And even though he ended up getting married five years later, he never regretted doing it, because he wanted to be as young as possible when his kids were grown.

I took a sip of wine.

I pulled out my laptop and typed into the Google bar: *finding a surrogate.*

I paused before hitting return.

For some reason, this felt strangely similar to that first night at my house in the Hills that started me off on this crazy journey of finding Hopwood.

I slammed my computer shut.

"One life adventure at a time," I told myself.

I took a deep breath and finished my wine.

And then I knocked my head against the pillow six times and went to sleep.

CHAPTER 23

"BY DEGREES"

*C*ongratulations, Hopwood!" It was Vernon Norris, leader of the council, on the other end of the phone. "Hopwood Hall has just received a grant of more than £250,000 to help in its rescue!"

I couldn't believe what I was hearing.

"Whooo hoooo!" I screamed, suddenly realizing the very polite and proper leader of the council was on the listening end. "Oh, sorry," I said, catching myself. "I guess I got a little carried away."

"It is quite all right," Vernon responded. "It is a brilliant bit of fantastic news. We knew you could do it. Your hard work, involvement, and dedication have helped make this happen. You should be proud of yourself."

Thanks to all my time with Bob, I learned that it's rare for a Brit to give you a compliment, so I didn't know quite what to say.

"Thank you," was all I could mutter, but on the inside, I was still whooping. This was a light at the end of the tunnel! The money was going to enable us to make critical structural repairs to Hopwood Hall, so that the house would finally be stabilized and watertight. This was a huge relief. With this grant, I knew Hopwood Hall would no longer be lost within five to ten years as Bob had originally predicted. Yes, there would still be a *lot* of work to do, but just in the nick of time, this grant would stop its imminent collapse.

I couldn't help but feel that maybe our resident ghost, Lady Hopwood, had been pulling some strings.

"I would like to give you more details in person," Vernon continued. "Are you available to meet me on Saturday during my surgery?"

I smiled to myself, suddenly feeling like a true Brit.

"Yes, of course," I said confidently. "Vernon, I would be more than happy to meet you during your surgery."

I couldn't wait for Saturday to arrive. It was also nice and calming to know in advance that I wouldn't be witnessing a hip replacement or vasectomy.

The first priority for the new money was to fix the roof. For three decades, intruders had been climbing onto the roof and stealing the lead from under the tiles. Without its protective layer of metal, the roof was as leaky as a sieve. To make matters worse, the house's drains and gutters were blocked with decades of rotting leaves, which meant there were giant pools of water on the roof that would trickle down into the rooms below—we're talking about timbers from the 1400s, carvings from the 1500s, streaming with water. All Bob and I could do was watch and pray that we'd be able to find a way to repair the roof before the whole building caved in. Until that was watertight, we would still have to run around in rainstorms putting buckets under the drips, and the Hall would remain in danger of complete collapse.

Right away, the council helped us find a firm who agreed to do the roof job and we should have been able to get started right away, except for one problem.

The rain.

Throughout the fall, into October and November, the rains kept coming in hurricane-like fashion. It seemed like we were living under a never-ending rain cloud. There was no way the work could start until the weather got better. So we waited. And waited. In the meantime, water began pouring into the Lord Byron Bedroom that had been one of the few areas in the house that had previously been dry. It was a disaster.

Bob and I decided that instead of starting work on the roof, we would instead focus on installing water and electricity to areas of the house where it would be safe to do so.

One dark December morning around 7 A.M., however, I got a call from Bob. I could hear the panic in his voice.

"Hopwood, get over here now!" he insisted. "The people from the electricity company are here early—they want to start work today!"

That's great, I remember thinking. *I wonder why Bob is upset?*

I got up, skipped a shower, and threw on my dusty work clothes and boots from the day before. Catching a quick glimpse in the mirror, I barely recognized myself.

Wow, I really am living a different life, I thought. My tan was fading fast—Lady Hopwood would have approved. My blond hair was becoming more of a British brown, and my clothes were streaked in mud, a tool belt fastened around my waist. If Jay could have seen me, he'd probably remain my best friend but professionally cut me as a client. And Jonny would insist on dropping me off at the day spa, but for two days. I missed my friends in LA but had no idea how I would ever explain to them my life in England these days.

As quickly as I could, I was out the door. Minutes later, I arrived at the Hall.

"You're not going to believe this," Bob told me when I arrived. "But it looks like we won't be able to get started on the electrics either. Phineas Shellburn won't let us dig across his land to put the cables in!"

I told Bob I was sure I could persuade Shellburn if I could just sit down and have a sensible discussion with him. He probably just didn't appreciate being surprised by the early arrival of the team from the power company. Even as I said the words, I knew that it was a long shot.

"It's too late already," Bob said, shaking his head. "The installers have already gone. We'll have to wait months to get another appointment now."

This new turn of events was infuriating. The lack of access was what had been slowly killing Hopwood Hall for three decades, holding it captive and squeezing the life out of it. Even with the grant and all the support and help, none of it would mean anything until we resolved the access issue with our neighbor.

I left Bob and went to the small makeshift desk area I'd set up in a corner of the Guards' Room to draft an email to Bev Percival at the council, giving her the update and seeing if she could maybe help put some gentle pressure on Shellburn.

Dear Bev,

I hate to be the bearer of bad news, but this morning we hit a major roadblock at Hopwood Hall . . .

Suddenly, just as my thoughts were beginning to flow, Bob burst in. At that moment, I happened to be typing on my laptop with my legs kicked up on a chair in front of me.

"I need your help out here," he barked. "What are you doing?"

"Working," I replied.

Bob looked at me perplexed and then mimicked me by sticking one leg in the air and leaning back as if he was floating in a pool. And then he put his hands in front and mimed as if he was typing.

"Is this what you Hollywood types call wooorking?!"

"Just because I'm not lifting a piece of machinery doesn't mean I'm not doing anything!" I blurted out. "Someone has got to keep things moving with the council and the grants and the community. In fact, saving Hopwood Hall is a lot like producing a movie—which, by the way, is hard work!"

"Right. Well, that sounds like retirement to me," Bob bit back. "I'll be waiting if you can give me a hand with the ladder. I need help—real help! Not your 'wooorking'!"

Bob stomped off and I sat there at my desk, bubbling with anger and unable to focus on the email I was supposed to be writing. It took me a few minutes to calm down.

As much as I was annoyed by his outburst, I also understood his frustration. As fast as we could move, it was as if the house was one step ahead of us, decaying faster than we could run to rescue it. Every time we had an up, it was followed by a down. Every day, something else gave way or broke down. It was just like Cazzy said, being responsible for a museum filled with precious artifacts, except in this case the roof was full of holes and it felt up to me, with no roofing experience, to figure out how to stop everything from getting wet and rotting in the middle of a hurricane, while racing against time. No wonder I'd lay awake at night every time it rained, praying that the roof wouldn't cave in.

I decided I needed a bit more time to regain my composure, so I took a walk over to the fireplace in the Reception Hall to have a look at the Hopwood family motto. The fireplace had become my favorite spot to stand and think and find answers whenever I felt the challenges of the Hall overwhelming me.

The towering limestone fireplace had been a fixture in Hopwood Hall that had welcomed and warmed family and friends for centuries as they entered from their likely cold and wet carriage ride. Absorbed in its hand-laid stone were thousands of conversations over hundreds of years, from both troubled times to celebrations, arguments to laughter and romantic fireside chats and whispers. The mantel is taller than I am at six-foot-two, with hand-chiseled details including the Hopwood family crest, large stags—the Hopwood family heraldic animal—and the family motto emblazoned in each corner: "By Degrees."

According to Geoff, there are a couple of ways of interpreting the phrase. One is to relate it to the Middleton archers, my ancestors from long ago, who knew that the margin of error for hitting or missing a target with an arrow was "by degrees." The other is in the most basic sense: that all progress happens little by little, step by step, never all at once. For my part, I had started to think of "By Degrees" as less of a motto and more of a mantra, something I needed to recite to myself every day. I imagined my predecessors, each of them across the many decades and centuries, finding solace from the words. Maybe every generation of Hopwoods had felt like Bob and me at times— overwhelmed and desperate—but reassured by the motto that slowly, bit by bit, we'd make a small amount of improvement. Standing in front of the fireplace, I vowed to try harder to live up to Bob's expectations and to improve my restoration skills.

It had been a long, cold day, and I realized I was tired. Bob was also getting ready to leave, so we agreed to call it a day. I apologized for my upset, and he did too for his frustration—not something that was typical for either of us—and we shook hands as friends again.

By the time I made it back to the Castleton I knew what I had to do. As committed as I was to the Hall and its future, it was almost Christmas. There was no way we could have a party at the Hall, not without Shellburn's permission. And as we weren't going to be able to start work on the roof or put the electrics in anytime soon, I was going to take a break. I cracked open my laptop and booked a return flight home to Michigan to see my family. I would come back to Hopwood Hall in the new year rejuvenated and ready to start again.

CHAPTER 24

THE DISCO MONKS

*A*s yet another new year dawned, I realized I had now achieved major life progress: I could honestly look myself in the mirror and know deep down that I was no longer the type of person who would collapse in frustration in the parking lot of a Home Depot if I was ever again confronted with even a beginner-level DIY project. I was no expert, and I knew I still had a long way to go, but such tasks no longer seemed so daunting to me.

What's more, Bob had stopped making jokes about me "wooork-ing" at my laptop ever since I'd spent a number of hours the first few weeks of the year emailing back and forth with the council to finally get his contract renewed. The next month was a blur of teamwork as we waited for the major roof and electrical work to begin.

In the meantime, Geoff invited me to join him in one of the history talks that he occasionally did at the request of the community—this time for the Middleton Archaeological Society. The talk was going to be held in the event room at the Olde Boar's Head pub—and it was going to be all about Hopwood Hall. Even though I knew the Hall was well loved in the area, I was still shocked to walk into a standing-room only crowd in the pub's atmospheric, dark-wood-paneled event room. It had been a former court in the sixteenth century and looking around it wasn't hard to imagine someone sitting in there on trial for being a witch. As the only American in the room, I couldn't help but say a little prayer that the group wouldn't suddenly turn and convict *me*!

"I'm amazed this many people care so much about the Hall to come out on a Friday night," I said to Geoff. He smiled with a happy look as he surveyed the crowd.

"Most of these people have a connection as deep as you do to the Hall, Hopwood," he pointed out. "When they were growing up, many were told stories and legends about it from their parents and grandparents just like you. Back in the day, sneaking through the woods to find Hopwood Hall was kind of like searching for the Wizard of Oz. Being connected to the Hall and its history also means they're part of something bigger than all of us."

Geoff was right. I often had people approach me and tell me similar stories of a parent or grandparent whose life had been strongly impacted by Hopwood Hall, with memories of playing in one of the gardens, or running alongside the brook, or peeking in through a window to see the inside.

After the talk was over, there was an auction to raise money for the restoration. A Middleton artist had donated a watercolor painting of Hopwood Hall to be auctioned off to the highest bidder. The artist had suggested an opening bid of £15. To our surprise, the supportive audience made bids back and forth to drive the price up, finally landing on the winner of the painting at £160. The highest bidder was a man named Ian.

When the room began to clear, Ian walked up to claim his new artwork. He was a tall husky man, with black graying hair and smiling eyes.

He introduced himself with his strong Northern accent and outstretched his hand.

"If there is anything I can ever do to help in the restoration of the Hall, please let me know," he told us.

It turned out Ian's mother remembered the place from when she was growing up in the area and had told him that if he helped to save it, it would make her proud.

The evening at the Olde Boar's Head confirmed to me the importance of the work and gave me a renewed sense of purpose. When Bob decided it was time to tackle the Hopwood Family Chapel,

Watercolor painting of Hopwood Hall Estate by local artist
Steve Whitworth *Steve Whitworth, artist*

which is located to the left side of the carriage entrance just as you come in, it felt like the perfect next project.

The Family Chapel is housed in a single room that dates to the 1690s, when John Hopwood, the squire of the times, decided he wanted a safe place of his own to worship. It has its own huge door with hand-forged rivets and hinges, covered in carvings with the family crest topped by a stag, all hand-carved into wood over the entrance. Inside is a simple room without the kind of ecclesiastical details you might expect, but Bob explained this was typical of private chapels in that time.

During the Victorian era, this room had been used as the billiards room—where the gentleman would come after dinner for a game or two. But when the order of monks moved into the Hall in the 1960s, they began using it as a chapel again for their daily rituals. The problem was, they also decided to clean up the place by covering over the original walls with a layer of modern cement.

"At the time, they didn't realize that the materials they were using wouldn't allow the brick underneath to breathe," Bob said, scratching his head. "If we want to save the Chapel, we're going to have to chip off the cement bit by bit to free the much older brickwork below."

Bob took a hammer and began tapping gently at the walls.

"If you tap it too hard, you'll damage what's underneath," Bob said, demonstrating how to carefully remove the cement.

I could tell this was going to take a lot of patience to remove these pieces in tiny, 2-inch sections. I took a deep breath and decided to appreciate the process.

One day as we were coming back from lunch and walking toward the Chapel, I happened to notice a large sheet of weathered old wood firmly nailed to a brick wall.

"What's behind that board, Bob?" I asked.

"I dunno. It's probably a closet. I've never looked," he muttered. "Too many other things to do!"

"You've never looked?!" I asked incredulously.

"Hopwood, you're like a little kid. You know that?" he said, exasperated. "Not everything is a secret room or a hidden passage-way!"

Despite his words, I couldn't help but smile with excitement. I loved it when it felt like Bob and I were on the verge of a discovery.

"Do you want me to get the crowbar?" he exhaled.

The board made a cracking noise as we pried it away from the wall to reveal a darkened doorway. Bob looked at me with a raised eyebrow.

"Hmm, maybe it's not a closet," he said.

The doorway was blockaded with a makeshift door that appeared to swing inward even though it was jammed shut. We both pushed on it with all our might but without luck.

"You're younger than I am," Bob said. "Give it a kick!"

With that, I leaned back and gave the best forward donkey kick that I could muster. The door flung open.

I was shocked to see a dark cavernous space beyond.

"What is this?!" I said to Bob.

"It looks like another room," he replied matter-of-factly.

We carefully stepped inside, shining our cell phone lights. Bob made his way across the space and located another board on the wall inside that he was able to pull free, revealing a window, which let the daylight flood in.

"Wow," I said as I surveyed the room, which had a small kitchen-ette and a shower in another adjacent space. It was a real *The Lion, the Witch and the Wardrobe* moment. I was only hoping Mr. Tumnus, the half man, half goat faun, wasn't going to suddenly spring out of a hole in the wall.

"You do look a bit like Mr. Tumnus," I said to Bob. "You know, with your beard. But without the goat legs."

Bob gave me a sidelong glance. He clearly didn't get the joke.

Meanwhile, I was entranced. On multiple occasions we had talked about how great it would be if one of the rooms were available to be used as an office or perhaps a place for me to temporarily live for a few years and keep watch over the Hall while she was being renovated. This space was like its own small apartment.

"It must have been home to one of the monks who lived here," Bob pointed out with a slight smile. "It will be the perfect place for your laptop work."

"Yes, Bob," I said. "Yes, it will."

But for now, we needed to get back to the business of chipping away to expose the original brick walls in the Chapel. Bob explained to me that it was possible that horse urine would have been used as a kind of shellac in a chapel of this age. I tried not to think too much about that as we started to expose bricks that at some point would've been holding up paneling soaked in pee.

Bob and I were working well together these days. I noticed that rather than get upset and frustrated with me as he had in the past, he was finally starting to trust me with tasks. In turn, I was feeling more confident, carefully chipping away at the cement rendering tiny piece by tiny piece as Bob had shown me, rather than racing to pull off large chunks at once.

"Not bad, Yankee boy," Bob told me at one point, which I took as a glowing compliment.

The task was mammoth so soon Bob brought in his brother, who also lived locally, to help tackle the ongoing work.

"Hopwood, come look at this!" shouted Bob and his brother as I emptied a wheelbarrow full of cement rubble into the dumpster outside.

Inside the Chapel, I could see that they had pulled down a section of the plaster drop ceiling that the monks had installed, presumably to save heat, to reveal several large wooden beams stretching across the ceiling.

I craned my neck trying to look up.

"Are those original beams?" I asked.

"Yes indeed," Bob said. "Likely from 1690. You see the skinny white lines on them? That's where they would've affixed the slats and plaster back in the day. It has been a long time since these beams have been seen by human eyes."

As the rest of the ceiling was pulled down, the Chapel began to take on a new dimension. The 1960s drop ceiling had stunted the room. With the extra several feet above the windows it changed the whole feel.

"Now, this is how this room was meant to have looked when it was built by John Hopwood," Bob said with a smile of accomplishment at the hard work.

As the cement rendering slowly fell away from the walls of the Chapel, we made another important discovery: a stone plinth that Bob was convinced was part of a foundation dating back to the 1400s, and perhaps earlier, when the Hall had first been established.

"They would have placed these hand-mortared rocks on the bottom of the structure," Bob explained, "building from the ground up, roughly stacking them to about two feet, then creating a somewhat level surface where a wood structure could then sit on top so that it wouldn't be in risk of rotting from the dampness of the ground below."

One day, as we continued to work in the Chapel, my phone surprisingly rang. It was Jay calling from LA.

"Why aren't you calling me back?" he demanded.

I had missed his two previous attempts earlier in the day most likely due to the lack of reception and I was so ensconced in the work I hadn't thought to see if I had any messages.

"Sorry," I said truthfully. "I'm learning so much; I just get swept up in the moment. Did you know that in the fifteenth century, people would've shellacked their wood paneling with horse urine?!"

It shouldn't have surprised me that my question was met with silence. Then I realized I was on the phone to Beverly Hills. And Jay's assistant was probably listening in, taking copious notes, which is standard business practice in LA.

I laughed.

"Are you still there?" I asked.

"Uh, yeah. Uh, the call seems to keep cutting out. Anyway, I was thinking maybe you should come back to LA for the Oscar parties. I know you're busy with Hopwood Hall, but it would be good for you to remind people you haven't dropped off the planet."

I had to stop and think. Did I really want to ditch everything I was doing at the Hall to pack up and fly all the way to LA for a party?

My hesitation must have upset Jay because he hung up.

Or so I thought he did. A few minutes later, my phone vibrated again, and it was him. This happened several times because I was in the Hall and my cell reception wasn't great. I was reluctant to step outside because as usual it was pouring rain.

The call kept dropping, and I was getting incredibly frustrated. Then I looked down at the fifteenth-century stone plinth and suddenly began to laugh. Here I was getting upset because the signal from my cell phone was having trouble penetrating through the six-hundred-year-old walls my ancestors had laid, to instantaneously beam up to space from England and back down to my manager's office in Beverly Hills, so that we could carry on a continuous conversation about the "importance" of me going to an Oscar party! The call dropping, the Oscar party. It all seemed ridiculous. The saying goes, "If these walls could talk . . . ," but I couldn't help but think that if these walls could laugh, then the joke would be on me.

With all the progress happening at the Hall it felt like my former life in Hollywood had faded away into the background. Increasingly, as I spoke to friends who were still there pursuing careers, I no longer felt like a main player in the film but more like an extra. And for the first time in my life, I didn't mind being on the sidelines. I actually might have preferred it this way.

CHAPTER 25

LIGHTS UP

*S*pring became summer, and suddenly progress at the Hall was moving at lightning speed. Okay, fine—*nothing* related to a historic home moves at lightning speed. But we had a major breakthrough.

In early July I received an email from Bev Percival at the council:

> Dear Hopwood,
>
> I am happy to report our legal department found a loophole clause that prohibits your neighbor Phineas Shellburn from disallowing electricity to be installed to Hopwood Hall. We have contacted him directly and made great inroads toward facilitating this progress. He understands the installation will be moving forward without any further delay. Unfortunately, we also contacted the electricity company who had originally been scheduled and they have informed us the earliest they can accommodate this type of

complicated installation will be next spring as they are currently
focused on another substantial job. If you have any thoughts, please
let me know, otherwise we will look to arrange it for next March.
   Best regards,
   Bev

This was a huge deal. There hadn't been working electricity in Hopwood Hall for more than three decades!

I immediately called both Bob and Geoff, and we decided to meet for a pint at the Hopwood pub to put our heads together. Clearly, installing electricity prior to another harsh winter would be a godsend for the Hall and would breathe new life back into her, as well as provide some heat in the winter for my aching toes.

"The problem is that there's a shortage of skilled electricians in the area who would take on this type of job," said Bob. "I'm happy to help look, but I think we're probably stuck till March."

I could tell he desperately didn't want to rain on our parade, but he was only being realistic. He knew the importance of this step, so his demeanor was a bit softer. If Bob had a soft side, this was it.

I stared into my beer and thought long and hard. Suddenly Geoff cleared his throat.

"What about that chap Ian we met at the talk about Hopwood Hall who bought the painting? I think I recall someone saying that he is an electrician," Geoff offered.

A lightbulb was about to go off. Literally.

I immediately sent an email to Ian to see if he was indeed an electrician and still interested in helping us. A few minutes later he replied and said he was happy to hear from us.

It turns out his mom was now very sick and near the end of her life. For him to be able to tell her he was involved in the rescue effort of the Hall would brighten her spirits.

My next email was to Bev Percival. As soon as we got the approval from the council for Ian to go ahead with the electricity, he began the installation work for us, stopping by the Hall every day at 2 P.M. after he finished his regular electrical jobs. Ian had his work cut out for him. He had to establish and connect to a main feed before running hundreds and hundreds of feet of cable through cramped and inaccessible places and spaces in a way that would be acceptable to the council and meet specific historic building guidelines. No easy feat.

I recognized Ian's passion for the project right away. Like me, his work on the Hall was almost a form of therapy, giving him a sort of mission during a difficult time. Even a few weeks later, after his mom passed away, Ian kept coming to the Hall.

"This is what mum would want," he said, with a quiver in his voice. "In fact, she left a small bit of money in her will to pay for some of the cabling. She wanted to leave her memory and spirit within these walls."

I couldn't help but get a bit choked up. It also made me feel responsible, very responsible, for bringing this restoration to fruition. Getting to know Ian, it became apparent he was a man of modest means. The money that his mother had left behind to help with the Hall, and the £160 he had paid for the painting, were significant amounts of money to them. This was a labor of love, and despite being from different parts of the world, we had this common goal that drew us in closer.

But it wasn't all sweetness and light. With Ian on the job, this also meant that Bob had a partner in making me the butt of his almost constant jokes. All of a sudden, there were two people laughing at me instead of one. I was the clueless Yank, no matter what I did. A blond fool from California who had his head in the clouds, bleached teeth, and bronzer on his face. Not exactly a complimentary image among the guys on a construction site.

"Hopwood, why don't you make yourself useful and go film a toothpaste commercial," Bob once cracked, which brought Ian and some of the other guys assisting to near tears of laughter.

And if I ever referred to something I was doing as "DIY," they would ask in between chuckles if that stood for "dim inexperienced Yank."

I laughed along, knowing it was the best form of acceptance.

It also seemed that Bob's gruff Manchester ways were beginning to rub off on me.

One day, Bob mentioned that since I was the best at working in the office (aka "staying out of everyone's way"), it would be great if I could put in an online order for some electrical supplies that Ian needed in a rush so they could be installed the following day. I ordered them shipped to the Castleton so there would be no delay.

Two days later the package hadn't showed up, even though it was marked online as delivered, so I called the delivery company. A very proper English-sounding man answered the line.

"Sir, we did deliver the package," he informed me. "But it shows here you were out, so we left the package in the recycling bin."

I was very confused.

"In the recycling bin?" I asked. "Like where we put things to be thrown away?"

"Yes sir," he said matter-of-factly.

Apparently, this is common practice in England to keep the package from getting wet or stolen. It's an unwritten rule, and every

Brit seems to know that if you're looking for your missing package to check the recycling bin.

I ran down to the dumpsters to see if indeed my package was happily sitting there among the trash, waiting for me to retrieve it. Unfortunately, I found the recycling bins near the street, having been emptied that morning.

"The recycling has been picked up and I didn't receive the package," I said. "So can you please rush me another? We really need the materials."

"Sir, I'm sorry, but we did deliver them to you."

I couldn't contain how baffled I was. I also couldn't help but think of Bob and Ian laughing at another one of my complete and utter failures.

"Well, you didn't deliver the package to ME!" I barked. "You delivered it to the recycling bin. You know, a place for discarded items and things people don't want any more? Oh, and did I forget to mention that my bin is tended to by someone else who has the sole mission of emptying it regularly into the back of their truck and driving away? Why would you deliver my package to the bin?!"

There was silence.

"For safekeeping," he responded after a moment.

"So let me get this straight. To keep it safe, you basically threw it away? What next? 'Ah, Mr. DePree, to prevent your car being stolen, we've pushed it down a mine shaft'?"

It was like Bob had inhabited my body and was making the words flow from my mouth—but the funny thing was I found it worked. The representative finally agreed to send me a replacement package. We were back in business. I felt proud of myself for standing up and pulling this off—clearly, the cat no longer had my tongue. And more important, I had passed the test from Bob.

Finally, in late summer, Ian announced he had completed his work. Electricity was installed. We rejoiced. Never before had I appreciated the miracle of electricity—it was as if it had just been invented and I got an insight into how the family must have felt back in the 1880s, when Thomas Edison's lightbulb first came to these shores. The new electric supply at the Hall allowed us to install security lights and cameras, which meant that the place would be much more secure from intruders. We could also put in heaters in certain areas to keep our fingers from freezing off in the winter. A couple of weeks after we had electricity, Ian even managed to hook up Wi-Fi—Hopwood Hall's first-ever internet connection in her six hundred years of existence. To celebrate, I went online and ordered a pizza delivery for Bob, Ian, and the rest of the crew.

Of course, they didn't leave a single piece for me.

In the fall, we installed toilets and sinks in the Hall. As luck would have it, I'd recently visited another stately fixer-upper, Wentworth Woodhouse—the largest privately owned house in Britain. The house was in the middle of its own refurbishment, and the trust that takes care of it offered us a stack of vintage sinks that they no longer needed. Bob and I loaded up his van and brought them back to Hopwood Hall. Now, not only could you now wash your hands and flush a toilet at the Hall, but with the addition of electricity and Wi-Fi, you could also watch Netflix! We were dragging Hopwood Hall into the twenty-first century.

Next, we began our most ambitious renovation project yet: the restoration of the roof. With our funds from Historic England and the council, we were finally ready to start. The roof repair was so extensive, with good weather and luck on our side, it was going to take us at least nine months to complete. Until we sealed the roof, however, there was no hope of saving the Hall. Any restoration we made to any one of the rooms would be pointless because once the rain got in, it would be ruined. With the roof finished, the renovations we made underneath it would be protected.

For the first time, we had a full crew working on the hall each day, complete with a foreman taking charge of everything. Although Bob and I were still involved, it felt great to have so many people on the job. The first step was to put up scaffolding on one side of the house so that the team could get up and down to the roof. It took a couple of days to connect all the iron rungs to wooden platforms, but as soon as it was complete, I decided to peek at the top of the house.

I began climbing confidently up the ladder, through a hole to the platform, up another ladder and then another. Six years ago, when I first came to Hopwood Hall, I would have been completely intimidated by such an activity—back then the highest I felt comfortable climbing was up my spiral staircase in my house in LA. But these days I thought nothing of scaling scaffolding and ladders, ducking through holes and balancing on platforms tens of feet high.

Up on the roof, I took a large lungful of air and surveyed the scene. The dozens of towering brick chimneys sprouting from the roof that I had first seen in the old black-and-white photo on my computer were now firmly planted in reality all around me. The fields in the distance were bright green and brown, the tree branches bare, crisscrossing the midwinter gray skies. Once upon a time, all the farmland that surrounded the house would have been part of the Hopwood estate, and although that was no longer the case, the house and the land still felt connected in some deeper and ancient sense. I'd never seen the area from this perspective before, and yet again, I felt grateful to the Hall and all the many ways she had literally and figuratively changed my outlook.

The roof, not surprisingly, was a wreck. There were holes in the lead covering where thieves had made off with their spoils, tiles that had broken and come loose in storms, and a giant lake of water in the middle that looked big enough to float a boat in. I knew that the first step was to remove all the tiles so that the missing lead that was supposed to be covering any gaps underneath could be revealed. Experimentally, I picked up a stray slate roof tile to see how heavy it was. *Oof.* It weighed a ton. Thank goodness Bob and I didn't have to do this on our own. Or, as Bob would say, that he didn't have to do it on *his* own.

In the days and weeks to come, Bob and I were at the Hall every day, as the crew climbed up the scaffolding, then onto the roof, plucking a tile at a time, balancing it on their shoulders, and then nimbly climbing down again to the scaffolded platform where the tiles were numbered, so we would know where on the roof they came from, and put in a stack. Bob estimated there were thirty tons of tile in the one section that was in most need of repair. On dry days, Bob would allow me to climb up to talk with the crew to see if I could help. I quickly realized that walking on a mossy slate roof carrying a heavy historic slate on my back was not one of my innate skills, and I left the experts to do their jobs. Once the tiles were safely stacked, the next step was to repair and strengthen the roof. And after that, the tiles could be put back in place.

The work would continue into the new year, but we were making an amazing start. I like to say "we," even though I mainly watched. I figure if people can say "we" won when their favorite sports team takes the championship, then I could fairly say "we" when talking about the roof.

Bob laughed when I told him my reasoning. "If you produce a

movie, I assume you aren't also the person who's setting up the lights, or who's running the camera, are you?"

Of course I wasn't. But I was surprised that Bob had come full circle and was now using movie analogies to explain how we were all working so well together.

"Bob, are you saying you think my participation in the rescue is actually helping?" I asked, cracking a smile.

Of course, I knew he would never admit anything like that.

"I'm just telling you to keep off the roof!" he snarled, smile disappearing, as he headed back up the ladder.

$\mathcal{A}$s we got closer to the holidays, I began daydreaming again about a Christmas party at the Hall. Everyone had worked so hard to get things to this point. Surely my neighbor Phineas Shellburn could let us have access to the Hall during the quickly approaching holidays, when the college would be closed and people couldn't come in via the campus. Given the council had made inroads in pressuring him to allow us to install electricity, I had renewed hope that perhaps he might now treat the situation differently. Last time I asked Shellburn about it, in the pub two years ago, it had been such a fiasco that all last year, I hadn't even bothered to make an appeal to him again. But this year, things were so far along with the progress of the renovation that it would have been a crime *not* to have a party.

Having failed to persuade Shellburn in the past, I knew I needed to strategize another attempt. Growing up, my mom had always told me that, if you want to impress, you should send a handwritten letter. So I took out a pen and a sheet of paper and decided to write him a note.

Dear Mr. Shellburn,

I hope you are well. I am writing to you with the great hope that you will find it in your heart to be able to help.

Since both of our families are from Middleton, and I know they have had some serious differences over the centuries, there is one thing I know that they both would have shared in common: their sense of community.

Over the past few years, people of all ages in the community have rallied together to help rescue a piece of their heritage known as Hopwood Hall. It is an important history to them as many of their ancestors lived and worked on the estate. We have worked tirelessly to stabilize the building, and install electricity and even running water.

Christmas will soon be here again, and it would be a dream to host a Christmas party here. It will be the first Christmas party at Hopwood Hall in a hundred years, so it is long overdue. If it is able to happen, I would also like to extend an invitation for you to please join us.

Ultimately, the decision to hold the Christmas party lies in your hands.

Please, Mr. Shellburn, would you be willing to grant us the access to cross over your land?

Sincerely,

Hopwood DePree

I sealed the envelope, put a stamp on it, and popped the letter in the postbox.

CHAPTER 26

CHRISTMAS SURPRISE

*P*HINEAS SHELLBURN CALLING flashed across the screen of my phone.

It had been about a week since I had mailed the letter.

"I've got to take this!" I explained to my clerk friend at the Hopwood gas station as I was laying two cans of beans and a bag of bread on the counter.

I dashed outside to a quieter environment and picked up the phone.

"DePree?" said the familiar gruff voice on the other end of the line.

"Mr. Shellburn?" I replied, trying not to sound too terrified.

"Look, I don't want to waste my time or yours," he said. "You've been a real thorn in my side, but I'm reluctantly going to agree to let you and your group cross over my land."

"So you're okay with allowing us access to Hopwood Hall?" I doubly confirmed, shocked at his change in demeanor.

"For the party, yes. But for the longer term, we'll need to discuss it more. I am not opposed to helping you in your mission to save the Hall, but I need to fully understand how that will affect me. We can talk about it further at a later date."

Clearly, I still had work to do smoothing over my relationship with my neighbor, but this felt like an important first step.

"Oh, that's incredible," I replied, finding it hard to believe. "Thank you. Is there a chance we might see you at the party?"

"I'll think about it," he replied, "My days of celebrating seem to be long since over, but I do know both of our ancestors did like a good knees-up."

"Well, if you can make it, we would love to have you there."

I was still trying to wrap my head around how and why Shellburn would change his mind when he gave me my answer.

"You should know that your friend Mary put a good word in on your behalf," he said. "She can be very persuasive, you know."

It turns out that sixty years ago, when Mary first moved to the area from Ireland, she babysat the young Phineas Shellburn to make ends meet. Over the years they had remained friends, and the last time they ran into each other at the grocery store, Mary mentioned that she knew me, and that my intentions with Hopwood Hall were entirely honorable.

"Until I spoke to Mary, I thought you were some kind of Hollywood guy who would dash back to America at the first opportunity. Now I understand that you really care about this community and you're here to stay. That makes all the difference to me. I'm now prepared to let old feuds lay in the past."

I knew deep down that this was the best acceptance I could ask for. If people in Middleton talked out of the side of their mouth about you, then you knew you were in trouble, but if they stood up for you, then you were going to be fine.

With Phineas Shellburn's temporary permission secured, there was nothing stopping us from finally hosting a Christmas party at Hopwood Hall. And in retrospect, as difficult as it was to wait this long, it was probably a good thing we did. We now had electricity. We had security lights and cameras. We had working toilets. Our party preparations could begin! For the first time since Edward and Robert Hopwood were killed in World War I, there was going to be a Christmas party for the entire community at Hopwood Hall. And for the first time since my dad died, I was planning a holiday celebration again. I felt more than ready.

Bev Percival organized for the council to send a structural engineer to survey the place, and she confirmed that the Guards' Room and the Reception Hall were fully stable and that we could host the party in those areas. Even better, we could allow guests into those areas *without* requiring them to wear hard hats and high-vis vests. They could wear Christmas sweaters! (Or should I say *jumpers?*)

Over the next few weeks, our team of regular volunteers helped to pick up debris and to push brooms. With the newly installed electricity, we were able to use heavy-duty vacuum cleaners to remove the decades of dust. People came every night after work to volunteer with the cleanup. They also made donations of unused Christmas decorations, dropping off lights, tablecloths, and punch bowls. I ordered battery-operated candles—due to fire regulations with such a historic building, I didn't want to take any extra risk— and put them in the fireplace to give the feel of a fire going. Ian set up all the lighting. Zena, our marketing magician, once again got the word out to the newspapers. A local florist donated flowers.

Kids from the nearby school made ornaments for the tree. Locals watched YouTube videos to learn how to make wreaths with ribbon and berries and clippings from pine trees in the Hopwood Woods.

Now the only thing we needed was a tree! Before I knew it, a truck pulled up and delivered not one but *two* trees, compliments of a local farmer. We hung flashing Christmas lights outside and put up the big wreath with a red ribbon over the fireplace.

As I was helping Ian hang the blinking Christmas lights on the outside of the Hall over the carriage entrance, I remembered that this was going to be his first Christmas without his mother. I knew what it felt like to go through the first holiday without a parent.

"I'm sorry your mom can't be here with us for the party," I told him.

Ian paused and then stepped down from the ladder.

"Would it be all right if I invited my mum's friend?" he asked. "She's nearly a hundred years old, and she used to work at Hopwood Hall in the 1940s when it was used as a base of operations during World War II. She hasn't been here since."

I couldn't think of anything better.

The night of the party, I ran back to the Castleton to get changed, throwing on a Christmas jumper and a Santa hat to get in the festive spirit. As I looked in the mirror before I headed out the door, I knew my dad would approve. The magic of Christmas was back in my soul, and I felt that my dad was right there with me.

As a precaution, the council was only allowing us to have sixty guests for safety reasons, and by the time I got back to the Hall, it looked like pretty much everyone we'd invited had showed up, the line of people waiting to get in snaking out of the carriage entrance doors and down the approach, just like a century ago. It was a crisp December day, and I could hear everyone chattering and laughing along with a general excitement to get the party started. We opened the huge medieval doors and people filed in, just like I had on my first visit nearly seven years ago. To ramp up the tradition once again, I asked them to sign a new guest book on their way in, hoping this would be the start of a whole library of guest books filled with signatures for years to come. Inside the Reception Hall, the candles were twinkling and sparkling. Ian's wife served mulled wine and homemade mince pies.

Within minutes, the room was filled to capacity. So many new friends and community members who had helped us get the Hall to this point were in attendance, locals from all walks of life and all ages. Many were older people who, like Ian's friend, remembered the Hall before it fell into disrepair. The mayor and members of the council. Vernon Norris. Even representatives from the top grant funders: Historic England, the National Lottery, the Architectural Heritage Fund. Bob and his family, my housemates from the Castleton, including Mary, and of course Geoff and his wife, Lyn. They couldn't believe after all this time of dreaming about the hall's revival that we were finally doing this. Even Jay showed up from LA. He had been in London on business and decided to come up for a visit.

Those who had prior obligations, such as Teddy, Cazzy, and Dr. Rolph, sent notes of congratulations and well wishes in hopes of joining the following year. My family had decided they couldn't make the long trek this time but told me they were very much there in spirit.

The only person missing that we hadn't heard from was Phineas Shellburn. Finally, about thirty minutes into the party, he showed up as promised, brandishing his walking stick in one hand and grabbing a glass of mulled wine with the other.

Now that Shellburn was here, I decided I wanted to make a toast. I stood up in front of everyone and cleared my throat.

"I want to thank a number of people. First of all, all the volunteers and local supporters who helped make this happen, because we wouldn't be here without you. I also want to thank our neighbor, Mr. Shellburn, who is allowing this party to happen."

Shellburn waved his cane in the air as the room erupted into hoots and hollers.

"I would like to read you a little passage that was written by a woman about a party that she actually attended here in the 1890s," I said. "'Preparing Hopwood Hall for Christmas began weeks before. The resident staff stripped off the dust covers in the drawing room, and the rooms were cleaned and polished. The bedrooms were prepared with snowy white linen. Fires were lit in the fireplaces until all the rooms in the house were warm and cozy and ready for the party. To picture the blazing logs in the inglenook. With a tall tree sparkling with tinsel and silver, laden with gifts, and to hear the carol singers coming up to the door, it isn't hard for those who can remember the Hall when it was filled with furniture, and people and family happiness.'

"So here we are, bringing back family happiness, with our family, all of you. I want to make a toast to all of you and to bringing back the tradition at Hopwood Hall. Merry Christmas!"

After my toast, the crowd clinked glasses. I then asked Ian's mother's friend, Brenda, to come up and say a few words. Brenda was a white-haired older woman with a big smile, dressed festively in a red sweater. She slowly made her way up to the front, clutching Ian's arm for assistance. I asked her if she could tell us about some of her memories of the Hall.

"I was fourteen when I came to work here in 1944, during the war," she described. "I can remember walking up to the house for the first time with my mother. I couldn't believe anywhere could have so many chimneys!"

Brenda had gotten a job with the Lancashire Cotton Corporation, which had moved here during World War II. She worked as a secretary, helping to keep the business running to make uniforms for the troops.

"Do you know I was standing in this exact room nearly seventy-five years ago when someone rushed in shouting, '*The war is over! It's over!*'"

As she told this story, everyone in the room was silent. I think we all had chills, and for once, it was not from the cold. It was as if we were all back in that room seventy-five years ago with teenage Brenda.

After she finished speaking, everyone clapped, and I went over to shake her hand and let her know how much it meant to me that she was here and that she had shared her story. Ian was beaming with pride, offering congratulations on a great night. I turned back to find Phineas Shellburn standing behind me, so we shook hands and I told him again how much I appreciated him making all this possible. I nudged shoulders with Bob and told him how much he meant to me, knowing that a hug or words of sincerity would only lead him to make one of his jokes.

"You did it, Hopwood, you did it!" Geoff said, clasping my hand and shaking it up, knowing how much this moment meant to me.

"Well done, Hopwood," Lyn agreed. "It's just so hard to believe we're actually standing here."

My old friend Jay told me, "I get it now. I totally see why you're doing what you're doing. This is important—keep going."

The rep from Historic England said how much he would like

to see the fireplace working again for the next Christmas party in the future and felt that his organization would likely provide some funding to do it, among other important improvements.

As he finished his sentence, for some strange reason, all the lights—including the LED candles—flickered at once. We both stopped and looked around.

"That's weird!" I laughed.

I couldn't help but wonder if perhaps it was a signal from Lady Hopwood and all the Hopwood ancestors helping us along the way.

As the rep from Historic England put on his coat and we wrapped up our conversation about the next phase of the rescue, he became very complimentary about my efforts to help save the Hall. Perhaps my former self, seven years younger, would have wanted this type of acknowledgment. But today, I felt different. Sure, it was nice to hear and to be validated, but at the same time I knew it took so many more than just me. It was the entire community, both living and dead, that had made this moment happen.

After all the guests had left, I had a few minutes alone at the Hall. I sat down in a chair next to the huge fireplace and looked around. Even though the Reception Hall was usually vast and drafty, I could have sworn it felt warm and cozy that night. Lights on the tall Christmas tree and candles glowed all around the room, illuminating the centuries-old brick- and stonework. I inhaled deeply. We'd brought back the Hopwood family Christmas to the Hall for the first time in one hundred years. A centuries-old tradition had been broken by the First World War when Edward and Robert were killed, but now the chain had been reconnected. And for the first time since my dad died, I celebrated Christmas and actually enjoyed it. I felt a profound happiness mixed with a little pride at what had been achieved. It might not have been Victorian Christmas at Hopwood Hall circa 1890—we had all been wearing jeans and jumpers, not black-tie—but it still felt like we were bringing things full circle. Here I was, sitting in the same spot my forebears had sat hundreds of years earlier at Christmastime. I wondered if they had felt similar emotions. I didn't feel dizzy at the thought of it, not even after the mulled wine! Instead, my head was clear, and for the first time in a long time, I felt stable, strong, content, and comfortable in my own skin.

My fiftieth birthday was right on the horizon in February, but I no longer feared growing older. In fact, I welcomed it, because I knew what I was supposed to be doing with my life. When I first came here almost seven years ago, Bob predicted that if nothing was done to save Hopwood Hall, then the place would be gone in five to ten years. That first day, the thought went through my mind: *I don't want to be the Hopwood who goes down in history as the guy who allowed the Hall to disappear during his lifetime.* Thanks to our work stabilizing the house, even if for some reason we were unable to do anything else to protect the Hall, the most important parts of her were going to be secure for *at least* another generation or two. And it had all been done "By Degrees."

Maybe someday I will have a little Hopwood Jr. or Hopwoodia of my own running around the Hall and sliding down the banisters. Maybe they will be the ones to eventually carry the house forward for the next generations.

Of course, I knew there was still a long road ahead. But, no matter what, thanks to the Hall, and its long, deep history, I had a new-found sense of perspective. I no longer measured time in weeks or months, or even decades. I counted in centuries now. I was aware that the story of Hopwood Hall was much, much bigger than me, and if I'm lucky, at some point in the future, when historians write about the place, they will write about our efforts, probably reducing the years of my life down to a single sentence:

"And in the twenty-first century, Hopwood DePree moved from Hollywood to rescue Hopwood Hall from being lost forever, with the help of the community."

But before my leaf on the family tree is finished, I'm hoping they'll be able to add at least three more words to the end of the sentence:

"And they succeeded."

But of course, since we're in Middleton, the three words they'll probably use instead are:

"They were ALRIGHT!"

Hopwood Hall Estate, December 2019 *Courtesy of the author*

EPILOGUE

I have a feeling this is going to be the best year yet!" I declared. It was early January 2020, and I was standing in the arrival hall at Manchester Airport, welcoming my sister Dori who had just flown in from Michigan.

The new year was bringing us lots of new momentum: Heritage organizations wanted to fund us, the local community and council were behind us, and everyone wanted us to succeed. Dori had even decided it was time to pack up her bags and move over to England to help me push Operation Save Hopwood Hall to the next level.

"Let's do this!" she exclaimed, while giving me a giant hug.

Little did we realize that a global pandemic was just a few months away from bringing the world to a grinding halt—and our project along with it.

Lucky for me, my sister just happens to have a master's degree in labor and industrial relations, which is, broadly, the academic study of helping businesses and organizations build a success strategy for management and operation—even in a crisis. Yes, it sounds a bit dry, which is why at parties she usually doesn't tell people what she does. Over the years of her career, however, she has also developed an amazing track record of writing grant applications that go on to be funded. In fact, she's the only person I've met in life who is truly passionate about writing grants, a process that can take months or even years, and which, as far as I'm concerned, is so tedious it makes an excellent replacement for the sleeping pills that are so difficult to get ahold of in England.

With Dori on board, we were going to be able to ramp up our funding, as we would thankfully no longer be dependent on me to spearhead grant applications. It was also incredibly validating to know that a member of my family would put her life on hold in America for six months to come and join me in this crazy pursuit in England.

From the moment I picked up my sister from the airport, we were off to the races. Dori came with me to Historic England meetings and those with other grant-giving organizations to discuss our future plans as a charitable venture. With every meeting, we were inching closer to the dream of creating a retreat where writers, actors, musicians, painters, cooks, environmentalists, and tech innovators could gather to learn, teach, and get inspired. My greatest hope was that the Hall would become a catalyst for people to find their true path in life, just as it had done for me.

We estimated that upkeep and staffing for such a venture was going to cost in the region of half a million pounds a year. We wouldn't be able to annually raise all of that in grants, so the idea was to rent the Hall out for weddings and other events to help cover costs. Thanks to a new friend, Des Styles, we had begun to make connections with potential investors. Des is a financial consultant who, totally coincidentally, lives about twenty-five minutes' drive from Middleton and whom we met after my aunt happened to sit next to him on a transatlantic flight, telling him all about the Hall. Des—a force to be reckoned with, in his early sixties with salt-and-pepper hair and a big-hearted laugh—had heard about the Hall and our plans to turn her into an arts retreat and immediately wanted to know more. He loved our vision and offered to connect us with other people in the financial world who might want to help with the project. A number of wine-fueled late-night dinners ensued where we pitched our ideas.

Dori and Des weren't the only new members of the team. Toward the end of 2019, I'd hired an assistant named Geraldine, whom I'd met while she was managing the Manchester Golf Club that is adjacent to the Hall. Gerry, as she prefers to be called, is a beaming blond local businessperson in her fifties who not only had a real talent for organization but was brimming over with enthusiasm about the Hall and our mission.

*B*y end of February, I was feeling more optimistic than ever. Everything was really ramping up. Nothing was going to stand in our way! At the rate we were moving ahead, I predicted I would be able to move into the Hall—or at least a small corner—by early spring, so that I could be onsite full-time to oversee the protection and progress of the project. As March began, I did my best to tune out the headlines that had begun to dominate the news about the creeping "novel coronavirus." I tried not to worry when toilet paper started vanishing from the supermarket shelves faster than anyone could restock it.

By mid-March, LA had already shut down, with New York quick

to follow. British prime minister Boris Johnson went on TV and advised everyone to pause "nonessential contact and travel." We understood things were serious, but at that point, the pandemic still felt far away—happening somewhere else, not the kind of thing that would be a problem in a small town like Middleton. Pubs and restaurants were still open, and hardly anyone was wearing a mask.

Then, on March 23, 2020, the UK went into lockdown.

"We're going to have to shut the Hall," Bob said with a crack of emotion in his voice on the end of the phone line.

I went over there to help close up shop. *How can this be happening?* I remember thinking as our construction team put down their tools and left the site to go home. But COVID-19 was a matter of life and death, and it was clear that shutting down was the only way to keep people safe from the deadly virus.

I watched as the taillights of the team's cars and trucks disappeared into the misty gray fog. The Hall was suddenly quieter than it had been in a long time. I realized I'd gotten used to the hustle and bustle of workers and volunteers. I felt my stomach sink as I locked the gates behind me. Yes, we had made great progress on the roof, but there was a long way to go. Critical work was still needed to continue to keep the Hall on the uptick and rebound. I hoped that in a couple of weeks, maybe a month, we'd be able to get back on the job.

"What are we going to do?" Dori asked, sitting on the sofa, looking very worried as BBC News flickered on the television in the background. Everything suddenly seemed at a standstill.

She and I were sheltering in south Manchester with our new friend Des. He welcomed us in and had plenty of extra room to safely spread apart in his five-bedroom home that also happened to be dotted with family photos of his pop-star son, Harry Styles. Like everybody else, Dori, Des, and I spent our days staring at the news channels, cooking, sleeping, and drinking while trying to determine what the future held.

After about a week of complete shutdown, my phone rang. It was Bob again.

"The council is saying that we can go back into the Hall to start up work." That was the good news. The bad news was that only essential tradespeople could return, and by the tone of his voice, I could tell that Bob didn't think I would be considered "essential." Sure, I had learned a lot since my days of only being trusted with a broom, and I could confidently try to help, but if it was only going to be a very limited A-team allowed onsite to progress the works, then I was not going to be part of it. I was sad but completely understood. Ultimately, like much of the world, I knew my work could be done at home, sitting at my computer in pajama pants.

"Well, this really is history repeating itself," Geoff said on the phone as I paced back and forth in Des's spacious green garden. "I know it all seems scary, but don't forget, this isn't the first time this has happened. In 1918, not long after the Hopwood sons were killed in the war, the influenza pandemic swept the country. Troops returning home to England from the trenches of Northern France added to the spread. And then if you go back even further, to the fourteenth century, when the Hall would have been just a hunting lodge, the Black Death killed millions. After that, there would be outbreaks of the plague every few years for the next three centuries. This isn't anything Hopwood Hall hasn't seen before."

Geoff reminded me that my ancestors must have found ways to survive and protect the Hall, even during immense challenges and times of uncertainty, and this inspired me to at least try to do the same.

Sadly, a few days later, we got word that the major grant providers, including Historic England, were immediately putting all grants on hiatus until further notice so they could get a better understanding of what was happening. Of course, Historic England was a crucial part of funding the next wave of works that were planned to commence in early spring. We had enough money to keep Bob and perhaps his brother Phil working a few days a week at the Hall, but as far as the new financing for the major works—everything had to be put on pause.

Meanwhile, Dori and I began talking about returning to the United States before flights got shut down altogether.

"You both should get on the next plane home," said a family friend who worked for the US government. "There's no way to know what might happen in the coming days."

Dori and I took the advice, booked our flights, and boarded a massive international jet in Manchester with only about ten other people on it. With so few passengers, the flight attendants didn't have much to focus on other than bringing us multiple dinners and snacks and plying us with drinks. On the nine-hour flight, Dori and I hatched a plan. We couldn't let the pandemic derail our mission completely. We may not be able to be onsite with our friends, but that didn't mean we couldn't brainstorm other ways to keep the project alive, promoting and continuing our efforts in other ways. We decided to use what we assumed would be a month at home to work on setting up a charity to support the Hall and creating proposals that could be used to apply for grants when they began funding again.

Little did we know we would actually end spending a full year in Michigan with our family while we waited for the pandemic to pass. As the months turned into a year, I reminded myself that, in the grand scheme of things, this was a mere blip in the life of the centuries-old hall. I also knew the project was in good hands with

Bob, Geoff, and the huge gang of local supporters, and the work that had been done on the roof was at least good enough that the interior wouldn't be ravaged by another year of weather.

By now, I had begun work on a book about my adventures to save Hopwood Hall.

"Writing a book is a great idea," Jay had said on the phone from his home office in LA. "That's what agents always tell clients to do if for some reason they end up going to prison. It's kind of like we're all in prison right now, so go for it!"

Following Jay's advice, I used my time to write, thereby keeping Middleton constantly in my thoughts, even from a distance of thousands of miles. And as most people discovered in the year 2020, there's a lot that can be achieved on Zoom.

"I was thinking I wasn't going to have to see your face for a while," Bob said as our first Zoom meeting launched. "And now here you are, staring at me in my living room. I'm not sure how I feel about that."

Thankfully, as the weeks went on, Bob and Ian were able to continue to work on basic repairs. Gerry, who lived locally, was my boots on the ground, and she turned out to be an amazing asset, forming a group of volunteers committed to cleaning up the gardens, pulling out three decades' worth of bramble and overgrowth. We managed to bring in funding for Bob to teach a course in how to make leaded windows; Ian and his wife and several other people signed up. After taking the course, everyone was working safely and separately on the small, square-shaped windows, with Bob then fitting them.

My meetings with Geoff and Lyn and the Friends of Hopwood

Hall Estate committee on Zoom to discuss plans, to figure out what was next and where do we go from here, continued. The Historic Houses group also met regularly on Zoom. Many historic home-owners were struggling with the dramatic sudden loss of income from canceled weddings and visitor tours that was so important to help to keep their estates operational. We became like a support group, everyone experiencing different aspects of the same problem. People agreed that in a time of so much illness and loss of life, these were secondary concerns, although very stressful.

Finally, in April 2021, after an incredible amount of offsite work by Dori and a UK-based solicitor aka lawyer, we were able to an-nounce that the Hall had been awarded charitable status by the Charity Commission for England and Wales. Called the Hopwood Foundation for Heritage, Arts, Education, and Inspiration, the mission of the nonprofit is to deliver educational and engagement opportunities to the public. Board members included Xa and Des, as well as a talented Manchester-based heritage architect and the chief operating officer of BBC England. Everyone was committed to helping take Hopwood Hall to the next level of rescue, allowing her to survive for generations to come.

In early May 2021, I finally booked my ticket back to England. Numbers of new COVID-19 cases were going down, as was the length of the UK mandatory travel quarantine. The majority of British people were now vaccinated, and businesses were prepping to fully reopen. It was time. I felt blessed to have made it through safe and healthy. Dori promised to join me in the fall.

As my flight came in to land at Manchester Airport, I realized it had been almost eight years since we'd first visited the Hall in May 2013. Back then, my sense of excitement as I looked out the airplane window and down on the unmistakably green fields of the English landscape was about getting to visit somewhere that was completely unknown to me. This time, as the plane descended toward the runway, I was heading toward somewhere I knew like the back of my hand, somewhere I now considered home.

After a five-day mandatory travel quarantine at Des's house, I returned to Hopwood Hall on May 13, 2021. By coincidence, it was exactly eight years to the day of my first tour with Geoff and Bob. Gerry and her newly established "garden group" of volunteers had strung both British and American flags throughout our office area, and a sign hung by the door that said WELCOME HOME, HOPWOOD. Fresh chocolates, scones, and tea were sitting on the table awaiting my arrival while they were all out working in the garden.

I heard a noise behind me and turned back to see Bob.

"Welcome back, Yank," Bob said gruff as ever. "When you're finished with your little tea party here, we've got plenty of work to do. So if you know anyone who's qualified, send 'em my way."

I laughed. Clearly nothing had changed. I wondered if Bob would EVER have anything nice to say about me.

"Oh, and tell Gerry next time just to drop off the scones at my house. Bringing them here is only going to attract mice," he added with a half smile as he put his hard hat back on.

A few minutes later, as I chomped on a scone, I heard a clanging noise at the gate and looked out to see Geoff. I was thrilled to be reunited with him, and even though he was wearing a facemask, I could tell he was smiling from ear to ear.

It was a strange turn of events to be the one who was opening the gate to show him around. We spent the next hour walking the Hall and grounds with Bob, seeing all the progress that he and the community volunteers had made over the last year. Bob showed us the Family Chapel windows that had been smashed out but now were replaced with beautiful leaded glass, handmade by the community, protecting the Hall from the harsh weather. The gardens had been cleared. Xa would be proud.

I couldn't help but feel a deep sense of solace in knowing that no matter what, through the ups and downs that this house had weathered over the centuries, including those in 2020, this rescue project would now continue onward and upward with or without me.

I could feel my eyes becoming a bit watery as I surveyed the scene. I looked to Geoff, who gave me an understanding nod. Bob put a friendly hand on my shoulder.

"Shall we have ourselves a brew?" he asked.

I smiled.

"Sure. It's been a while since I've had a real English tea. I've missed it," I said as the three of us turned and walked back into the Hall, ready for whatever the future would bring next.

ACKNOWLEDGMENTS

*T*here are so many people who have helped me along the way on this journey that I could probably fill an entire book with personal thank-yous. However, due to space (and my mind being mush from writing the book), I am limited to keeping individual names to the unmentioned behind-the-scenes people who specifically assisted in the development and production of said book. Please forgive me if I have gotten bleary-eyed and failed to mention you. With that, I must say a huge THANK YOU to:

Everyone and everyplace already named within the narrative—obviously you have been a key driver in this adventure.

The people of Middleton, Rochdale Borough, Greater Manchester, and across the UK for their unflinching support, encouragement, and friendship—without you there would be no story to tell. Hopefully you all know who you are, and how appreciative I am.

My family for their ongoing positive thoughts, especially my mother, who left her budding journalism career to instead focus on raising me as a child. It is only because of your sacrifices that I was able to write this book.

Eve Claxton, my editor/collaborator/friend who was with me throughout the process and a joy to work with—even across continental time zones, lockdowns, and, of course, technology issues.

My literary agent, Jen Marshall, who sought me out and led the way to turn the thought of a book into reality.

The entire team at HarperCollins and William Morrow: executive editor Rachel Kahan, who championed the project and was an inspiration every step of the way; marketing director Kayleigh George; publicist Alison Hinchcliffe; production editor Shelby Peak; copyeditor Amy Vreeland; cover designer Yeon Kim; and Ariana Sinclair, for all her assistance.

Jay Froberg and the whole company at ROAR for their support throughout this entire journey.

My loyal core staff: Zena Howard, for her expert eye in communications; Fred Leao Prado, for his creative passion; and Geraldine Connor, for keeping things moving with a smile, even when the walls and ceilings were about to fall down.

Researcher Sarah Palmer and the generous visual contributions from numerous sources, as individually named in the credits, including local libraries, image collections, artists, and photographers.

Director Chris Head for his guidance and coaching in pushing me to first share my story onstage with a live audience, which led to turning it into a book.

The Edinburgh Festival Fringe, Surgeons' Hall, theSpaceUK, for giving me a home to tell the story; as well as the wonderful people and places on the tour along the way at the Greater Manchester Fringe, the International Anthony Burgess Foundation; the Brighton Fringe, Sweet Venues; and the Camden Fringe, Etcetera Theatre.

ACKNOWLEDGMENTS

The UK media, which has been amazing and has championed the Hopwood Hall Estate rescue project and continues to do so. Beginning as a local story in Rochdale Online; to Charles Moore and Robert Mendick at the *Daily Telegraph*, who were behind the first national coverage; to Kim Hjelmgaard, who wrote an article for *USA Today* that caught the attention of a literary agent in NYC who contacted me to set up a meeting to discuss the book that you now hold in your hands. In between we were blessed with journalists and outlets who took the time to thoughtfully share the story and visit Hopwood Hall: Helen Pidd, *The Guardian*; Anna Tyzack, *The Telegraph*; Ian Youngs and Colin Patterson, BBC; Tom Grater, *Deadline*; Gabriella Swerling, *The Times*; Darren Boyle, *Daily Mail*; *The One Show*; *Good Morning Britain*; ITV News; Phil Trow and BBC Radio Manchester; Radio 5's Nihal Arthanayake; *Spear's Magazine*; Stephen Beard for Marketplace; Mercury Press; Getty Images; *Middleton Guardian*; *Historic House* magazine; Jacey Normand, Dom Callaghan, and the fantastic teams at *Inside Out*; *North West Tonight*; and Helen Johnson and colleagues at *Manchester Evening News*.

My hometown media in West Michigan, which has been incredibly important too: Greg Chandler, Grand Rapids Press; *The Holland Sentinel*; Michele DeSelms; FOX WXMI; Rachael Ruiz, NBC WOOD-TV; Val Lego, ABC WZZM; and, of course, Hollywire in my other "hometown" of LA.

The Friends of Hopwood Hall Estate/Friends of the Hopwood Foundation—where would any of this be without you?

The Trustees of the Hopwood Foundation for Heritage, Arts, Education & Inspiration, who have provided the sense of stability and clearheadedness that have allowed me to have the inner peace to be able to write.

The many owners of UK's amazing historic homes who have

become dear friends, mentors, and a support group that has helped me navigate and understand the guardianship of heritage.

My incredible friends and cheerleaders for their belief in me from Holland, Michigan, to Los Angeles to New York and everywhere in between.

Rochdale Borough Council

Rochdale Development Agency

Middleton Township Committee

Heritage Open Days

Historic Houses

Historic England

National Lottery Heritage Fund

Architectural Heritage Fund

English Heritage

UK Visas & Immigration

Edgeleigh Consulting

Heritage Trust Network

The Circles of Art

Hopwood Hall College

Lawrence Atkinson

Joel Stein

Des Styles

Dina Chapman

Scott Brooks and family

Angie Hindmarch

Sarah Callander Beckett

Ben Cowell

ACKNOWLEDGMENTS

The DIT

Lila DePree

Chris Roach

Mark Stephenson

Richard Lysons

Jenny Driver

Janet Byrne

Andi Wilkinson at Made By Factory for launching HopwoodHallEstate.com

All our social media followers and viewers who have encouraged me to share the adventure. Your kind comments and support make my soul shine.

I hope I got everyone in there. If this were an Oscar speech, they probably would have shut me down and started playing the music by now!

ABOUT THE AUTHOR

HOPWOOD DEPREE grew up in Holland, Michigan, where one of his neighbors once said, "He wasn't that great of a kid."

As a young adult, he fled for the bright lights of LA, where he successfully landed a job in front of a restaurant as a dancing chicken. The next day he was fired for not being "enthusiastic enough."

He managed to graduate from the University of Southern California, beginning his career as an actor and independent filmmaker with his first film, *Rhinoskin*, a comedic documentary that followed his hapless adventures attempting to break into the entertainment industry. Having charged up $20,000 on his credit cards to make the film, he crossed his fingers and hoped for the best. Fortunately, he found critical success on the film festival circuit and went on to write, produce, and act in independent and studio film and television productions, often having the lucky opportunity of being able to, incredibly and fortuitously, work alongside Emmy and Academy Award–winning and –nominated artists. Hopwood has performed stand-up comedy at notable venues in both LA and the UK, including the Edinburgh Festival Fringe, where only a few people walked out (they later said they had food poisoning). Hopwood continues to write and produce content and has been filming his journey of the rescue of Hopwood Hall Estate to share with those following him on YouTube, Patreon, and across his other social media outlets (hint, hint—this is a shameless subconscious plug to follow along if you like).